LATINASIAN CARTOGRAPHIES

LATINIDAD

Transnational Cultures in the United States

This series publishes books that deepen and expand our understanding of Latina/o populations, especially in the context of their transnational relationships within the Americas. Focusing on borders and boundary-crossings, broadly conceived, the series is committed to publishing scholarship in history, film and media, literary and cultural studies, public policy, economics, sociology, and anthropology. Inspired by interdisciplinary approaches, methods, and theories developed out of the study of transborder lives, cultures, and experiences, titles enrich our understanding of transnational dynamics.

Matthew Garcia, Series Editor, Professor of Latin American, Latino & Caribbean Studies, and History, Dartmouth College

For a list of titles in the series, see the last page of the book.

LATINASIAN CARTOGRAPHIES

History, Writing, and the National Imaginary

SUSAN THANANOPAVARN

RUTGERS UNIVERSITY PRESS
New Brunswick, Camden, and Newark, New Jersey, and London

Library of Congress Cataloging-in-Publication Data

Names: Thananopavarn, Susan, 1974– author.
Title: LatinAsian cartographies : history, writing, and the national imaginary / Susan Thananopavarn.
Description: New Brunswick : Rutgers University Press, 2018. | Series: Latinidad: transnational cultures in the united states | Includes bibliographical references and index.
Identifiers: LCCN 2017012060 (print) | LCCN 2017032588 (ebook) | ISBN 9780813589862 (E-pub) | ISBN 9780813589886 (Web PDF) | ISBN 9780813589855 (hardback) | ISBN 9780813589848 (paperback)
Subjects: LCSH: American literature—20th century—History and criticism. | American literature—Hispanic American authors—History and criticism. | American literature—Asian American authors—History and criticism. | American literature—21st century—History and criticism. | Literature and society—United States—History—20th century. | Literature and society—United States—History—21st century. | Racism in literature. |
National characteristics, American, in literature. | BISAC: LITERARY CRITICISM / American / Asian American. | LITERARY CRITICISM / American / Hispanic American. | HISTORY / United States / 20th Century. | HISTORY / United States / 21st Century. | SOCIAL SCIENCE / Discrimination & Race Relations.
Classification: LCC PS153.H56 (ebook) | LCC PS153.H56 T47 2018 (print) | DDC 810.9/868073—dc23
LC record available at https://lccn.loc.gov/2017012060

A British Cataloging-in-Publication record for this book is available from the British Library.

∞ The paper used in this publication meets the requirements of the American National Standard for Information Sciences—Permanence of Paper for Printed Library Materials, ANSI Z39.48–1992.

www.rutgersuniversitypress.org

Manufactured in the United States of America

For Adrian, Claire, and Eve

CONTENTS

LATINASIAN CARTOGRAPHIES

INTRODUCTION

Asian American and Latina/o Voices Writing History, Remapping Nation

It must be odd
to be a minority
he was saying.
I looked around
and didn't see any.
So I said
Yeah
it must be.

—Mitsuye Yamada, "Looking Out," *Camp Notes and Other Writings*

In the confusion, Pedro ran, terrified of being caught. He couldn't speak English, couldn't tell them he was fifth generation American. *Sin papeles*—he did not carry his birth certificate to work in the fields. *La migra* took him away while we watched.

—Gloria Anzaldúa, *Borderlands/La Frontera: The New Mestiza*

Mitsuye Yamada's poem "Looking Out" invites us to think critically about the idea of a racial "minority" as an unnamed speaker remarks, "It must be odd / to be a minority," and the narrator agrees, not considering herself a minority within her own community.[1] "Looking Out" is part of an autobiographical collection of poetry about Yamada's experiences as a Japanese American during World War II. Along with her family and approximately 120,000 other Japanese Americans, Yamada was incarcerated as an enemy alien during the war; when she was still a teenager, her family was sent to the Minidoka War Relocation Center in Idaho, far from their California home. Read in this context, the title of the poem invokes the image of a young girl gazing outwards from a position of captivity, perhaps from behind a barbed-wire perimeter fence like those used in many of the western camps that housed Japanese Americans during the war. The girl does not identify with the label "minority," since inside the camp she is in the majority, nor does she consider her identity as a Japanese American "odd." Displacing the oddity of minority status onto a hypothetical other, she concurs with the male figure in the poem: "Yeah / it must be." In another situation, this deferral might indicate a simple difference in perspective, an ironic nod to the slippage of language and meaning created by different points of view. Within the context of the incarceration camps, however, the fact that the girl is "looking out" means that she is being observed from a position of power. The "he" in the poem has the freedom of movement conferred by his status as a white male looking in, and the category of "minority" is one in which the narrator is imprisoned. The fact that she is not technically in the minority in her immediate environment proves that the term is less about numbers and more about power: who has the power to fix the captive other with his gaze. And the use of the word "odd" confirms this power, for the white male names the Japanese American girl "odd" in a way that places her outside the racial (and gendered) norm. The poem's perspective shift challenges this norm, even as it draws attention to the real, barbed-wire consequences of the power of the majority/minority construction, a construction that defines who is an American by default, and who must be subject to definition by others.

Chicana writer Gloria Anzaldúa also disrupts dominant assumptions of who is American as she tells the story of Pedro, a fifth generation U.S. citizen who is caught "*sin papeles*"—without papers—in the fields where he works as a laborer. If Yamada's poem must be read within the context of her experiences during World War II, this passage from Anzaldúa's *Borderlands/La Frontera* recalls Anzaldúa's own childhood along the United States-Mexico border, a place that she has famously referred to as an open wound, "*una herida abierta* where the Third World grates against the first and bleeds."[2] Within this border space, citizens like Pedro are "terrified of being caught" and run from *la migra*—the immigration officials—despite their status as native-born U.S. citizens.[3] The passage relies on the reader's knowledge of Pedro's constitutional rights: the Fourth Amendment to the United States Constitution prohibits unwarranted search and seizure. Unless driving a car or travelling by air (both considered voluntary activities), United States citizens are not required to carry identification with them. Pedro does not "carry his birth certificate to work in the fields," but no American is required to carry a birth certificate to go to work; the statement both explains his arrest and highlights the injustice of such a requirement. Likewise, Anzaldúa leaves the phrases "*sin papeles*" and "*la migra*" untranslated to show their importance and common usage for Pedro and his community. Pedro's terror "of being caught" is a terror that has nothing to do with his legal rights. As a fifth generation American, he is by rights an American citizen. Instead, his terror is a result of the dominant construction of the non-English speaking Latina/o as alien to the nation. This construction is more powerful than the presence of witnesses who are also presumably U.S. citizens—"*La migra* took him away while we watched"—and results in the tragic deportation of a man to a country that is not his own.

Both "Looking Out" and Pedro's story critique dominant constructions of America that exclude Asian Americans and Latina/os from the United States imaginary. They call into question narratives of outsider encroachment that position Asian Americans and Latina/os as external to the nation, forever in the "odd" position of racial "minorities" or "illegal" residents, without recognizing centuries-old patterns of migration, colonization, and military contact between Asia, Latin America, and the United States. They also interrogate the erasure of Latina/os and Asian Americans from official histories of the United States. As Anzaldúa shows, five generations of residence in the United States are not enough to prevent the arrest and deportation of a Latino field worker, nor were generations of Asian Americans in the United States enough to halt the imprisonment of Japanese Americans during World War II. Asian American and Latina/o histories are missing from mainstream histories of the United States, an absence that has deeply impacted civil rights since the nation's inception. Along with other Asian American and Latina/o writers in the twentieth and twenty-first centuries, Yamada and Anzaldúa ask important questions of their readers: what is an American? What does it mean to be a racial minority in the United States, particularly one defined as alien to the nation? And what can Asian American or Latina/o perspectives show us about dominant constructions of "America" and its historical and contemporary power structures?

LatinAsian Cartographies addresses these questions by placing Latina/o and Asian American literary texts in dialogue with foundational narratives of United States history, including narratives of American exceptionalism, wartime patriotism, Cold War anticommunism, and global free trade. It contends that the Asian American and Latina/o presence in the United States, often considered marginal in discourses of U.S. history and nationhood, is in fact crucial to understanding how U.S. national identity has been constructed historically and continues to be constructed in the present day. Although Asian Americans and Latina/os tend to be defined legally and socially as outsiders to the nation—as illustrated by Yamada's imprisoned Japanese American girl and Anzaldúa's deported field worker—this project seeks to turn this model inside out by placing Asian American and Latina/o histories at the center of U.S. national identity. Specifically, this book examines how Latina/o and Asian American literature can rewrite official national narratives and situate U.S. history within a global context that transforms dominant ideas of what it means to be American.

This examination of Asian American and Latina/o narratives is both comparative—illustrating similarities in Asian American and Latina/o experiences of U.S. imperialism, nativistic racism, Cold War divisions, and globalization—and intersectional, theorizing the transpacific zones of Asian-Latina/o interaction created by centuries of migration and colonization. Latina/o studies scholar María DeGuzmán has employed the term *Latinasia* to describe the transnational convergence of Asians and Latin Americans or Latina/os over the course of the last three centuries: "that is, the enormous influx of Asian immigrants and the movement of Latina/o peoples across the Americas, south to north and west to east."[4] Extending the idea of Latinasia to *LatinAsian* cultural productions, this book focuses on authors who write from within this historic convergence. The national geography that emerges from these perspectives is akin to Mary Louise Pratt's concept of the *contact zone*, a space in which people with distinct histories and identities collide. In the contact zone, people from different areas of the world come together in highly asymmetrical societies, usually involving various degrees of "coercion, radical inequality, and intractable conflict."[5] In this book, I propose that the United States may productively be understood as a LatinAsian contact zone, a place in which people of Latin American and Asian descent not only constitute groups with unique histories, but intersect in ways that reflect centuries of global labor migration and U.S. military intervention abroad.

From within the LatinAsian contact zone, suppressed aspects of U.S. history appear as central components of national formation. Mapped by Latina/o and Asian American authors, the LatinAsian contact zone contains the stories omitted in dominant historical discourse, drawing attention to the foreign and domestic policies that have had far-reaching implications both in the past and for the present. By tracing these historical and literary intersections, *LatinAsian Cartographies* joins a growing interest in comparative Latina/o and Asian American studies and fills a gap in the academic scholarship. Sociological studies that compare Latina/o and Asian American experiences are primarily concerned with how their subjects negotiate the black/white racial binary in the United States, while historians have focused on the similar experiences of particular Asian and Latina/o groups, such as Filipino Americans and Puerto Ricans, or, as in the case of Mae M. Ngai's book *Impossible Subjects: Illegal Aliens and the Making of Modern America* (2003), on the common experiences of Asian Americans and Mexican Americans as a result of twentieth-century U.S. immigration policies.[6] In literary criticism, Crystal Parikh's *An Ethics of Betrayal: The Politics of Otherness in Emergent U.S. Literatures and Culture* (2009) explores the trope of betrayal in Asian American and Latina/o literature and cultural narratives. Parikh focuses on how Asian American and Latina/o authors and subjects position themselves in terms of national belonging, treason, betrayal, and espionage. *LatinAsian Cartographies* builds on Ngai's and Parikh's work on the importance of legal and social exclusion in understanding Asian American and Latina/o histories, focusing on literary historical narratives and national memory rather than the idea of betrayal. In challenging nativism by claiming that the United States is in fact a LatinAsian nation—that Asian American and Latina/o literary narratives are important because they have the power to disrupt dominant histories of the United States—this work forges new connections between the fields of Asian American and Latina/o studies.

IMMIGRANTS AND ALIENS: HISTORICAL AND LEGAL CONSTRUCTIONS OF OTHERNESS

According to the United States Census Bureau, the growth of Asian American and Latina/o populations is one of the most important demographic changes of the twenty-first century. Summarizing the latest population estimates for nation, states, and counties, a widely publicized 2013 Census Bureau report highlighted the following four points:

- Asian is fastest growing group
- Hispanic population surpasses 53 million
- 11% of counties are now majority-minority
- The nation ages, but some areas become younger"[7]

Such reports emphasize the importance of Latina/o and Asian American studies for understanding the contemporary United States. They also serve as a reminder that race and ethnicity are highly charged issues in the United States, often suppressing other demographic narratives. In this report, Asian Americans and Latina/os are not only perceived as external to the United States majority; they are considered a threat to the majority status of the non-Hispanic white population as the fastest-growing part of a spreading "majority-minority." Even the statement "the nation ages" is less about aging than it is about race, as the report reveals that the non-Hispanic white population, on average, is more than ten years older than any other group; the "areas" that are becoming younger are geographically defined, but importantly, they are also demarcated by race and ethnicity.

These demographic reports are more than just statements of facts. To borrow a phrase from historian Hayden White, demography, like historiography, is both a social science and also a "species of the genus narrative."[8] The same data could have told that more than 63 percent of the U.S. population identifies as non-Hispanic white, forming by far the most numerous racial group.[9] It could have addressed the question of wealth distribution to show that the median wealth of non-Hispanic white residents of the United States is more than 20 times that of black residents and 18 times that of Hispanic residents,[10] or it could have shown that white residents are overrepresented in Congress, with 96 percent of senators and 81 percent of representatives identifying as white in 2012.[11] However, the narrative that is increasingly pulled from demographic reports in the twenty-first century is one of racial encroachment phrased as a growing *majority-minority*, a term that the census defines as "meaning that more than 50 percent of [an area's]

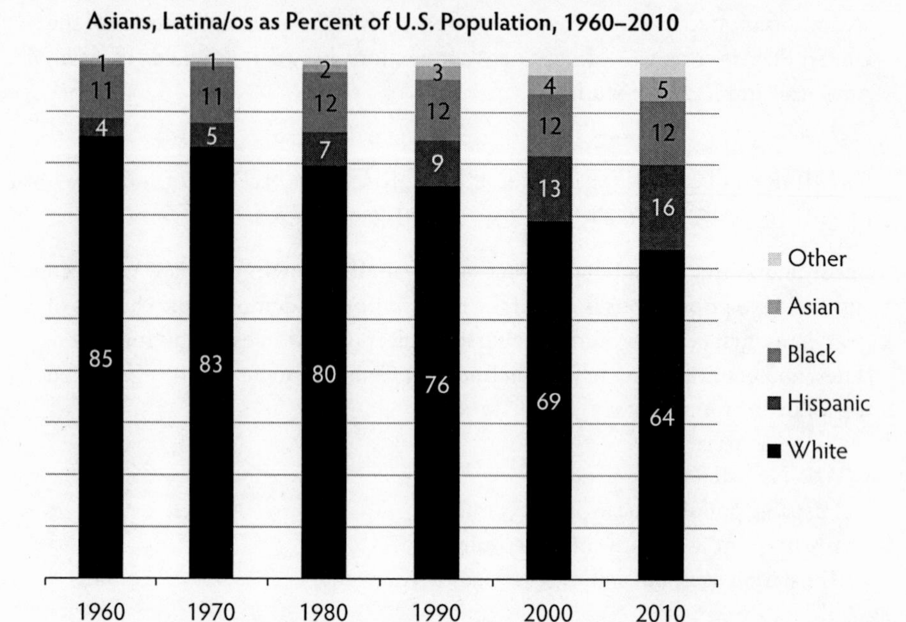

FIGURE 1. Asians and Latina/os are the fastest growing racial demographics in the United States ["Statistical Portrait of Hispanics in the United States," Pew Research Center, Washington, D.C. (April 19, 2016), http://www.pewhispanic.org/2016/04/19/statistical-portrait-of-hispanics-in-the-united-states-key-charts/].

population is other than non-Hispanic white alone."[12] A 2012 political cartoon by Pulitzer prize-winning cartoonist Joel Pett dramatizes this white anxiety that increasing numbers of minorities endanger the existing racial order. In the cartoon, a nurse in the hospital's newborn nursery has labeled each infant with a sign on its bassinet; half the signs read "Us," and the other half read "Them." To a man holding a news report stating "Minority Births Are Up," the nurse quips, "It's so you'll know which ones to fear."[13] Demographic reports that use the idea of a majority-minority imply that the majority white population should "know which ones to fear." And the minorities that are tagged as fastest-growing, most likely to tip the scales that determine whether an area is predominantly white or other, are Asian and Hispanic.

Twenty-first century unease about the growth of Asian and Latina/o populations in the United States has deep historic roots. Despite the Statue of Liberty's well-known inscription welcoming the world's "huddled masses yearning to breathe free," dominant society in the United States has never been enthusiastic about demographically significant numbers of immigrants, especially poor immigrants and refugees.[14] Concerns about lower-class immigrants have often intersected with racial and ethnic anxieties, and nineteenth and early twentieth century immigrants from Eastern and Southern Europe and Ireland were frequently met with hostility and legal attempts to limit their participation in society. For European immigrants, however, a paradigm of ethnicity defined race as a social category that could be overcome through cultural assimilation.[15] From the eighteenth century, authors like J. Hector St. John de Crèvecoeur answered the question "What is an American?" in theoretically flexible terms for these immigrants:

> He is an American, who, leaving behind him all his ancient prejudices and manners, receives new ones from the new mode of life he has embraced, the new government he obeys, and the new rank he holds. He becomes an American by being received in the broad lap of our great *alma mater.* Here individuals of all nations are melted into a new race of men, whose labours and posterity will one day cause great changes in the world.[16]

In this view, race is a matter of cultural prejudice and conventions that can be discarded at will, and indeed, must be discarded to enter into the new, wholly American "race of men." St. John de Crèvecoeur likened human beings to plants, theorizing that they would take on the characteristics of their new soil; a stunted plant transplanted to good soil would inevitably thrive. It was his image of melting, however, that became a crucial part of the American imaginary, re-appearing most significantly in Israel Zangwill's 1908 play *The Melting-Pot,* which promulgated the famous statement that "America is God's Crucible, the great Melting-Pot where all the races of Europe are melting and re-forming."[17] Zangwill's four-act elaboration of this idea resonated across America, and his images and terms have been utilized in public debates for more than a century. As theorist Werner Sollors has stated, whether critics agree with Zangwill or not, the debate on ethnicity and race has largely been shaped by the image of the melting pot and phrases and ideas from this "rarely read, yet universally invoked, play."[18]

Yet European origin remained key to both St. John de Crèvecoeur's and Zangwill's definition of an American. The former "endeavored to shew you how Europeans became Americans"[19]; for the latter, the races that God placed in his crucible were "all the races of Europe." The ethnicity paradigm of race relied on the ideas of cultural pluralism and assimilation and was not available to those identified as *racial* minorities: African Americans, Native Americans, Asian Americans, Latina/os, and other nonwhite minorities. Studies like Noel Ignatiev's *How the Irish Became White* demonstrate that assimilation in the United States has never been only a matter of shedding one's ethnic identity; it is also about making a move to whiteness and white privilege. While groups like the Irish could (and did) make this move, people of color could not.[20] For this reason, although the U.S. Census Bureau makes a distinction between race and ethnicity (i.e., white is a "race," but Hispanic is an "ethnicity"), it is more politically and sociologically consistent to discuss both Latina/os and Asian Americans according to Michael Omi's and Howard Winant's concept of *racial formation*, which they define as "the sociohistorical process by which racial categories are created, inhabited, transformed, and destroyed," and in terms of historically situated *racial projects* through which "human bodies and social structures are represented and organized."[21] Through these concepts, we can trace a historical continuity in which neither Asians nor Latina/os have been admitted as potential Americans to the crucible, and through which they are frequently represented and organized today as existing outside the constructed "majority" of non-Hispanic whites.

In reserving a disposable ethnic identity for Europeans only, the idea of the melting pot both excluded racial minorities and left unspoken the basic structure of U.S. racial politics along a black/white binary. The black/white binary was written into law early in United States history; the Nationality Act of 1790 restricted the right to naturalized citizenship to "free white persons" of good moral character, a deliberate exclusion of African American slaves and indigenous American peoples. This right was extended after the Civil War to include "persons of African nativity or descent," thus defining citizenship in the United States starkly in terms of white or black.[22] As Latina/o studies scholar Suzanne Oboler and Parikh have observed, the 1896 *Plessy v. Ferguson* case further codified the black/white binary, as it signaled the partial political incorporation of African Americans to the state even while it legalized racial discrimination; the court's "separate but equal" decision paradoxically acknowledged the rights of African Americans as citizens at the same time as it established the national community as one that "could be invoked primarily in white-only terms."[23] Outside of this black/white binary, however, Asians and Latina/os were considered foreign to the United States imaginary. From nineteenth century exclusion laws to the racially targeted immigration politics of the twenty-first century, dominant discourses in the United States have legally and rhetorically defined Asian and Latina/o Americans as permanent outsiders. This construction has prevented many Latina/o and Asian residents of the United States from becoming citizens, creating "illegal aliens" who were and are prohibited by law from accessing the full privileges of citizenship. It has also gone beyond the technicalities of citizenship to encompass perception and rights in the public imagination. Ngai argues that the legal racialization of Asian Americans and Latina/os has in fact produced the paradoxical phenomenon of "'alien' citizens—Asian Americans and Mexican Americans born in the United States who possess citizenship but remain alien in the eyes of the nation."[24] Parikh extends this idea to Latina/os as a whole (not only Mexican Americans), asserting that both Latina/os and Asian Americans "have been plagued by images of alienness, treason, and duplicity."[25] Parikh traces these images to the social and legal structures of racism within the United States, imperialism abroad, and exclusionary immigration policies that together form a "history that haunts the nation and structures present-day Asian

American and Latina/o alienation."[26] If the nation is an imagined community, as anthropologist Benedict Anderson and others have claimed, then Asian Americans and Latinos have historically been excluded from the national imaginary of the United States.

"INCAPABLE OF ASSIMILATING": ASIAN AMERICAN EXCLUSION

The exclusion of Asian Americans—which as cultural critic Kandice Chuh has argued renders the very category "Asian American" contradictory, as it both claims subjectivity and refers to the impossibility of the Asian American as citizen-subject[27]—can be traced to the nineteenth century, when Asians became the only people in United States history to be prohibited from immigration and naturalization solely on the basis of their race. Until 1924, immigration to the United States was numerically unrestricted and even encouraged as part of the free global movement of labor.[28] Asian exclusion, which was legislated in a series of laws in the late nineteenth and early twentieth centuries, was the exception to this rule. These laws were in part a response to anti-Chinese sentiment that had developed with the first mass immigration of Chinese laborers to California during the 1849 gold rush, a time in which cries of "California for Americans!" spurred white mob violence against both Chinese immigrants and Latin American participants in the gold rush.[29] The perception that Asian and Latina/o labor threatened "free white labor" is key to understanding how both groups were defined by dominant U.S. society in opposition to white interests. Unlike the experience of nineteenth century European immigrant groups, the prejudice encountered by Asian and Latina/o immigrants did not disappear in subsequent generations. Rather, both Asians and Latina/os were considered obstacles to the white Easterners and immigrants of pioneer legend.

In the case of the Chinese, white hostility led to the formation of anti-Chinese leagues, vigilante violence against Chinese laborers, and the passage of numerous laws targeting Chinese residents of California. Many of these laws were aimed at driving out Chinese residents through taxation and restriction of enterprises like mining and laundry businesses. Such California state and city laws included the Foreign Miners' Tax, which penalized Asian and Latin American miners; the San Francisco Cubic Air Ordinance, which criminalized Chinese tenement housing; the Sidewalk Ordinance, which banned Chinese merchants from carrying laundry or vegetables in baskets hanging from shoulder poles; various laundry ordinances that penalized Chinese businesses by outlawing wooden buildings and taxing hand-delivered laundry; a Queue Ordinance targeting Chinese hairstyles; and even a Cemetery Ordinance that disallowed traditional Chinese burial practices.[30] Moreover, in the nineteenth century California amended antimiscegenation laws to prohibit "Mongolians" from marrying whites and passed a school law barring "Mongolians and Negroes" from public schools.[31] Although all of these laws were eventually found unconstitutional, in the years they were enforced they imposed a significant hardship on Asian American residents of the United States. They also both reflected and created a national perception that the Chinese, along with other Asian peoples, were outsiders, unassimilable to American ways of life. This perception was reinforced by the passage of federal laws preventing Chinese immigration, including the Page Law of 1875 that prohibited the immigration of Chinese women by classifying them as prostitutes and the 1882 Chinese Exclusion Act that excluded the entry of Chinese laborers for a period of ten years.[32] The Chinese Exclusion Act was renewed by a series of laws, including the Geary Act of 1892 that allowed the deportation of Chinese residents who failed to register with the government, and it was not repealed until 1943.[33]

The official basis for these laws was the idea that Asian people were inherently foreign, unable to assimilate to life in the United States. This view was expressed strongly in the 1893 United States Supreme Court decision in *Fong Yue Ting v. United States,* which upheld the Geary Act and the right of the United States government to deport unregistered Chinese residents:

> After some years' experience, ... the government of the United States was brought to the opinion that the presence within our territory of large numbers of Chinese laborers, of a distinct race and religion, remaining strangers in the land, residing apart by themselves, tenaciously adhering to the customs and usages of their own country, unfamiliar with our institutions, and *apparently incapable of assimilating with our people,* might endanger good order, and be injurious to the public interests.[34]

In other words, people of Chinese ancestry, forced by discriminatory laws and vigilante violence to live in segregated areas, and prohibited from marrying or going to school with white Americans, were deemed unfit for American inclusion because of their incapacity to assimilate into white American life.

These discriminatory laws, initially aimed at the Chinese, were eventually extended to include all immigrants from Asia. Despite the opposition of the Japanese government, the United States Immigration Act of 1917 established a "barred Asiatic zone" that stretched from Afghanistan eastward to the Pacific Ocean.[35] Laws were enacted that retroactively defined all Asians as racially ineligible for naturalized citizenship on the basis of the Nationality Act of 1790, which reserved naturalization for free white persons and persons of African descent. Because Asians were aliens ineligible for citizenship, the courts reasoned, they could have no vested interest in promoting the welfare of the United States and should not be allowed to immigrate at all. In two Supreme Court cases, *Takao Ozawa v. U.S.* (1922) and *U.S. v. Baghat Singh Thind* (1923), Asian residents of the

United States challenged the prohibition to naturalization on the basis of their contributions to U.S. society (including military service), but their racial ineligibility for citizenship was upheld. The *Thind* case is particularly illuminating, as Baghat Singh Thind, a U.S. citizen and World War I veteran, fought denaturalization on racial grounds by claiming that he was descended from Aryans and was thus Caucasian, or white under U.S. law. The Supreme Court disagreed, stating that "the great body of our people instinctively . . . reject the thought of assimilation." Thind and all South Asians were subsequently denaturalized.[36] The fact that the Supreme Court had to fall back on "instinct" to deny Thind the right to naturalize shows how legal criteria were stretched to accommodate the existing racial order.

Legal criteria were also stretched in the case of Filipino migrants to the United States in the 1920s and 1930s, at a time when the Philippines was under U.S. colonial occupation. Just as nineteenth century rhetoric claimed that Asians and Latino workers threatened white jobs, in the early twentieth century "the charge that Filipinos threatened white American workers' jobs and wages was ubiquitous."[37] This rhetoric was fueled less by real competition between white and Filipino laborers and more by an entrenched narrative of foreign encroachment. Racial violence was exacerbated by specious claims that Filipino men posed a threat to white women. This narrative of "oversexed" Filipinos, like similar myths about African American men in the South, led to lynchings and attacks throughout the west coast in the 1920s and 1930s.[38] Legal proceedings against Filipino migrants were difficult to enact since Filipinos were colonial subjects and therefore U.S. nationals. However, a national desire to exclude them eventually resulted in the Tydings-McDuffie Act of 1934 (or Philippine Independence Act), which granted independence to the Philippines after ten years but immediately changed the status of all Filipinos from "nationals" to "aliens."[39]

In all of these legal proceedings, the courts used shifting criteria to establish that Chinese, Japanese, Indians, Filipinos, and other Asians were neither white nor black and were thus aliens permanently ineligible for citizenship. The fact that the courts established Filipino subjects as aliens while they were also U.S. colonial subjects, a clear violation of democratic principles, demonstrates U.S. commitment to maintaining that racial order. These laws had a tremendous impact on Asian Americans. Since alien land laws prohibited non-naturalized residents from owning land or property, they disenfranchised large numbers of Asian American farmers on the west coast as well as small business owners.[40] The hand of the law also reached into domestic life. In a striking instance of both racial and gendered state power, the Cable Act of 1922 ruled that women who were United States citizens could have their citizenship stripped by marrying Asian immigrants, as "any woman citizen who marries an alien ineligible to citizenship shall cease to be a citizen of the United States."[41]

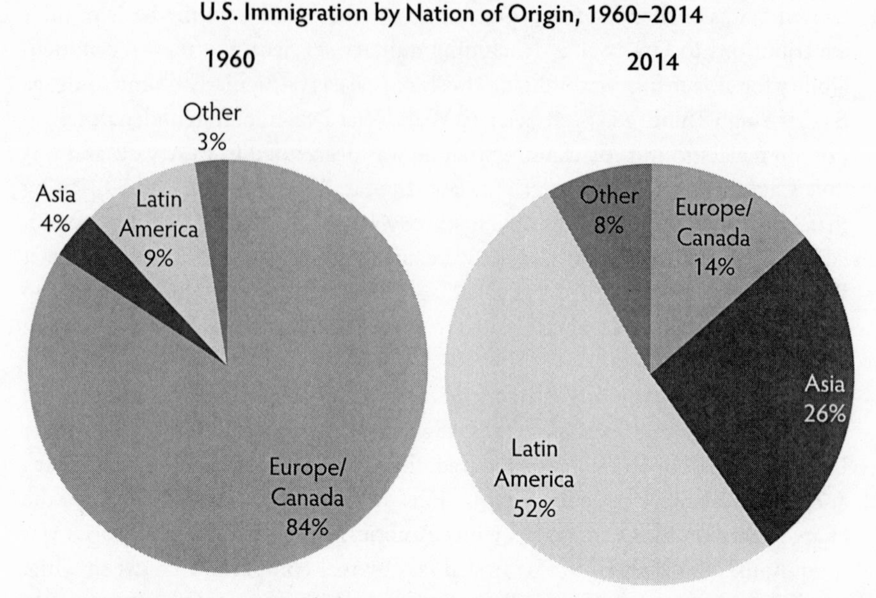

FIGURE 2. The passage of the Immigration Act of 1965 enabled a significant increase in immigration from Asia and Latin America [Asia here refers to East or South Asia only; "Origins of the U.S. Immigrant Population, 1960–2014," Pew Research Center, Washington, D.C. (September 26, 2015), http://www.pewhispanic.org/chart/origins-of-the-u-s-immigrant-population-1960-2013/].

The overall effect of these laws was to keep the number of Asian Americans very low well into the twentieth century. The Supreme Court case *United States v. Wong Kim Ark* had established in 1898 that all persons born in the United States were U.S. citizens regardless of whether their parents were eligible for citizenship. However, with laws that heavily restricted and criminalized immigration from Asia, the number of Asian Americans in the United States remained small until laws beginning in the 1940s began gradually chipping away at legal barriers to immigration. The Chinese exclusion laws were repealed in 1943, and the racial bar to naturalization was repealed entirely with the 1952 McCarran-Walter Act. But it was not until the Immigration Act of 1965 abolished the national origins quota system (which based immigration numbers on existing populations within the United States) that Asian immigrants were finally accorded many of the same rights as immigrants from Europe. With this act, every country not in the Western hemisphere was granted an equal allocation of visas, and a preference system was established that prioritized family reunification and professional or labor skills.[42]

Immigration law was not the only area in which Asian Americans were excluded from the United States imaginary. As is the case with other racial minorities, the protection of United States citizenship has not always guaranteed Asian Americans the same legal rights as other citizens. During World War II, approximately 120,000 Japanese Americans in California, Washington, and Oregon—including the adolescent Yamada—were removed without trial to camps in remote areas of the United States; more than half of these were U.S. citizens.[43] Despite private and military investigations that found no particular cause for concern or "disloyalty" among Japanese American residents of the west coast, and the objections of the attorney general, widespread racist sentiments against Japanese Americans prevailed. General John L. DeWitt, the army officer in charge of military security on the west coast, wrote:

> The Japanese Race is an enemy race, and while many second-and-third generation Japanese born on United States soil, possessed of United States citizenship, have become "Americanized," the racial strains are undiluted. . . . It, therefore, follows that along the vital Pacific Coast over 112,000 potential enemies, of Japanese extraction, are at large today.[44]

Legal challenges to the incarceration of Japanese Americans resulted in decisions that emphasized the importance of military necessity over the constitutional right of citizens. In one case, *Korematsu v. United States*, the U.S. Supreme Court ruled that "the identification and exclusion of a single racial group was allowable through the war powers of Congress and the president."[45] Forty-six years later, the efforts of Japanese American citizens and civil rights activists to obtain redress for this violation of their rights resulted in the passage of the Civil Liberties Act of 1988, which extended a federal apology and authorization of reparation payments to survivors of the camps. It also came with a formal acknowledgement that the forcible removal of Japanese Americans from their homes during the war was a decision based solely on their race.[46]

Laws excluding Asians from the United States and failures to protect Asian Americans within the law had cultural consequences. As Ngai has argued, the racial formations produced by these acts guaranteed a social and cultural climate that cast Asians as permanent outsiders; they wore a "badge of foreignness that could not be shed."[47] The consequence of permanent foreignness is evident in the particular tenor of anti-Asian violence and discrimination in the United States, which often operates on the assumption that Asian Americans are "less than fully American."[48] It also may carry forward to the twenty-first century emphasis on Asian demographic growth within the United States, not as a natural consequence of lifting numerical restrictions on some of the most populous countries in the world, but rather as part of a trend towards a so-called majority-minority, whose main consequence is decreasing the relative percentage of the white population.

"NOT A WHITE PERSON, NOR AN AFRICAN, NOR OF AFRICAN DESCENT": LATINA/OS IN THE UNITED STATES

If Asian Americans have been considered foreigners from the East, Latina/o populations in the United States have often been cast as the foreigners from the South, also historically excluded from the imagined community of "Americans." In the case of Latina/os, this exclusion both justified and erased the facts of U.S. occupation of former Mexican and Spanish land and dependence on Latina/o labor. In her book *Ethnic Labels, Latino Lives: Identity and the Politics of (Re)Presentation in the United States,* Oboler notes that the category "Hispanic" is inextricably linked to United States imperialism in Latin America and the Caribbean. She asserts that "internal social and racial group differentiations notwithstanding, people of Latin American descent in the United States have long been perceived homogeneously as 'foreign' to the image of 'being American' since the nineteenth century, regardless of the time and mode of their incorporation into the United States or their subsequent status as citizens of this nation."[49] Like the emergence of the category "Asian" in the United States, the homogenization of people of diverse origins into the category "Hispanic" has had less to do with social status, race, or nationality than with the construction of the United States polity as an entity based on the exclusion of certain others. As DeGuzmán explains, this exclusion was a key part of American exceptionalism: the need to understand the United States as a liberal antithesis of imperial Spain. DeGuzmán has traced the ways in which Anglo-American cultural productions since the eighteenth century have Orientalized and primitivized Spain in an attempt to frame "Anglo-American empire as an antiempire, innocent of the barbarities of the Spanish Empire."[50] Such anti-Spanish (and anti-Catholic) constructions grew to encompass post-independence Latin America, including Latina/os and the Spanish language itself.[51] As Anglo-American empire expanded in the Western hemisphere, so did the distinction between the two Americas, English America and Spanish America.

Historically, the construction of Latina/os outside the United States imaginary has depended on at least three ideologies: the idea of manifest destiny that drove U.S. expansion in the Southwest; the Monroe Doctrine and its justification of United States imperialism within the Western hemisphere; and the twentieth and twenty-first century construction of the "illegal alien" as a central trope of immigration politics. Each of these overlapping ideologies has contributed to the idea of a hemisphere divided into two Americas: a northern Anglo America and a southern Latin America, with Latina/os in the United States considered a foreign presence even in land that was once part of Mexico. Journalist John O'Sullivan coined the phrase "manifest destiny" in 1845 during the United States' annexation of Texas, when he famously warned European nations against any interference that would limit or check "the fulfillment of our manifest destiny to overspread the continent allotted by Providence for the free development of our yearly multiplying millions."[52] As historian Thomas R. Hietala has observed, this reconciliation of democracy with empire provided Americans with a legitimizing myth of Christian, democratic development at the same time that it "implicitly sanctioned the dispossession of all non-Anglo peoples on the continent."[53] Over the next decade, the U.S. occupation of the Southwest was justified in Congress by repeated comparisons between Indians and Mexicans, whose conquest was held to be in their own best interests. In the words of one New York congressman in 1847, the Mexicans of the borderlands were "a perfidious and mixed race—a community of pirates and robbers," and it was the duty of the United States to "civilize, Christianize, and moralize" them and "teach them what they so much stand in need of—a knowledge of humanity, industry, and justice; to their own great advantage, and to the advantage of all nations that have any intercourse of correspondence with them."[54] Another senator noted in a Senate speech in 1847 that "Mexico and the United States are peopled by two distinct and utterly unhomogenous races"; the Mexicans resembled "our own savage tribes" and were therefore "utterly unfit for the blessings and the restraints of rational liberty."[55] The idea of manifest destiny went hand in hand with the notion of the inferiority of the Indian and Mexican inhabitants of the Southwest and justified the annexation of Texas and the eventual occupation of a third of formerly Mexican lands.

The Treaty of Guadalupe Hidalgo, which ended the Mexican-American war in 1848, provided legal protection for Mexicans living in newly acquired territories of the United States, granting them the right to citizenship and the right to maintain ownership of their lands. However, although this treaty theoretically provided Latina/os in the United States with legal rights, in practice these protections were often challenged or violated. Corrupt lawyers, biased judges, pressure exerted on Mexicans to give up their land, and confusion about titles and land rights ultimately led to widespread dispossession of Mexican Americans from their land. Small village farmers' communally owned grazing lands were systematically expropriated, and by the turn of the twentieth century, many poor Mexicans had become seasonal migrant workers.[56] Not all Mexicans were equally dispossessed. Prewar Spanish colonial society in the Southwest was highly socially stratified, and many of the landed elite families forged alliances with Anglos, claiming a racial superiority based on a shared European "pure" ancestry. However, these "Spanish Americans," or "Hispanos," also came up against the nation's belief in a white, Protestant superiority and were eventually largely dispossessed of their land. In an early example of resistant Latina/o literature, California author María Amparo Ruiz de Burton wrote her novel *The Squatter and the Don* (1885) from the perspective of these wealthy Mexican Americans, demonstrating how the terms of the Treaty of Guadalupe Hidalgo were consistently violated by Anglo squatters and a hostile U.S. Congress. As Oboler has stated, "notwithstanding Mexicans' adherence to the social and racial dynamics that once differentiated their status and power in Spanish colonial and postcolonial societies, they, like other Latin American populations, came to be perceived homogeneously, and as culturally and racially inferior in the U.S. context."[57]

An 1897 legal case, *In re Rodriguez*, demonstrates the ways in which Latina/os and Asian Americans were subject to similar racial challenges in the nineteenth century, despite the legal protections afforded to Latina/os by the Treaty of Guadalupe Hidalgo. In this case, a Mexican man who had lived in Texas for ten years petitioned to become a citizen of the United States; his application was contested because, as two attorneys of the court noted, "he is not a white person, nor an African, nor of African descent."[58] In other words, Rodriguez's right to naturalize was called into question on the same grounds that Asians in the United States were defined as "aliens ineligible for citizenship." In Rodriguez's case, the court upheld his right to naturalize because of the Treaty of Guadalupe Hidalgo and other U.S.-Mexican treaties. Ngai observes, "Mexicans were thus deemed to be white for purposes of naturalization, an unintended consequence of conquest."[59] However, this definition was unstable and highly contingent on circumstances. As Oboler asserts, the very fact that Rodriguez's right to naturalize was initially denied on racial grounds, and he had to use racial terms to argue his case, "shows that the definition of the domestic boundaries of the national community in black/white terms had also become a legitimate justification for reinforcing nationality to render Mexican Americans invisible both as *citizens* and as *native-born members* of the nation."[60] Moreover, by the twentieth century the status of Mexican Americans outside the black/white binary was being actively used to justify discrimination against them. Ironically, because legally Mexican Americans were deemed "white," they had no legal basis to claim the violation of their Fourteenth Amendment rights when they were barred from white schools or restaurants, or when they were tried in a court of law by an all-Anglo jury; as whites, they could not technically experience racial discrimination. It was not until the landmark 1954 case *Hernandez v. Texas* successfully established that Mexican Americans were subject to discrimination as a "class apart" that they were granted the legal protection of the Fourteenth Amendment.[61] As a conquered people, Mexican Americans were accorded the legal right to citizenship and naturalization, but in practice this right was contested and unstable, subject to the shifting definition of "white" and the many legal loopholes afforded by an ill-defined place in the black/white binary.

The further expansion of the United States into Latin America after the Spanish-American war solidified the idea of peoples of Latin American descent as "other" Americans. DeGuzmán observes that after the Monroe Doctrine of 1823, "the United States representationally homogenized Latin America, subsuming difference between former parts of the Spanish Empire into one unified threat or opportunity for its own step-by-step expansion."[62] While initially welcomed by many Latin American countries as a way to establish their independence from Spain, the Monroe Doctrine effectively established the dominance of the United States within the Western hemisphere, particularly in the Latin American nations to the south. The end of the Spanish-American war and the 1898 Treaty of Paris, which granted the United States possession of Puerto Rico, Guam, and the Philippines and political control over Cuba, placed Puerto Ricans in the position of a colonized people, with neither the protection of an independent nation-state of their own nor the status of fully incorporated Americans. The structural similarities between Filipino/as and Puerto Ricans in their relationship to the United States were not lost on congressmen at the time, one of whom stated baldly: "I am opposed to increasing the opportunities for the millions of negroes in Puerto Rico and the 10,000,000 Asiatics in the Philippines of becoming American citizens and swarming into this country and coming in competition with our farmer and mechanics and laborers."[63] At the same time as anti-Chinese leagues throughout the American West sought to protect the interests of "free white labor" through the exclusion of Asians, Puerto Ricans were being typed as another labor threat, one that racially classified them as "negroes" along with African American former slaves. Like Mexican Americans, Puerto Ricans' racial category was unstable; what was certain was that they were outside the white imaginary of the United States.

The construction of the "illegal alien" in the twentieth century added to the perceived division between legitimate (Anglo) Americans and illegitimate (Latina/o) Americans in the United States. Ironically, the numerical restriction of immigration that came with the Johnson-Reed Immigration Act of 1924 did not apply to residents of the Western hemisphere, who were deemed necessary for the free movement of labor, but it nevertheless created a class of undocumented migrants from Mexico due to its bureaucratization of the immigration process. Mexicans in the 1920s crossing the United States-Mexico border faced a formal admissions process and inspection that was often both humiliating and expensive. Bathing, delousing, line inspections, and interrogation practices became the norm for anyone arriving at the Mexican border other than by first-class rail. These racially motivated practices (which were being eliminated at Ellis Island at the same time as they were introduced at the Mexican border) were accompanied by a head tax and visa fee that priced many Mexican migrants out of formal admission to the United States.[64] At the same time, in 1924, for the first time, Congress criminalized unlawful entry to the United States, making undocumented migrants subject to deportation and criminal prosecution.[65] Historian Natalia Molina has traced how these legal moves coincided with cultural representations of Mexicans as "birds of passage" who constituted a workforce that was desirable primarily because it was deportable.[66] "Repatriation" movements throughout the twentieth century, most notoriously the deportation of approximately one million Mexican Americans during the Great Depression, demonstrated that Mexicans in the United States were considered ideal workers precisely because they had no legal stake in the country and could be deported when economically or politically convenient.[67] While undocumented immigrants from Europe were often legalized as "deserving" through administrative reforms, such reforms were rarely applied to Mexicans, who were usually considered "undeserving" of relief. The result of these laws and representations was that by the mid-twentieth century, Mexican Americans were defined by and against the category "illegal alien," a category that ethnic studies scholar Lisa Marie Cacho notes is one of permanent criminalization. The category "illegal alien," Cacho writes, strips Mexican Americans of moral credibility as well as political rights and engenders violence that is based on the presumption that they are "ineligible for personhood."[68] In the twenty-first century, this conflation of undocumented status, criminality, and race has extended to Central Americans and other Latina/os. Calls for increasing the militarization of the United States-Mexico border explicitly aim to keep out migrants from Honduras, Guatemala, and El Salvador, rendering even child migrants "ineligible for personhood," as in the 2014 public outcry against tens of thousands of unaccompanied children fleeing violence in Central America.

To some extent, the Cold War granted Cuban Americans an exceptional status with respect to these tropes. The first wave of refugees to arrive in the United States in the early 1960s coincided with the height of U.S. anticommunist ideology. As political scientist Sheila Croucher explains, "widely publicized accounts of Cubans risking their lives to escape tyranny" were convenient to an administration invested in discrediting communism.[69] The Kennedy administration welcomed this first wave of refugees both politically and financially, providing Cuban exiles with more than $2 billion in housing, health care, job placement assistance, monthly stipends, and loans for education and businesses in one of the most costly and long-running refugee program in national history.[70] This investment in Cuban American success has partially set Cubans apart from other Latina/os in national perception as embodiments of the American Dream. The fact that many of the first wave of Cuban exiles were light-skinned elites allowed them to claim a place in the "melting pot" usually reserved for white European immigrants. Yet even so, Croucher and others have demonstrated that the Cuban American success story depends on a heavy elision of the racial and class diversity of actual Cuban migrants from the 1960s onwards. While this narrative has benefited Cuban American elites (and the ideological aims of the U.S. state), it has not reflected the economic struggles of many Cuban Americans, nor has it exempted them from being conscripted into the general categories "Hispanic" or "Latino."

Despite the apparent exception of the Cuban American success story, the creation of these categories—"Hispanic," "Latino," and "Asian American"—has overwhelmingly coincided with historic attempts to exclude people within these groups from citizenship and belonging in the United States. Civil rights movements in the 1960s and afterwards have used these categories to describe common experiences of oppression and mobilize politically to demand equal treatment under the law. They are sources of pride and solidarity as well as labels imposed from the outside. Still, from the politically charged immigration rhetoric of today, to census reports that define Asian and Latino population growth in terms of encroachment, the dominant constructions of both groups have been that they are essentially foreign, outside the black/white binary and outside the imagined community of the United States.

NATIONAL AMNESIA: RACE AND THE ERASURE OF HISTORICAL MEMORY

The construction of Asian Americans and Latina/os as alien to the United States has meant that Latina/o and Asian American histories have also been marginalized within discourses of United States nationalism. In his seminal work *Imagined Communities: Reflections on the Origin and Spread of Nationalism*, Benedict Anderson explores the reliance of modern nationalism on history, narrative, and selective amnesia. The secular nations that sprung from eighteenth-century revolutions, Anderson explains, relied on the idea of creating something new and breaking from the old ways of Europe, but they also relied on the careful construction of national genealogies. Embedded for the first time in secular and serial historical time, these nations required imaginings of fraternity and origins that preceded the foundation of the nation itself, even when the society was "fractured by the most violent racial, class and regional antagonisms," as in the nineteenth century United States.[71] Anderson argues that such covering over of the racial and class fractures of the past, explaining them, or erasing them entirely is part of the "characteristic amnesia" that accompanies the birth of modern nationalism, and narrative is the key mechanism by which this is accomplished.[72] Nations, like people, have a need for a "narrative of 'identity,'" for what cannot be remembered must be narrated.[73] In this view, the construction of history works back from the present moment, as the end must not only justify the means, it must also render the means into a meaningful and coherent narrative that extends backwards into history and forward in time according to the desired trajectory of the nation.

In the United States, the narrative myth of "a nation of immigrants," expressed most eloquently by President John F. Kennedy as justification for the immigration reforms of 1965, establishes the United States as a nation defined by democracy, openness, and freedom of choice. As Ngai has observed, it is an idea legally grounded in a relatively open process of naturalization (with major historical exceptions) and the principle that confers automatic citizenship to all children born in the United States; however, its rhetorical power is derived in large part from the ways in which it establishes the United States as exceptional and desirable, a place to which others come by choice to start a new life.[74] The power of this narrative obscures the historical origins of many Americans in circumstances of coercion and exclusion, not to mention the presence of Native Americans on the continent before the arrival of the first European immigrants. Ngai contends that the idea of a "nation of immigrants" was framed in terms of a Euro-American pluralism; Kennedy's published work, *A Nation of Immigrants*, included just two paragraphs on Asian and Latino immigration to the United States.[75] The implied European origin of the nation's immigrants, an ideal rooted in dominant images circulating since St. John de Crèvecoeur, had significant consequences for immigration policy, especially for Mexican (and later Central American) migrants, who began to appear symbolically as a racialized "illegal" foil for the "putatively legal, desirable, and freedom-loving European seeking entrance through the main gate."[76] It also tended to erase narratives of coercion, exclusion, and United States imperialism from dominant national histories.

Yet precisely because of these elisions, understanding Asian American and Latina/o histories in the United States is crucial to understanding the construction of the nation as a whole, both past and present. On the one hand, these histories are necessary to "write back in" the missing pieces of American history and remind us that the nation's pluralist origins have never been exclusively Euro-American or even solely drawn along the black/white binary. Rather, the long history of Latina/os and Asian Americans in the United States has been erased because it does not fit dominant nationalist narratives, much as the famous photograph of the "Golden Spike Ceremony," taken to mark the completion of the transcontinental railroad in 1869, deliberately excluded more than 12,000 Chinese workers despite the fact that they made up the majority of the Central Pacific Railroad's workforce.[77] Correcting dominant histories to include the Asian Americans and Latina/os who have resided in the United States for centuries, to establish that founding ancestors included Latina/o and Asian men and women, is an important step to countering current narratives of encroachment and nativism.

These missing histories include foundational narratives of Asian American and Latina/o achievement in the face of legal and social oppression, but they also include challenges that have shaped American society as a whole. Historian Gary Okihiro contends that while that minority "contributions" to American history are significant, the deeper significance of suppressed histories lies in the ways in which civil rights movements have changed dominant society; in the case of Asian Americans, he writes of their "opposition to the dominant paradigm, their fight against 'the power,' their efforts to transform, and not simply reform, American society and its structures."[78] Okihiro states that indeed, all "marginal" groups in the United States—he includes African Americans, Latinos, Native Americans, Asian Americans, women, and gay and lesbian groups in this definition—are the source of the "core ideals and values of the nation," their struggles a key part of the preservation and advancement of the true principles of democracy and equality.[79] As suggested by the title of Okihiro's 1994 book, *Margins and Mainstreams*, in this view so-called marginal histories are important not only to recognize the existence of minority groups, but because in fighting their legal and social exclusion, these groups have actively shaped mainstream American culture.

Asian American and Latina/o historical scholarship and literary production in the United States are thus engaged in a two-part project of historical recovery: the project of ripping aside "that veil drawn over 'proceedings too terrible to relate,'" to use Toni Morrison's exhortation to writers of color, and conversely, of documenting resistance, achievement, and the furthering of democratic principles through civil rights movements.[80] In addition to these important endeavors, Latina/o and Asian American cultural productions also *decolonize* history from inaccurate and damaging misrepresentations in dominant historical narratives. Here, I take the word "decolonize" from historian Emma Pérez's discussion of the "decolonial imaginary as a rupturing space, the alternative to that which is written in history."[81] For Pérez, writing about Chicana history in the U.S. Southwest, the political project of the historian is "to write a history that decolonizes otherness."[82] Historic images of the "yellow peril" or the "illegal alien" have been written into dominant histories in ways that misrepresent Asian Americans and Latina/os, casting them in the historic trope of outsiders to the legitimate nation. Latina/o and Asian American histories and literature decolonize otherness by contesting these historical representations. Literary critic Patricia Chu states that Asian American literary narratives both claim America for Asian Americans and engage in "scrutinizing or rewriting accounts of Asian ethnicities" that may be inaccurate or stereotypical.[83] For both Pérez and Chu, re-writing is an important political act. Whether writing against biased historical accounts or racial stereotypes in dominant culture, they view historical representation as a contested and colonized domain.

As part of the decolonization process, Asian American and Latina/o cultural productions often engage in interrogating the nation-state itself. In fact, given the remarkable heterogeneity of the very categories "Asian America" and "Latina/o" (in terms of gender, class, national origin, sexuality, age, generation, and language), many theorists define their use primarily in terms of strategic opposition to dominant national narratives. For example, cultural critic Lisa Lowe defines Asian American culture as an "alternative formation," a site "where the palimpsest of lost memories is reinvented, histories are fractured and retraced, and the unlike varieties of silence emerge into articulacy."[84] According to Lowe, because of its forced distance from dominant U.S. culture, Asian American literature forms a dialectical critique of national culture, challenging hegemonic views about nativism and assimilation, as well as silences about state violence and oppression. Latina/o studies theorists have proposed Latina/o cultural production, too, as a site of resistance and new possibilities for American studies. This critique emerges most strongly among Latina/o border theorists; in Gloria Anzaldúa's famous theorization of the United States-Mexico border, the space is both a "1,950 mile-long open wound" and a place for the uprooting of "dualistic thinking": a site of militarism and injustice, but also a site for healing the split between the white race and peoples of color.[85] Following Anzaldúa and others, Latina/o studies scholar José David Saldívar has posited that cultural productions from the United States-Mexico border engage in a critique of "linear narratives of immigration, assimilation, and nationhood" in American studies.[86] Indeed, Saldívar theorizes the border as a space of mixing, crossing, and resistance that calls into question the dominant trope of nationhood itself as a primary cultural organizer.[87]

In this vein, besides correcting historical erasures and misrepresentations, Latina/o and Asian American writers interrogate widespread ideas about collective national identity, including master narratives like the immigrant melting pot, manifest destiny, and American exceptionalism (the idea that unlike European nations, the United States has never engaged in imperialism). Asian American and Latina/o histories are thus central to understanding national identity in the United States as a contested domain. And because national identity is contested in the present, these histories are not only a matter of the past. The strategic exclusion of Asian Americans and Latina/os from national belonging in the legal realm and their depiction in mainstream representations as perpetual foreigners are integral aspects of current border politics, foreign policy, and domestic power structures. Historical theorist Hayden White writes that the invention of official histories has much to do with envisioning the present and the future of a group: "history is memory cultivated in the interest of producing a 'collective' past on the basis of which a collective identity can be forged."[88] Latina/o and Asian American histories challenge and complicate ideas of an American collective identity, in all senses of the term.

This challenge to nationalist myths and struggle against widespread cultural amnesia are crucial to the creation of a more equitable and just future. In *Memory, History, Forgetting,* philosopher Paul Ricoeur demonstrates the importance of creating debate by distinguishing between historical narratives and judicial narratives, especially with respect to the great crimes against humanity of the twentieth century. While a judge must establish a verdict, the work of the historical narrative is to produce a healthy *dissensus* and thereby educate the public; in the words of White, "the task of the historian is to keep memory of [events] alive, rather than to try to wrap them up, classify them, and return them to the archive."[89] Ricoeur observes that the defect inherent in the imaginary unity of nationalism is that it "erases from the official memory the examples of crimes likely to protect the future from the past and, by depriving public opinion of the benefits of *dissensus* . . . condemn[s] competing memories to an unhealthy underground existence."[90] By this token, the cultural productions of Asian Americans and Latina/os in the United States are an important part of producing a *dissensus* about American history. Some of the most vocal opponents of the racial profiling of Muslim Americans after the attacks of September 11, 2001, and the resulting "War on Terror" were Japanese American citizens recalling their racially motivated incarceration during World War II. Latina/o and Asian American voices can help the public recall past injustices, providing alternative views of the past that speak to the present and future directions of the nation.

And while much of this important work lies in the realm of historians, a key part of it cannot be done with facts alone. Literary theorist Paula M.L. Moya reminds us that racial schemas, or people's common understandings of how race and racism operates, are both emotional and epistemological. Borrowing from poet Lorna Dee Cervantes, Moya observes that "racism is not intellectual"; one might argue that no emotionally charged category is intellectual, including national identity.[91] Facts do not often change minds or deeply impact people's ideas about nationalism, racial hierarchies, or social inequalities unless those people have a personal stake in confronting their own often-erroneous beliefs. Literature written by racial others, however, can provide that personal stake; according to Moya, "literature's constitutive heteroglossia enables an author and a reader to engage dialogically at a deep emotional and epistemological level with the difficult questions around race, culture, and inequality that are inevitably raised by a good multicultural work of literature."[92] Unlike historical facts, literature has the effect of providing a reader with a radically different point of view and also providing him or her with an emotional stake in the condition and well-being of characters in a poem, play, novel, or story. Moya is not naïve; she does not posit that the "questioning" prompted by literature leads "ipso facto to epistemic and emotional growth."[93] Rather, reading such literature lays out conditions in which such growth can happen. Moya's theories do not only apply to white readers; they apply to any readers, including those from an "inside group" engaging dialogically with historical events and those who experience different forms of racial oppression. Whereas Moya is primarily interested in readers creating more accurate racial schemas in their everyday lives, I am interested in the ways in which Asian American and Latina/o works can help readers re-imagine the past and come to a new understanding of "America" as an ideal and a present-day reality. It is no accident that writer Toni Morrison's exhortation to writers of color to "rip aside that veil" calls to mind a veiled dancer or painting, not a work of scholarship. Art can convey emotional truths that the logical mind is reluctant to process.

For this reason, it is unfortunate that Latina/o and Asian American narratives tend to be taught separately from American history and literature as a whole—or banned from being taught altogether, as in the case of the 2010 Arizona Bill HB 2281 that prohibits ethnic studies classes in public schools. Both historical and literary narratives are key to a full understanding of U.S. national identity, now and in the future. As anthropologist Renato Rosaldo writes, "when one moves beyond [the] notion of our history and their history and sees instead interconnected histories that interact and mutually shape one another, subordinated histories and dissident traditions become a pathway, not to separatism and fundamentalism, but to a renewed vision of national histories."[94] Breaking down notions of "our" and "their" is the work of radical literature, to rip aside the veil that separates the subject from the object and to reveal to us not only the missing histories, but also why they matter.

REIMAGINING THE PAST: LATINA/O AND ASIAN AMERICAN COMPARATIVE WORK

LatinAsian Cartographies focuses on aspects of American history and structures of knowledge that have been uncovered and/or reinterpreted by Asian American and Latina/o authors, from nineteenth and early twentieth century imperialism to the effects of neoliberal economic policies at the turn of the twenty-first century. The literary texts I address have been carefully selected to emphasize overlapping and intersectional experiences and critiques. Thus, each chapter brings together one Asian American text with one Latina/o text of roughly the same time period, and the book moves chronologically through U.S. history and literature, ending with an Asian Latin American text that prompts us to consider the United States within a larger transpacific framework. The advantage of this method is that it allows Asian American and Latina/o literature to act as theory; in the words of literary critic Donald Goellnicht, I understand these texts as "theoretically informed and informing," repudiating the binary opposition that establishes texts by peoples of color as objects of inquiry on which Anglo/white theory is applied and instead acknowledging within them the epistemological "power usually reserved for European texts."[95] This method allows the reader to see the connections between these critiques and the historical amnesia on which so much of U.S. national identity is founded. Of course, such an approach cannot hope to be comprehensive. *LatinAsian Cartographies* should not be read as a catalogue of Asian American and Latina/o literature, but as a conceptual remapping of the Americas through the strategic juxtaposition of texts-as-theory.

With this intent, Chapter 1 examines ideologies of U.S. imperialism in Asia and Latin America through works by Filipino American author Carlos Bulosan and a "founding father of Chicano literature," Américo Paredes. Generations of scholars have insisted on the importance of imperialism in Asia and Latin America to U.S. history, yet dominant discourse in the United States continues to minimize or deny that it ever occurred. In Chapter 1, I explore the role of literary narratives in recovering the violence of U.S. imperialism in the Philippines and along the United States-Mexico border. The idea that the United States is a nation of voluntary immigrants—that there has been no American

Empire, or slavery, or indigenous presence—erases human rights violations in a way that both impairs our understanding of history and enables the suffering that occurs in the aftermath of imperial conquest. Anthropologist and physician Paul Farmer calls this suffering "structural violence," a violence that manifests itself in disease, poverty, and widespread inequality and depends on legitimizing structures of forgetting. I contend that literary texts can participate in what Farmer calls the "enterprise of ... fighting amnesia" and therefore delegitimizing structural violence.[96] The texts that I examine, Bulosan's *America Is in the Heart* (1946) and Paredes's *George Washington Gómez* (published in 1990, but written fifty years earlier), document the structural violence of U.S. imperialism in the Philippines and in the American Southwest, respectively, as well as the ways that it has been rationalized by those in power. They illustrate how Asian American and Latina/o literary texts have important roles to play in countering the erasure of this history from textbooks, political discourse, and public policies that deeply affect people today.

In the next chapter, I turn to expressions of patriotism in times of war. Chapter 2 focuses particularly on civil rights-era authors Luis Valdez and Mitsuye Yamada and their critiques of nativistic racism against Chicanos and Japanese Americans during World War II. This chapter addresses what legal scholar Angelo Ancheta calls "patriotic racism," a form of nativistic racism directed towards members of internal minority groups who are associated through cultural elements, social ties, and physiognomy to foreign—and enemy—combatants. Patriotic racism is linked with national identity, as it is an attempt by the dominant society to express national loyalty through racial hostility towards domestic groups perceived as foreign regardless of their actual citizenship status. Mexican Americans and Japanese Americans became targets for patriotic racism during World War II in the "zoot suit riots" and the wartime incarceration camps. In his play *Zoot Suit* (1978), playwright Luis Valdez considers the historical moment of the riots to be of key importance to the Chicano movement. Poet Mitsuye Yamada and other Japanese American writers also take the experience of the Japanese American incarceration to be pivotal to understanding the material, psychological, and social conditions of Japanese Americans in the United States. Chapter 2 examines works by Valdez and Yamada to demonstrate how the experiences of Latina/os and Asian Americans are often subject to intense pressures around questions of insider/outsider and loyalty/disloyalty, particularly in times of war or other external threat.

Chapter 3 explores structures of knowledge produced by Cold War military actions in Korea and Cuba through the critical novels of Susan Choi and Achy Obejas. Perhaps nowhere is national amnesia more evident than in the history of the Cold War, when the United States fought "secret wars" in Asia while militarily supporting so-called counterinsurgencies in Latin America. Chapter 3 investigates the role of Asian American and Latina/o writers in recovering these secret histories. It also explores the predicament of groups within the United States, such as Korean Americans and Cuban Americans, who have been subject to Cold War anti-Communist ideologies and dependent on these ideologies for visas, citizenship eligibility, and membership in the nation. Both Susan Choi's *The Foreign Student* (1998) and Achy Obejas's *Memory Mambo* (1996) recover secret histories of U.S. military involvement in Asia and Latin America; they also take on the task of deconstructing the Cold War as an ideological project, one that was (and is) complicit with internal racism, earlier imperial practices, and gendered violence. Partially based on real-life histories—the story of Choi's father in Korea and the U.S. South, and the story of Obejas's own immigration from Cuba to Chicago—these narratives question the bilateral framework of the Cold War. They tell the stories of individuals caught in the violent turmoil of war and its aftermath, emphasizing the disconnect between Asian/American and Latin/American experiences and the ideological justifications that have been put forth for U.S. intervention in these wars. Ultimately, this chapter argues that Asian American and Latina/o cultural productions since the last decades of the twentieth century act as important counternarratives to the Cold War rhetoric of containment, insurgency, and dualism that shaped twentieth century politics, served as justification for domestic racism and gender oppression, and continues to inform U.S. policy in the age of "wars on terror."

To re-imagine national identity is to pay close attention to borders; in Latina/o studies, border theory has sought to place the United States-Mexico border at the center of a new American studies paradigm. Chapter 4 examines how Latina/o and Asian American literature of the past few decades reconceptualizes U.S. geography in the age of globalization. In this chapter, I delve into Pratt's concept of the "contact zone" to examine the consequences of understanding the geography of the Americas as a *LatinAsian* contact zone. Chapter 4 addresses the way two writers engage the idea of the LatinAsian contact zone to critique the United States's role in globalization policies. Karen Tei Yamashita's *Tropic of Orange* (1997) reconfigures the United States within the geography of the Pacific Rim, a LatinAsian configuration that incorporates North and South America as well as Asia. In her novel, people and commodities move across both East/West and North/South borders; a sinister infant organ smuggling ring symbolizes the cannibalistic tendencies of U.S.-originated policies like NAFTA (the North American Free Trade Agreement). With "traffic" a key trope of this novel, *Tropic of Orange* demonstrates how a focus on the porous borders of the United States can place domestic power inequities in a critical global context. Cristina García's novel *The Lady Matador's Hotel* (2010) also focuses on the movement of people and children across borders; set in a fictionalized Guatemala, the novel connects U.S. involvement in military atrocities in Latin America to the availability of Guatemalan children for international adoption. Chapter 4 argues that the cannibalistic themes of these two novels are not a coincidence.

Rather, the literary depiction of the U.S. consumption of Third World children symbolizes the racial politics of the United States as a global presence.

The conclusion of this project explores the ways that LatinAsian cartographies can challenge national frameworks by placing the United States within a long history of transpacific migration between Asia, North America, and South America. In this final chapter, I discuss the stories of Chinese-Peruvian-American author Siu Kam Wen. Asian American literary scholars rarely consider works written in languages other than English, while Latina/o literary critics often overlook the texts and experiences of Asian Latina/o writers. As a LatinAsian American writing in Spanish, Siu forces a consideration of how U.S. history fits within a broader framework of "the Americas," in which transpacific migration has linked Asia and Latin America for more than four centuries. Specifically, I examine Siu's short story collection *El tramo final* (1988) as a text that rewrites the history of a multicultural Peru in dialogue with China and the United States. The works of Siu complicate ideas of Asian American and Latina/o identity, dislocating race from cultural and national identity and stretching our idea of Asian and Latina/o America to incorporate the migratory movements of Asians along both East-West and North-South axes. LatinAsian cartographies point to conceptual geographies that are in fact much larger and more fluid than the borders of actual nation-states.

In making these connections, I emphasize not only the similarities and intersections, but also the particularities of what are often very different historical experiences and trajectories. Since its inception during the civil rights era, the field of ethnic studies has found strength in a comparative approach that emphasizes cross-ethnic alliances; the demand for increased visibility and equal rights is one that can benefit from the solidarity of others. Yet there are also dangers in comparative work that this study seeks to avoid. Above all, my intention is not to elide the specific historical circumstances that make each group's experiences unique; besides the fact that such a move would render broad claims about these experiences moot, comparisons between historical incidents of violence run the risk of trivializing specific traumas if they imply an equivalence between traumas of very different scope or scale. It is this fear that prompted Latina feminist Cherríe Moraga to write in *This Bridge Called My Back*, "The danger lies in ranking the oppressions. *The danger lies in failing to acknowledge the specificity of the oppression.*"[97] In this passage, Moraga is addressing the different but intersecting oppressions that come with lesbianism, "being brown," being a woman, and "being just plain poor." For her, the price of ranking the oppressions, of failing to acknowledge their specificity, is exclusion along one or more lines; the stakes for developing an "authentic, non-hierarchical connection among oppressed groups" are high and can only be accomplished with an emotionally honest grappling with the oppression and division that can occur within groups.[98]

Any comparative effort must therefore avoid "ranking the oppressions"—that is, trivializing the cost of violence and racism by applying an arbitrary and non-equivalent scale—as well as homogenizing, or "flattening," experiences in a way that overlooks conflict between and within groups. How to avoid homogenizing experiences is a question that concerns comparative historians as well as feminists of color. Writing about whether one can compare or even contextualize the Holocaust, for example, Ricoeur argues that such work is possible only by acknowledging the "moral singularity" of events. Historical events can be compared, and done so in a way that enhances our present-day vigilance, as long as one recognizes there is an "absolute incomparability of the irruptions of horror. . . . There is no scale of the inhuman, because the inhuman is outside of any scale."[99] In other words, historical comparison does not preclude a stance that takes "irruptions of horror" to be morally singular, inexcusable, and unrankable. In this study, I follow Ricouer's distinction between moral and historical singularity. The deaths of up to a million Filipinos during the Philippine-American war were an event of moral singularity which we can absolutely condemn; yet discussing this war in the context of other U.S. imperial endeavors, including the U.S. invasion and occupation of the Southwest after the Mexican-American war, can shed light on the rhetoric and operations of U.S. imperialism and the ways it may be operating now and in the future.

Nor does comparative work necessarily elide differences and antagonisms, particularly class-based differences, between groups. In discussing comparative projects in African American and Asian American studies, literary critic Colleen Lye notes that many Afro-Asian comparative studies appear to be strategic responses to a growing class (and racial) divide between African Americans and Asian Americans in the United States: these often conflictual class relations expose "the limits of the notion of parallel minoritization at the heart of coalitional politics."[100] Sociologist Eduardo Bonilla-Silva reports, for example, that in polls many Asian Americans are found to hold negative attitudes towards Latina/os, while Latina/o attitudes towards Asian Americans were highly varied.[101] These tensions between groups are noteworthy but do not mean that comparative work is unproductive; the socially constructed nature of all racial and ethnic groups means that tensions can also be found within groups, especially groups as diverse as "Asian Americans" and "Latina/os." Here I turn to social scientist Laura Pulido's discussion of the ways in which minority groups in the United States experience "differential racialization." Comparative ethnic studies recognize that the process of racialization is specific, involving historical particularities, geographical variations, economic and labor conditions, and more.[102] Racialization can also change over time and vary by region within the United States. The task of comparative ethnic studies is to explore the complex ways in which differential racialization works within U.S. society. These complexities include relationships between minority groups as well as with dominant society; they include racial hierarchies but also points of intersection and alliance.

In this study, I seek to draw attention to potential sites of connection while acknowledging the differential racialization of Asian Americans and Latina/os in the United States. I also strive to keep each text historically grounded in its particular context. As such, I heed Lowe's call to "diversify our practices to include a more heterogeneous group and to enable crucial alliances—with other groups of color, class-based struggles, feminist coalitions, and sexuality-based efforts—in the ongoing work of transforming hegemony."[103]

PLURALISM WITHOUT FORGETTING: NEW HISTORICAL DESTINIES

As United States Census Bureau reports remind us, Latina/os and Asian Americans are the fastest growing "minority" groups in the United States. Given this fact, it is vital that we incorporate Latina/o and Asian American histories as an integral part of our national identity in a way that transforms current paradigms rather than simply "tacks them on" as exceptions to the rule. In *Imagined Communities*, Anderson considers race as antithetical to nationalism: "The fact of the matter is that nationalism thinks in terms of historical destinies, while racism dreams of eternal contaminations."[104] Understanding Asian Americans and Latina/os as outsiders to the nation places them in the category of contaminations, just as the framing of the growing pluralism of the United States in terms of a new "majority minority" threatens the historical destinies imagined by dominant national narratives. A recent study by two psychologists at Northwestern University examined white reactions to media reports about racial demographic changes in the United States. Far from ushering in greater tolerance and acceptance of others, these media reports generated the opposite effect: "we found consistent evidence that exposure to the changing racial demographics of the United States, and, most notably, the impending 'majority-minority' U.S. population leads White Americans to express greater racial bias."[105] Specifically, white Americans exposed to reports of a growing "majority-minority" were more likely to prefer interactions with other white people, express an anti-minority bias, and express more negative attitudes towards Latina/os, African Americans, and Asian Americans. In particular, the psychologists report that the act of grouping all "non-white Hispanic alone" residents of the United States into a monolithic "minority" group creates an increase in racial hostility towards all non-white racial groups by "evoking group status threat in White Americans."[106]

Latina/o and Asian American writers provide an important alternative to the stories of racial encroachment that have come to characterize twenty-first century dominant discourses of race. They take us inside the World War II incarceration camps, where being a "minority" is not an objective matter of numbers but rather a term enabling the abuse of power, and to the fields on the United States-Mexico border, where Spanish-speaking U.S. citizens live in a colonized space as outsiders on land they have tended for generations. In dialogue with each other and with dominant historical discourses, the authors in this study create a new "LatinAsian" view of the United States that emphasizes previously suppressed aspects of national history. Bringing home the impact of United States imperialism, nativistic racism during World War II, Cold War operations in Latin America and Asia, and the politics of national borders in an age of globalization, these authors intervene in dominant national narratives to re-imagine these histories from the perspective of those "looking out." Ultimately, they can disrupt narratives of racial encroachment, countering the discourse of the "majority-minority" and transforming our understanding of what it means to be American.

1 • UNITED STATES IMPERIALISM AND STRUCTURAL VIOLENCE IN THE BORDERLANDS

> Erasing history is perhaps the most common explanatory sleight-of-hand relied upon by the architects of structural violence. Erasure or distortion of history is part of the process of desocialization necessary for the emergence of hegemonic accounts of what happened and why.
>
> —Paul Farmer, "An Anthropology of Structural Violence"

> To survive in this new land, we have to forget. The stream changes course, and slowly our ghost catches up. Now we must remember in order to survive.
>
> —Marlon Fuentes, *Bontoc Eulogy*

The 2010 decision by the Texas Board of Education to eliminate the word "imperialism" from its U.S. history curriculum echoes historian William Appleman Williams's famous statement over fifty years ago that "one of the central themes of American historiography is that there is no American Empire."[1] Despite the work of generations of scholars, dominant discourse in the United States continues to minimize or deny the impact of imperialism in Asia and Latin America on United States history.[2] In the case of the Texas school board, the excision of "imperialism" and its replacement with the word "expansionism" suggests the neutrality and even inevitability of U.S. military aggression.[3] Gases and liquids "expand" according to the laws of nature. "Empire," on the other hand, contradicts the preferred nationalist discourse, which in the school board's terms is one that explicitly celebrates "the rich diversity of our people as a nation of immigrants."[4]

The idea that the United States is a nation comprised of voluntary immigrants—that there is no American Empire, or slavery, or indigenous presence—has consequences for national policy toward immigrants, as well as toward those frequently considered immigrants regardless of citizenship status.[5] Specifically, the denial of U.S. imperialism in Asia and Latin America erases human rights violations in a way that not only impairs our understanding of history, but also actively enables the suffering that occurs in the aftermath of imperial conquest. Anthropologist and physician Paul Farmer calls this suffering "structural violence," an excess of disease, poverty, and disenfranchisement that occurs when "inequality is structured and legitimated over time."[6] As a medical doctor working in Haiti, Farmer is particularly concerned with tuberculosis and AIDS as ways in which structural violence, as the legacy of imperialism, "harvests its victims"; disease, often seen as simply biological, is also both political and historical. In this chapter, I explore how literary texts can participate in what Farmer calls the "enterprise of . . . fighting amnesia."[7] Two literary texts of the mid-twentieth century, Carlos Bulosan's *America Is in the Heart* and Américo Paredes's *George Washington Gómez,* document the structural violence of U.S. imperialism, as well as the ways that it has been rationalized and strategically forgotten. They illustrate how Asian American and Latina/o literary texts have critical roles to play in countering the erasure of this history from textbooks, political discourse, and public policies that deeply affect the human rights of today's world.

Bulosan's semifictional autobiography and Paredes's semi-autobiographical novel are each foundational texts in their respective literary canons. E. San Juan, Jr., calls *America Is in the Heart* a "classic testimony," and Sau-ling Cynthia Wong notes its widespread use as a textbook in Asian American and ethnic studies courses.[8] As one of the only—and certainly one of the most comprehensive—first-hand depictions of Filipino American migrant labor in the early part of the twentieth century, *America Is in the Heart* is important as a historical document as well as an early example of Filipino American literature. Meanwhile, it would be difficult to overstate the importance of Américo Paredes's scholarly work to Mexican American border studies. In his monograph *The Borderlands of Culture: Américo Paredes and the Transnational Imaginary,* Ramón Saldívar describes a trip he took with the elderly Paredes in the late 1990s:

> Everywhere he went . . . when people heard he was coming, they crowded around him to shake his hand, speak with him, and touch the legendary man. This was true at the planned receptions on the campuses of the University of Texas at Brownsville and at Texas Southmost College. But it also happened spontaneously at the airport in Harlingen, at the Luby's Cafeteria in Weslaco, and at the high school in Edcouch-Elsa. I came to think of the five days in the Rio Grande Valley as the Américo Paredes Adoration Tour. For me it offered a glimpse of what it must be like to serve as a roadie for a rock star—a traveler in the shadow of fame.[9]

As Paredes's first novel, one recovered and published late in the scholar's career, *George Washington Gómez* has the distinction of predating his transformative studies of folklore and resistance among Mexican Americans along the border. Rolando Hinojosa describes it in an introduction to the text as "an historical work," a text that is "dated authentically" to express the views of a young writer who was to become one of the fathers of the modern Chicano movement.[10] Needless to say, there is no shortage of literary criticism devoted to these two canonical texts. Yet I suggest that examining them together takes each beyond its respective discipline; such a move insists that U.S. imperialism, occupation, and exclusion are not only Asian American issues or Latina/o issues, but integral parts of U.S. history as a whole. In his introduction to *The Ethnic Canon*, David Palumbo-Liu makes a strong case for "critical multiculturalism," an exercise that questions the historical basis of power structures in the United States.[11] Placing these literary traditions in dialogue highlights the importance of multiethnic literature in confronting silences within dominant U.S. historical narratives; it situates U.S. history within a global context, interrogating the politics of our national memory.

Although Bulosan and Paredes wrote in different states for different audiences, their contemporaneity also illustrates intersections between Asian American and Latina/o experiences in the early twentieth century. In Bulosan's text, the narrator works with Filipino and Mexican sugar beet workers in California, teaching about labor unions and finding a common language in Biblical freedom narratives.[12] Throughout *America Is in the Heart*, Filipino characters encounter Mexican workers laboring in similar conditions and subject to similar racial discrimination. In *George Washington Gómez*, a key scene also juxtaposes Asian and Latina/o characters, as it features a white doorman singling out Mexican American and Japanese American students for scrutiny according to the racial hierarchy of the time.[13] Although the Japanese Americans are ultimately deemed acceptable, while the darker skinned Mexican Americans are rejected, the scene illustrates the (often arbitrary) application of Jim Crow laws to both Asian Americans and Latina/os in the early twentieth century. Later in his life, Américo Paredes was to become even more intimately acquainted with discrimination against Asian Americans. Having married the half-Japanese daughter of a Uraguayan ambassador during his World War II military service in Japan, Paredes found his wife blocked from entry to the United States by Asian American exclusion laws. The couple made plans to settle in Mexico before the "law changed" and his wife became eligible to apply for a permanent visa.[14]

Bulosan's and Paredes's experiences with racial exclusion and discrimination distinguish their texts from other leftist, socialist-leaning literature of the 1930s and 1940s. These works, such as John Steinbeck's Pulitzer Prize-winning *Grapes of Wrath* (1939), focus on class exploitation and the lack of a social safety net for disenfranchised Americans; Marxist philosophy and socialist ideals were widespread literary themes in pre-McCarthy-era America.[15] Bulosan's and Paredes's texts extend this critique, drawing attention to the ways in which racial conflict can exacerbate conditions of exploitation. When the narrator of *George Washington Gómez* describes the Depression-related plight of the "people of Oklahoma, who were leaving their land, getting on their trucks and going west"—people who could be the "Okies" of Steinbeck's novel—he remarks on their relatively privileged position, observing that "to a Mexicotexan laborer, anybody who owned a truck was rich."[16] For Paredes, the Great Depression intensified injustice and oppression already experienced by Mexican Americans in the 1930s. Bulosan's class analysis is also complicated by race, as evident in his protagonist's ambivalence about joining the Communist Party. In *America Is in the Heart,* Bulosan questions whether communism is truly "relevant to the needs of the Filipinos in California," who could not own land, practice law, or become citizens.[17] Both Bulosan and Paredes felt strongly that the racial struggles of their people were an important aspect of their class stratification. For these writers, conditions of poverty were inextricable from racial hierarchies, and their works illustrate the ways in which racism has blocked traditional mechanisms of class mobility like education, property ownership, and political participation.

Reading these works, it becomes clear that U.S. imperialism in Asia and Latin America in the nineteenth and early twentieth centuries created colonial situations that complicated class relations and defied the standard immigration rhetoric based on voluntary European immigration. For Filipino Americans, immigration to the United States was inseparable from the history of the U.S. colonization of the Philippines; scholar Victor Bascara summarizes this relationship succinctly by borrowing the postcolonial catchphrase "We are here because you were there."[18] Mexican American border populations have also experienced a colonial/postcolonial relationship with the United States, along with the military occupation of the Southwest as a result of what the Texas School Board euphemistically calls "westward expansion." Bulosan's and Paredes's works resituate U.S. history within this global context, illustrating how literature can resist the erasure of this colonial legacy. They bear witness to the structural violence that occurs as part of the aftermath of imperialism—the lack of access to health care, adequate housing, or employment—and in doing so counter the silence on which these structures of violence depend. *America Is in the Heart* and *George Washington Gómez* fight structural violence by fighting amnesia, insisting that we remember U.S. imperialism in Asia and along the United States-Mexico border as events that haunt the nation to the present day.

EMBODYING THE COLONIAL PAST: CARLOS BULOSAN'S *AMERICA IS IN THE HEART*

When *America Is in the Heart* was published in 1946, Carlos Bulosan had already established a literary reputation in the United States as a Filipino American author. This was a rare achievement for a man of his background; unlike many early Asian immigrant writers, who came from wealthy Asian families, Bulosan was born into an impoverished family in the Philippines and migrated to the United States in the 1930s along with his brothers in search of employment. Hospitalized for years in Los Angeles County Hospital with advanced tuberculosis, he read extensively during his convalescence and credits this self-education for his success as a writer. This success was considerable; in 1943 Bulosan achieved national recognition for his essay "Freedom from Want," which was based on President Franklin D. Roosevelt's "Four Freedoms" speech and was chosen by the *Saturday Evening Post* as a companion piece to Norman Rockwell's famous illustration.[19] When Bulosan hastily drafted *America Is in the Heart,* his tuberculosis had become critical, and he had been told he had little time to live; "racing with death," Bulosan says he wrote six hundred pages of the book in just twenty-eight days.[20] Advertised as his autobiography, *America Is in the Heart* describes the author's early life in the Philippines and his migration to the United States as a laborer. Briefly, the text is comprised of two parts, the first describing the narrator's childhood in the Philippines, his family's growing poverty and struggles with illness, and his own early education within the U.S. colonial apparatus. The second, much longer part of the book describes his migration to the United States, chronicling in painful detail the racial discrimination, poverty, and despair experienced by many Filipino laborers during the early part of the twentieth century. Despite these grim events, the text is curiously idealistic. Juxtaposed with accounts of discrimination and lynchings, labor activism, and Marxist class analysis is the narrator's professed faith in America, his "desire to know America, and to become a part of her great tradition, and to contribute something toward her final fulfillment."[21] Thus, Bulosan's testimony of racism and litany of injustice ends with this statement: "I knew that no man could destroy my faith in America that had sprung from all our hopes and aspirations, *ever*."[22]

Literary critics and ethnic studies scholars have often struggled with the apparent contradiction between the text's scathing critique of racism and its emotional, patriotic appeals to an idealized America. Bascara aptly describes the text as "something of a Mona Lisa smile for Asian American studies," in that "its ultimately undecidable meaning provokes compelling speculations."[23] One such speculation considers the text a work of fiction rather than autobiography, enabling the reader to distinguish between Carlos, the naïve protagonist of the work, and Bulosan, the more cynical author. From the time of the book's publication, it has been evident that many events in the narrative do not correspond to the known events of Bulosan's life, and that the text is in fact less a strictly factual autobiography and more a "composite portrait of the Filipino American community,"[24] or more militantly, a "popular-front allegory" with the protagonist representing the 30,000 Filipino laborers in the United States.[25] Assuming this discrepancy is a deliberate move on the part of the author, Marilyn C. Alquizola insists that *America Is in the Heart* must be read as a work of fiction, one in which the ironic distance between the author, who describes horrific instances of racial oppression, and the narrator, who professes undying faith in America, is meant to provoke suspicion in the minds of its readers.[26] The appeal of this interpretive strategy is evident in the way that it not only accounts for certain life-narrative discrepancies, but also plausibly dismisses the text's assimilationist tendencies, framing them within a post-World War II publishing climate that would not have tolerated overtly anti-American sentiments.

The publishing climate certainly influenced the form of the book's critique. In Bulosan's posthumously published novel *The Cry and the Dedication* (1995), an American doctor in the Philippines fiercely confesses, "I hate the Filipino people," and a revolutionary replies that he understands why his Filipino American friend was bitter about white Americans: "Even in our own land you try to run our lives."[27] In 1946, the year that *America Is In the Heart* was published, there could be no such open references to the American occupation of the Philippines. Throughout World War II, the U.S. publishing industry was heavily invested in promoting ideals of democracy and antifascism that it wanted to characterize as "American" ideals. As part of this war effort, the heads of every major publishing house in the United States joined together to form the Council of Books in Wartime, a committee with the slogan "Books Are Weapons in the War of Ideas." Between 1942 and 1946, the Council of Books in Wartime sent more than 120 million books representing 1,180 titles to members of the U.S. Armed Forces, and over 3.6 million books to civilians in "freed European and Asiatic countries."[28] A 1942 letter sent by President Franklin Roosevelt to Council Chairman W. W. Norton illustrates the gravity with which this wartime mission was undertaken; Roosevelt wrote, "a war of ideas can no more be won without books than a naval war can be won without ships. Books, like ships, have the toughest armor, the longest cruising range, and mount the most powerful guns."[29] Through books, he stated, "we have appraised our enemies and discovered our allies." As part of this effort, Bulosan's own collection of stories about life in the Philippines, *Laughter of My Father* (1944), was radio broadcast to American troops around the world in an attempt to win sympathy for the Philippine allied forces in the Pacific.[30] In this publishing climate, the oft-repeated faith in America expressed in *America Is In the Heart*—and Bulosan's description of his battle against unjust landowners in the Philippines and the United States as a war against "fascism" rather than against U.S. imperialism or systematic racism—allowed the text to fit within approved wartime rhetoric.

It also placed the book squarely within a long-held American literary tradition of dissent in the name of patriotism. Cultural critic Sacvan Bercovitch has identified this tradition as the "American Jeremiad," a form of protest that simultaneously laments the faults of America while celebrating its ideals. It is a protest that is both ritualized and limited. As Bercovitch says of early American writers of the Jeremiad: "the dream that inspired them to defy the false Americanism of their time compelled them to speak their defiance as keepers of the dream."[31] For Bulosan, adhering to this American literary genre allowed him to express his own discontent at the violation of Filipino rights while pledging his devotion to an American ideal that existed, as he says in the book, not in real life but "in the heart." Within the structure of the American Jeremiad, there could be no direct reference to the Philippine-American War or the U.S. colonization of the Philippines; such critiques would undermine the ideal democracy that the United States had to represent during wartime. Yet critic E. San Juan, Jr., names the U.S. invasion of the Philippines as crucial to developing an interpretive framework of the novel, calling the Philippine-American War and its aftermath the repressed theme of the text, "what the bulk of this narrative wants to forget but cannot."[32] Understanding the context of the narrative within this theme elucidates key aspects of the text, including Bulosan's unusual identification with tribal Filipino peoples and his decision to use English "as a weapon" in his fight for justice. It also illuminates what I call the metatheme of the text: the structural violence that visits bodily harm on the characters in this memoir and prematurely ended the lives of Bulosan and many other Filipinos during this time period from poverty-related disease and violence.

The Philippine-American War officially lasted from 1899–1902, though fighting continued for years after President Theodore Roosevelt officially declared the war to be over. By all accounts, it was a particularly brutal war. Scorched-earth policies, mass concentration camps, and water torture were among the strategies employed by American forces who were daunted by the ability of guerrilla soldiers to draw from the nationalistic support of villagers. In 1901, the deaths of 54 American soldiers initiated what Philippine scholar Luzviminda Francisco calls a "reign of terror," in which General Jake Smith ordered his men into Philippine villages to "kill and burn, kill and burn, the more you kill and the more you burn the more you please me." General Smith defined the age limit for killing as "everything over ten," and ordered that the area be made a "howling wilderness" such that "even the birds could not live there."[33] Similar massacres in Panay and Batangas occurred in response to suspicions of insurgency, while detention camps for villagers resulted in thousands of deaths from disease and starvation. The atrocities committed in the Philippines by American soldiers during the war were so egregious that they met with massive opposition in the United States among organizations such as the Anti-Imperialist League and the Black Citizens of Boston. Politicians, worried about re-election, suppressed information about the war, with the result that it is now impossible to precisely pinpoint how many Filipinos died during the campaign. Francisco dismisses estimates of 250,000 as "chosen and repeated in ignorance"; based on U.S. military documents and conservative estimates of known slaughters, she puts the figure at closer to a million deaths or one in every five men, women, and children on the islands.[34]

Such an overt and brutal act of military aggression required substantial ideological justification, and indeed, racial ideologies in the United States and in the Philippines attempted to reframe and in many cases erase what had happened from the historical record. In remarks to a Methodist delegation on the eve of the war, President William McKinley describes spending a sleepless night praying to "Almighty God" about what to do with the Philippines after the Spanish-American War. Finally, the situation was revealed to him with the following clarity:

> (1) That we could not give them back to Spain—that would be cowardly and dishonorable; (2) that we could not turn them over to France and Germany—our commercial rivals in the Orient—that would be bad business and discreditable; (3) that we could not leave them to themselves—they were unfit for self-government—and they would soon have anarchy and misrule over there worse than Spain's war; and (4) that there was nothing left for us to do but to take them all, and to educate the Filipinos, and uplift and civilize and Christianize them, and by God's grace do the very best we could by them, as our fellow-men for whom Christ also died.[35]

McKinley's remarks reveal the interests of the United States in the Philippines, interests that were at once based on military strategy, economic policy (the Philippines were the gateway to China), and assumptions of racial superiority. His remarks also indicate the direction of future U.S. policy in the Philippines: once "pacified," the Filipino people were to be "civilized" through Christian education. In 1901, in a striking demonstration of the rhetorical connection between colonialism and education, the United States refitted a military transport ship to carry 509 American teachers to engage in this mission of "civilization" and "uplift." Calling themselves the "Thomasites," after the *USS Thomas* on which they crossed the ocean, these men and women saw their task as spiritual regeneration and approached it with missionary zeal.[36]

In this spirit, the United States soon established a colonial education system with the express aim of the "benevolent assimilation" of the Filipino. Philippine historian Renato Constantino describes the recasting of history for the Filipino student: "He had to forget his past and unlearn the nationalist virtues. . . . The new Filipino generation learned of the lives of American heroes, sang American songs, and dreamt of snow and Santa Claus. The nationalist resistance leaders . . . were regarded as brigands and outlaws. The lives of Philippine heroes were taught but their nationalist teachings were glossed over. Spain was the villain, America was the savior."[37] McKinley's plan of educational uplift strategically replaced the memory of a nationalist war, in which a million Filipinos were killed, with a narrative in which the United States had liberated the Philippines from imperial Spanish rule.

Meanwhile, within the United States, political leaders were emphasizing capitalist enterprise and opportunity to a public skeptical about the cost and morality of engaging in the colonial administration of a distant territory. The Philippine Exposition at the 1904 World's Fair in St. Louis was designed by President Theodore Roosevelt and then Governor-General William H. Taft to display the natural resources of the Philippines to an American public and to highlight the investment potential of "bring[ing] the two peoples together to promote friendly and trade relations."[38] More than 19 million people visited the St. Louis World's Fair, and by far the most popular exhibit was the 47-acre Philippine Reservation, which featured supposedly authentic villages inhabited by more than a thousand Filipino tribal peoples and guarded by Filipino soldiers. Steeped in the anthropological evolutionary theories of the time, the exhibits placed Filipino ethnic groups in rings of increasingly "primitive" villages; scientists were on hand to measure physical characteristics of the villagers, including skull size and shape, according to the scientific methods of the day. Historian Paul Kramer observes that the Fair's original intent, to portray the Philippines as a pacified and civilized nation—a good trade investment—was in fact defeated by its sensational depictions of "savages" that appealed to the public's touristic desires and made the exhibit a conflation of "spectacle, commercialism, and late-Victorian sexual repression."[39] This was particularly true of the Igorot village, which featured barely clothed men and women and scheduled displays of dog-eating for journalists and tourists.[40] On both sides of the Pacific, the United States was engaged in empire-building through racialized narratives of progress; while schoolteachers in the Philippines were recasting the United States in the role of democratic liberator, public discourse in the United States was identifying Filipinos with Igorot tribal peoples, who titillated public interest even while they apparently justified a mission of civilizing uplift.

The first third of Bulosan's *America Is in the Heart* takes place within the context of these racialized narratives. Thus, it is perhaps not surprising that the young narrator Allos (Bulosan's childhood name) begins his own colonial education with an American schoolteacher who rescues him from a poverty-stricken existence posing for white tourists' photographs.[41] Allos describes how he marked his face with dirt and stripped off his clothes to pass for an Igorot child in order to draw the gaze and coins of American tourists. Critic Kandice Chuh has called attention to the sexualized aspects of Allos's participation in this ritual; the tourists' interest in "young Igorot girls with large breasts and robust mountain men whose genitals were nearly exposed" clearly marks the intersection of colonial exploitation and sexuality.[42] Equally striking, however, is Allos's self-identification with Igorot tribal people, an alliance that is in tension with his later adoration of Miss Mary Strandon, his white American schoolteacher. Seeing Igorot men for the first time in a market place, he notes that they "had long black hair like mine."[43] Later, going to school, Allos is teased for having long hair and is called "Igorot boy" by his classmates.[44] When he is taken in by Miss Strandon and learns English along with an Igorot servant, Allos learns to identify with the story of Abraham Lincoln rather than with the "half-naked" Igorots posing for tourists; however, repeated comparisons between himself and the Igorots undermine this division. In his film *Bontoc Eulogy* (1995), Marlon Fuentes describes the ways in which Igorots functioned as a foil for the Western education apparatus. In the film, Filipino schoolchildren are taught to display scholarly interest in tribal peoples, but only from afar; Fuentes' narrator explains, "As a child, when I shared my interest in the Igorots with my friends from school, they asked me if I ever wore a G-string or if I danced around a blazing fire at night beating a brass gong or whether my mother served dog meat at home." This teasing, which reflects the narrative of progress so evident in the structure of the 1904 World's Fair, resonates with the teasing Allos endures when he is mistaken for an Igorot boy at his own school. Yet the Igorot people in *America Is in the Heart* are, in contrast, depicted with dignity and nostalgia.

Allos's identification with these people both resists his colonial education and draws attention to the absence at the center of the text, the U.S. invasion of the Philippines. Very early in the narrative, Allos describes an Igorot meal that his father cooks for him. This roasted shrimp delicacy that Allos shares with his father on a hunting trip is one his father learned to make from Igorot people in the mountains of Baguio. His father explains, "I lived with them when the revolution was broken in southern Luzon. I fought with them, and we were called guerrillas. Someday you will understand, and maybe when you grow up you will see my Igorot friends . . ."[45] This revolution remains unnamed in the text, but considering that the dialogue takes place between 1916 and 1920 and refers to events that predate the birth of Allos's oldest brother, it almost certainly refers to the Philippine-American war and its aftermath.[46] This supposed piece of cultural information is accompanied by an enigmatic reference to future enlightenment. But what exactly does Carlos's father mean when he says, "someday you will understand?" If young Allos is to understand guerrilla warfare, the Philippine-American War, and the initiation of U.S. imperialism by visiting his father's Igorot friends, such an illuminating event never occurs in the narrative. Nevertheless, progress towards greater understanding of some kind is a key theme in the text; critic Meg Wesling refers to the "dialectical tension of knowing and not knowing that structures the entire novel's progression, as the story that Carlos tells is one of his gradual enlightenment towards the knowledge through which he makes meaningful the struggles of his life."[47] Wesling also observes that this structure, based on the ideals of Western colonial education, contradicts the lived realities of Carlos's life much as the democratic ideals used to justify the invasion of the Philippines contradicted the realities of "exclusion, disenfranchisement, and forced, or 'necessitous' mobility."[48] Caught in a narrative structure that must emphasize educational uplift through stories of American heroes, Bulosan cannot explain what it is his father wishes when he says "someday you will understand." However, throughout the narrative of his life in the Philippines, Bulosan resists American colonial rhetoric by identifying his childhood persona with the Igorot people. In contrast to the World's Fair ideology that emphasized the "savage" aspects of Igorot tribal peoples eating dog meat for tourists, Bulosan's text associates Igorots with resistance to U.S. imperial invasion and a future revelation about this resistance.

This element of resistance is reinforced by Allos's growing desire to fight against the injustice that plagues his family. According to Allos, his conscious life began in response to his family's tragic loss of their land to moneylenders, a loss that occurs because the family must borrow heavily to send his older brother to school.[49] This schooling is ostensibly "free," but its true cost is high: "When the free education that the United States had introduced spread throughout the islands, every family who had a son pooled its resources and sent him to school."[50] Although the education was free, the room, board, and other living expenses were not. The brother, Macario, eventually graduates and gets a job as a schoolteacher, but his salary is too little, too late. The family's loss of their land was not unusual in the early years of the U.S. occupation; Bulosan explains, "There were no usury laws and we the peasants were the victims or large corporations and absentee landlords."[51] More than anything, this loss plunges the family into poverty and adversely affects their health and their very lives. As a child in the Philippines, Allos witnesses the death of his baby sister from a hemorrhagic fever, one of many relatives and friends whom Allos believes "would have lived if there had been a doctor to take care of them."[52] During his own lengthy convalescence from a fall—injuries sustained as part of the dangerous job of climbing coconut trees for the copra (coconut oil) industry—Allos begins to form revolutionary ideas. Inspired by a Bible that his brother has brought home for him, especially "the story of a man named Moses who delivered his persecuted people to safety," Allos asks whether there is a man like him in the Philippines:

> "Yes, Allos," he said. "His name is José Rizal."
> "What happened to him?"
> "The cruel Spanish rulers killed him."
> "Why?"
> "Because he was the leader of our people."
> "I would like to know more about Rizal," I said.... "I would like to fight for you, our parents, my brothers and sister."
> "You will suffer," Macario said.
> "I am not afraid," I said.[53]

Because the overall narrative is structured as a story of gradual revelation and self-discovery, this episode foreshadows the narrator's later suffering on behalf of his people. By paralleling his own life with that of José Rizal, a Filipino nationalist executed by the Spanish in 1896, the narrator effectively displaces the violence onto the "cruel Spanish rulers." In keeping with Constantino's description of the colonial educational system, Spain is cast as the villain in this dialogue, yet significantly America is not the savior. Although it remains unstated in the text of *America Is in the Heart*, the cruelty experienced by Allos and his family was inflicted by the U.S. invasion of the Philippines and the implementation of a colonial system that widely disenfranchised the Filipino peasantry. The "free" educational system that cost many peasants their livelihood, the absentee corporations (largely American-owned) that took their land, and the growing poverty that made health care inaccessible to the poor were part of the restructuring of Philippine society under U.S. colonial rule. Likewise, the suffering foreshadowed when Macario states, "You will suffer," is not inflicted by armed rebellion against the Spanish, but by poverty-related disease and racial violence in the United States.

The extent of this structural violence becomes evident during his life in the United States, not only in the racial discrimination Carlos and other Filipinos face—the low wages, the poor working conditions, the landlords that will not rent to Filipinos—but also in the two years that Carlos spends in the Los Angeles County hospital with advanced tuberculosis, likely contracted from another brother in the Philippines who died of tuberculosis around that time. As Bulosan has repeatedly stated in letters and memoirs, this time in the hospital was transformative in his "discovery of America" through self-education, yet it also foretold his death. After a woman from Social Services comes to interview Carlos extensively about his childhood poverty, she declares that he is "ineligible to go to a sanitarium for technical reasons," and an appeal brings a statement from a second social worker that "You Filipinos . . . ought to be shipped back to your jungle homes!"[54] When the doctor states that the refusal of further medical care is equivalent to "hanging him on a tree," the text deliberately links lack of health care to racial violence, evoking the specter of lynching to protest a possibly preventable death from tuberculosis. Before streptomycin, the only treatment for tuberculosis was rest, a healthy environment, and good nutrition, none of which are possible for Carlos; leaving the hospital, he cannot even find a decent place to live that will rent to Filipinos. Bulosan himself eventually endured eleven operations for lung and knee lesions before dying of tuberculosis, alcoholism, and exposure on a Seattle street at the age of 42.[55]

The deaths of Bulosan and his family members can be understood as structural violence, as part of conditions set into motion during the U.S. invasion of the Philippines. The rhetoric of civilizing uplift employed by President McKinley promoted a national amnesia about this invasion, and a publishing climate bent on promoting American democratic ideals silenced Bulosan on the subject of imperialism, except as practiced by the Spanish. However, it appears in his rejection from further health care: the "technicality" of his rejection is possible because of the ambiguous legal statutes that allowed Filipinos to migrate to the United States as nationals but left them ineligible for citizenship. It also appears in the social worker's implication that his disease is due to the inherent poverty of his homeland, rather than through structural conditions of colonialism, and the suggestion that he go back to his "jungle home." Ultimately, Carlos's illness and Bulosan's death are examples of structural violence that stem from the historical context of imperial conquest, war, and impoverishment, even while the denial of their basic human rights depends on the erasure of this context to operate.

Bulosan resisted this structural violence through his writing. In *America Is in the Heart*, young Allos meets an Igorot boy who is reading about Abraham Lincoln as part of his colonial education in the Philippines. This boy, Dalmacio, is reading about the former president of the United States in order to learn English, because as he says, "English is the best weapon";[56] this passage suggests that Bulosan believed resistance was possible even using the tools of colonial rule. Allos's father wished for him to meet his Igorot friends to "understand" something unspecified about resistance. Significantly, the first Igorot friend Allos names in the text points him to resistance through the English language. For Allos, who is to find his life's work in writing about racial injustice to Filipinos in the United States, his identification with Igorot tribal people shapes his later destiny as a writer. As a writer, he must conform to the tradition of the American Jeremiad, which dissents even as it re-affirms the ideal that is America. However, the fact of U.S. imperialism haunts the text. It resurfaces in Allos's identification of himself with the Igorots who fought in the Philippine-American war, his resolve to fight against injustice framed as Spanish imperialism, and his documentation of the structural violence that depends on erasure to inflict its heavy toll.

FROM GRINGO SCHOOL DAYS TO MILITARY ESPIONAGE: AMÉRICO PAREDES'S *GEORGE WASHINGTON GÓMEZ*

The U.S. invasion and colonization of the Philippines was an outgrowth of the Spanish-American War, and 1892 has been taken by many scholars to be the "moment" of U.S. imperialism. This time period saw the acquisition of several U.S. territories as spoils of war in Asia and Latin America, as the United States gained domination of the former Spanish colonies of the Philippines, Puerto Rico, and Cuba. Yet the idea of manifest destiny was not new, and Mexican American literature is an important reminder that the expansion of the United States into its new territories in Asia and Latin America was part of a much longer historical trajectory of territorial "expansion." A political cartoon from 1898 in the popular magazine *Puck* clearly illustrates this continuity. Titled "A Trifle Embarrassed," it features Uncle Sam and his star-spangled wife at the gates of the "U.S. Foundling Asylum," preparing to receive a basket of new babies. The

FIGURE 3. "A Trifle Embarrassed," illustration by Udo J. Keppler, in the August 3, 1898 edition of *Puck*. The original caption reads: "Uncle Sam—Gosh! I wish they wouldn't come quite so many in a bunch; but, if I've got to take them, I guess I can do as well by them as I've done by the others!" (Library of Congress, Washington, D.C. http://loc.gov/pictures/item/2012647587.)

bawling, dark-skinned infants in the basket, bearing the tags "Philippines," "Puerto Rico," "Hawaii," and "Cuba," are offered up to the United States by anonymous white arms tattooed with the words "Manifest Destiny." Inside the compound, older children identified as "Texas," "Cal," and "Mexico" dance in a circle, along with an unnamed child with brown skin and black braids, presumably representing the indigenous Indian population. The cartoon follows a visual strategy common in the late nineteenth and early twentieth centuries: depicting new territorial acquisitions as infants in need of paternal support and guidance. Significantly, the infants in the basket outside the gate are howling, their little faces contorted with misery, while the children inside the gates are playing happily, having already benefitted from U.S. patronage. The cartoon is also a perfect illustration of the ways in which the events of the Spanish-American War continued to follow a rhetoric already established in the conquest of the U.S. Southwest during the period euphemistically known as "westward expansion."

Américo Paredes's novel *George Washington Gómez* was finished in 1939, seven years before the publication of *America Is in the Heart*. The novel was not published until 1990, however, because of Paredes's difficulty in finding a publisher for the text at the time that it was written.[57] Not surprisingly, both Paredes and Bulosan had difficulty articulating their critiques of U.S. imperialism due to the publishing constraints of the time. Unlike *America Is in the Heart* but similar to Bulosan's later, posthumously published work, *George Washington Gómez* is overtly oppositional to U.S. imperialist policies and the hegemonic ideas that support them. Like Bulosan, Paredes was deeply aware of the structural violence that occurs as part of an imperial legacy. In his short story "The Hammon and the Beans" (published in 1963), Paredes writes about the death of a young Mexican American girl in the shadow of the U.S. military occupation of the Texas-Mexico border. The doctor, who ascribes her death to "Pneumonia, flu, malnutrition, worms, the evil eye.... What the hell difference does it make?" angrily claims that "in classical times they did things better. Take Troy, for instance. After they stormed the city they grabbed the babies by the heels and dashed them against the wall. That was more humane."[58] In Paredes's work, death and disease are explicitly linked to military occupation. In *George Washington Gómez,* however, the focus is on forgetting, as the novel demonstrates the ways in which educational systems have been complicit in rationalizing imperialism as a mechanism of colonial hegemony. From its opening scenes of border violence, which feature Texas Rangers terrorizing the Mexicotexan people, to its direct criticism of the Monroe Doctrine, the novel resists the easy narratives of westward expansion that so often characterize U.S. history lessons. An anti-heroic story, the narrative particularly illustrates the dangers of the deliberate amnesia that accompanies success in the dominant culture.

George Washington Gómez is the coming-of-age story of a young boy in the fictional town of Jonesville-on-the-Grande, which resembles Paredes's hometown of Brownsville, Texas. From the moment of his birth, the child is placed in the midst of conflict: "Born a foreigner in his native land, he was fated to a life controlled by others. At that very moment his life was being shaped, people were already running his affairs, but he did not know it.... Nobody had asked him whether he, a Mexican, had wanted to be born in Texas, or whether he had wanted to be born at all."[59] Ramón Saldívar aptly analyzes the birth and naming of the child in terms of the Althusserian interpellation of the subject, as each of his family members chooses a different name in order to fit him within differing social roles: religious, revolutionary, and familial/ancestral.[60] Finally, the child is given two names, George Washington, meant to signify a "great man among the Gringos," and Guálinto, his grandmother's mispronunciation of the Anglo name, which also suggests Indian ancestry. As Saldívar observes, each name "signals a different set of speech genres and promises to inscribe the child into a particular discursive history"; in particular, the binary opposition between the names George and Guálinto signifies the tension between the draw of the U.S. dominant culture and the resistance among the Mexican American people of the border.[61]

The naming of Guálinto Gómez and the early scenes of the novel are set in the historical time frame of 1915–1917, a period of extreme violence along the United States-Mexico border in Texas.[62] This violence occurred as a result of the execution and suppression of a planned uprising, the Plan de San Diego, which called for a rebellion to occur on February 20, 1915, against "Yankee tyranny." The uprising was to consist of an unusual coalition of "Mexicans, blacks, Japanese, and Indians" and aimed to create an independent republic in the Southwest spanning from Texas to California.[63] Despite the international context of the Plan, which included involvement by Mexican revolutionaries and German supporters, the rebellion seems to have been carried out entirely by Mexicans and Mexican Americans in Texas. According to historian David Montejano, it was rooted in "the prejudice and contempt that Mexicans in the region were subjected to," including the displacement of Mexican American landowners, vigilante lynchings, police abuses, and Anglo racism.[64] In fact, the rebellion resulted in an increase in violence toward Mexicans; raids were met with brutal repression by Texas Rangers, who conducted manhunts for the raiders and also engineered executions of "escaped" prisoners, burned homes of suspected sympathizers, and forced uninvolved Mexican ranchers into towns to better control them. Ultimately, the U.S. armed forces were called in—nearly all troops available for combat duty—and approximately fifty thousand troops were stationed along the border. This, combined with action by Mexican army and state officials, stopped the widespread violence, but sporadic executions of Mexicans and Mexican Americans continued. In all, between three hundred and five thousand Mexicans were killed in the Rio Grande Valley, as well as sixty-two Anglo settlers and sixty-four soldiers.[65] The rebellion also had consequences in terms of land ownership; the role of the Texas Rangers was not limited to killing and suppressing Mexican "banditry" but also paved the way for the widespread transformation of the land into Anglo farming communities, a transformation that ultimately further disenfranchised Mexican Americans along the border.[66] Moreover, as historian Benjamin Heber Johnson observes, it "ushered in a system of harsh racial segregation in south Texas, one explicitly modeled on the south's Jim Crow."[67] For Paredes, born in 1915, the uprising cast a shadow on his childhood in Brownsville, Texas; it lived on in folklore about Texas Rangers, or *rinches*, that Paredes was later to document in his scholarly work, as well as in the material consequences of racial segregation for Latinos along the border.

Despite the importance of the Plan de San Diego uprising to Texan history, it remains largely suppressed even in local histories of Texas. The title of Johnson's historical account of the rebellion, *Revolution in Texas: How a Forgotten Rebellion and Its Bloody Suppression Turned Mexicans into Americans,* emphasizes the obscurity of the incident. Researching the incident, Johnson questions the lack of historical recognition for one of the largest race riots in U.S. history:

> The uprising was thus violent, large, and had important consequences. Then why had neither I nor my parents, all of us natives of Texas and products of its school system, ever heard of it? . . . Although there were some sources available . . . it became clear that the events had been largely ignored by historians and the general

> public alike. In fact, I learned later, some of this was due to the fact that the Texas legislature deliberately suppressed evidence of the Texas Rangers' brutality, refusing to publish copies of hearings into their conduct and allowing Rangers to threaten their chief opponent in the legislature with death.[68]

The action of *George Washington Gómez* writes this segment of history back into the consciousness of the reader. As Johnson observes, the novel is ambivalent about the motives of "Los Sediciosos," some of whom are portrayed as righteous fighters, and some of whom are guilty of excessive cruelty.[69] However, the novel clearly indicts the Texas Rangers for their brutal suppression of the Mexicotexan people. Gumersindo, Guálinto's innocent, naïve father, is shot in the back by a Ranger in a staged "escape" attempt; guilty of nothing but a family association with rebels, Gumersindo is left to die alone in the dirt. With this episode, Paredes highlights the wanton killings of Mexicans by Texas Rangers and Anglo vigilante groups, a tradition of border violence and vigilante (in)justice that has continued into the twenty-first century in groups such as the Minutemen Project.[70] He also structures the novel in a way that emphasizes the importance of remembering this forgotten episode of history, for although Guálinto grows up in the wake of this murder, it is his father's dying wish that his son never know who had killed him, so that he can grow up with "no hate." The tension between the father's wish to erase this moment and the uncle's conviction that "he must know," that "it is his right to know," ultimately becomes the driving force of the novel.[71] Paredes places the reader in the same position as Feliciano, Guálinto's uncle, who knows the truth but cannot inform Guálinto; like Feliciano, readers are left to observe the further injustices that are perpetrated through the protagonist's ignorance of his own history.

Even more than reinserting a history that is largely absent from public awareness, Paredes uses the novel to criticize the rhetoric of violence that has accompanied misrepresentations of Mexican American history in the United States. If the Philippine-American War has been nearly erased from U.S. national consciousness, Mexican-American border conflicts are often framed as justifications for violence against Latinos living on the border; the notorious cry "Remember the Alamo" is a familiar example of this kind of polarizing remembrance. Paredes's later scholarly work, the enormously influential *With His Pistol in His Hand,* was written in response to what José David Saldívar calls "the ideological rhetoric of white supremacy [that] dominated Southern and Southwestern politics and eventually became institutionalized in state discourses, laws, and narratives regulating relations of whites with nonwhites, especially blacks and Chicanos."[72] This rhetoric generally sought to justify violence toward ethnic Mexicans on the basis of cruelties committed by Santa Anna during his battles with the independent Republic of Texas in the 1830s. In his scholarly work, Paredes observes the irony of judging Mexican people by the actions of a military dictator whose atrocities were resisted by Mexicotexans fighting for Texas and by his own men:

> The truth seems to be that the old war propaganda concerning the Alamo, Goliad, and Mier later provided a convenient justification for outrages committed on the Border by Texans of certain types, so convenient an excuse that it was artificially prolonged for almost a century. And had the Alamo, Goliad, and Mier not existed, they would have been invented, as indeed they seem to have been in part.[73]

The invention of Texas history, with its glorification of the Texas Rangers and corresponding denigration of Mexicans as "weak," "cruel," and "cowardly," was an injustice that Paredes dedicated his entire career to combatting. In the novel *George Washington Gómez,* the institutional consequences of these historical elisions and misrepresentations are most evident in Guálinto's school days. Through the drama of what he sardonically titles "Dear Old Gringo School Days," Paredes uses Guálinto's experience with state education both to challenge hegemonic interpretations of history and to demonstrate their material power in society.

Perhaps nowhere is state hegemony more apparent than in Guálinto's elementary school, which sorts children by language into "high" and "low" grades such that Mexican American children are guaranteed to fail. Presided over by the self-hating, malicious Miss Cornelia, a middle aged lady "of Mexican descent" with political connections, first grade for Guálinto is a torturous experience, during which he is encouraged to reject his knowledge of Spanish, even while enduring public ridicule for his parents' presumption in giving him the name of an Anglo president.[74] Within the school system, the Mexican American teachers are instrumental in the failure of their students; meanwhile, well-meaning white teachers are ultimately ineffectual. The text is both sympathetic and cynical about the white teachers at the school, who are described as "earnest young women from up north, too religious to join the GPA and too inhibited to become . . . vocal social reformer[s], but still entertaining some ideas about equality and justice."[75] When students question textbook portrayals of Mexicans as "treacherous and bloody" or statements that Mexicans are "dirty and live under trees," the Anglo teachers are in a bind:

> The teacher cannot criticize a textbook on Texas history. She will be called a Communist and lose her job. Her only recourse is to change the subject, telling a joke, something to make her students laugh. If she succeeds the tension is over, for the moment at least. Despite the textbooks, she does her best and that is often good enough.[76]

Yet the powerlessness of even the well-meaning teachers in the Jonesville school system makes them unwilling representatives of Anglo hegemony. Their best is often *not* good enough, as illustrated in the text by two incidents involving Guálinto's high school teacher, Miss Barton.

In the first incident, Paredes uses Guálinto's classroom as a vehicle to directly challenge the rhetoric of manifest destiny in U.S. historiography. After Guálinto challenges her paternalistic explanation of the Monroe Doctrine, Miss Barton explains that the United States was "acting as a big brother to a weaker nation." She utilizes the image of a bully taking candy to emphasize this point, saying "suppose that next door to you lives a little fellow. He's about to eat a piece of candy when suddenly a big boy your size comes into the little boy's yard and tries to take his candy away from him. What would you do? You would jump over the fence and drive the bully away, wouldn't you?"[77] This explanation, though couched in childish language, is entirely consistent with the political rhetoric of the time period, as in the political cartoon portraying territories and future acquisitions as infants to be looked after by "Uncle Sam." Yet Guálinto turns the analogy on its head when he sarcastically replies, "Sure . . . and after I drive the big bully away I take the candy from the little fellow and eat it myself."[78] Guálinto's engagement with Miss Barton demonstrates the ways in which paternalism is another form of power. His challenge to dominant historical interpretation highlights the hypocrisy behind the Monroe Doctrine's promises of paternal protection, as well as the illogic of manifest destiny's rationale of conquest in the name of enlightenment.

More than any other moment in the novel, this scene identifies the importance of Latina/o literature in redefining U.S. history. Even as Bulosan's mention of José Rizal implicitly questions the justice of U.S. imperialism in Asia, Paredes's description of the Monroe Doctrine overtly questions the rationalization of U.S. occupation of the Southwest. This challenge is especially acute in the context of early historiographies of the Mexican-American War. According to historian Richard Griswold del Castillo, the rhetoric of manifest destiny was not only employed by politicians in the nineteenth century to justify the war itself, but it was repeatedly invoked in subsequent interpretations of the war and its concluding legal document, the Treaty of Guadalupe Hidalgo. Early histories of the Mexican-American War reflected this rhetoric by casting the border dispute that began the war as an act of Mexican aggression against the United States; as Griswold del Castillo observes, their interpretation of the border's location was only valid according to a logic that traced the land back to French occupation.[79] In other words, because the Mexican congress had never acknowledged the Rio Grande to be the border between Mexico and the United States, Mexico's "invasion" of the United States could only make sense if the United States discounted the validity of Mexico as a sovereign nation, instead relying solely on prior treaties with France and Spain. Histories written in the early twentieth century took this logic even further. Justin Smith's two-volume *The War With Mexico*, for example, published in 1919, concluded that the war was both "beneficient" and "reasonable" on the part of Americans, given the moral result of a lack of civilization in Mexico: "Being what they were, they had forfeited a large share of their national rights."[80] The assumption of the moral superiority of the United States, along with the presumption that European powers had the sole right to dictate national borders—that they were the "big brothers" and other nations the "children"—colluded to form the dominant historiography of the time.

Guálinto's challenge to this historiography thus directly addresses the terms of his own experience as a Mexican American child growing up in formerly Mexican territory. Keeping the metaphor of "big brothers" and "children," he subverts the moral authority of protectionism by recasting the United States in the role of a "bully" taking candy from other children; moral authority becomes greed, acquisition for the sake of material gain rather than benevolent enlightenment. In this scene, the U.S. education system, far from asserting complete hegemony over the students, is revealed as weak in the face of Guálinto's superior logic. When the class is over, Miss Barton sits staring, "the tired look in her eyes more pronounced than usual," while in class she soldiers on, congratulating Guálinto on his debating skills and "gaily" saying, "It's nice to discuss things if we do it nicely."[81] Here, the repetition of the vague word "nice" demonstrates the teacher's linguistic and ideological impotence in the face of the glaring contradictions of dominant historical narratives.

While Guálinto successfully challenges the Monroe Doctrine in school, outside of the classroom the impotence of his well-meaning teacher reveals the collusion of this rhetoric with the institutional racism of Depression-era Texas. When the Mexican American students are barred from entering the restaurant Miss Barton has chosen as the site of their senior class party, a pseudo-Mexican restaurant catering to white tourists, Guálinto is confronted with the reality of Mexican American disempowerment. In this instance, the teacher's outraged demands to talk to the manager end in tears; she has no power to change the situation, and she lacks the strength of character to call off the whole party. Reduced to giving the Mexican American students their money back, she "stood looking after them, her handkerchief to her mouth. Then she blew her nose and went inside."[82] Guálinto, whose light skin enables him to pass for white, joins the Mexican American students in solidarity, but they remain shut out of their own graduation party. The rhetoric that divides him politically from the white students may be easily dismantled with logic, but the consequences of that rhetoric—the disenfranchisement of Mexican Americans in the land of their ancestors—are not so easily dismantled. After this incident, Guálinto is haunted by nightmares of being chased through the chaparral, "running, running, pursued by a mob of people, all of them slavering like mad dogs and howling 'Alamo! Alamo! Alamo!'"[83] The Alamo, in white supremacist rhetoric a symbol of U.S. entitlement to Mexican land, here becomes a symbol for U.S. aggression against Mexico and Mexican Americans. Thus, although Guálinto has the admirable ability to challenge the well-meaning Miss Barton, her impotence in the face of institutional racism and her unwillingness to fight the rhetoric of manifest destiny ultimately undermine his classroom victory. The U.S. education system, for Guálinto, is not an empowering experience. Throughout the ironically titled section "Dear Old Gringo School Days," Guálinto's growing racial consciousness is countered both by school policies designed to disenfranchise Latinos and by teachers whose understanding of U.S. history and society is either actively hostile or passively ineffectual.

This power of the text to demonstrate the cultural hegemony of dominant historical narratives is reinforced in a surprise ending in which Guálinto betrays his people by becoming a counter-intelligence spy for the U.S. military. In the last pages of the novel, Guálinto even changes his name in response to the racist logic of his father-in-law, a former Texas Ranger, who complains: "You look white but you're a goddam Meskin. And what does your mother do but give you a nigger name. George Washington Go-maize."[84] By legally eliminating Washington from his name, Guálinto capitulates to a logic that once again associates his father's dream with presumption, this time ascribing the dream to African Americans, who are at the same time dismissed with a racial epithet. By also ridding himself of the nickname Guálinto, the mature George rejects his Mexican-Indian heritage as well. Thus, with one legal name change, the protagonist betrays his father's dream, rejects any racial solidarity with African Americans, and "whitens" any Indianness his name may suggest. Even worse, the fact that he makes this change in response to his father-in-law's comments signifies that he has chosen the beliefs of the Texas Ranger over his own father, who was murdered by a Ranger. The magnitude of this betrayal is such that despite clearly autobiographical elements, during his lifetime Paredes vehemently rejected any identification of the novel as autobiography, for of course Paredes himself was a self-described "fiery, loud radical."[85]

The abruptness of the last chapter, in fact, begs the question: why end the novel in this way at all? Ramón Saldívar characterizes it as a deliberate revision of the European model of a bildungsroman: "Like the hero of classical nineteenth-century bourgeois narrative, Guálinto's narrative is one of emergence as he undergoes an education in moral choice."[86] Unlike a classic coming-of-age tale, however, Guálinto's moral choice is destabilized by the social conditions of structural racism along the United States-Mexico border in the early twentieth century. This reading is consistent with the idea of Guálinto's interpellation into society, which was symbolized by the multiplicity of his names. It also places *George Washington Gómez* in the position of subverting the European genre of bildungsroman by making his coming-of-age profoundly dissatisfying to the reader. Significantly, this destabilization occurs precisely at the point of Guálinto's acceptance of the dominant education system: his decision to go to college.

The turning point occurs at Guálinto's graduation, the commencement speech for which is given by K. Hank Harvey, a white American scholar who is considered "the foremost of authorities on the Mexicans of Texas."[87] Harvey, who does not speak Spanish, fulfills an economic need for the state of Texas "to point out the local color, and in the process make the general public see that starving Mexicans were not an ugly, pitiful sight but something very picturesque and quaint, something tourists from the North would pay money to come and see."[88] Invited by the school to speak to the graduates, Harvey exhorts them to remember "the names of Sam Houston, James Bowie, and Davey Crockett," to "remember the Alamo wherever they go," and to emulate the example of previous patriots who have "forever erased Mexican cruelty and tyranny from this fair land."[89] The figure of Harvey is based on the real figure of J. Frank Dobie, a Texan historian whose work reinforced negative stereotypes of Mexicans and enshrined the Texas Rangers as heroes in the dominant U.S. imagination. In later years, Paredes spoke almost fondly of Dobie, calling him a "lovable, nice old fraud."[90] This term of endearment does not, however, mitigate the criticism inherent in the label "fraud," and it is significant that this thinly fictionalized portrait of Dobie, written before Paredes had met the man, was left unchanged in 1990 when Paredes submitted the work for publication. Clearly, Dobie/Harvey's work is emblematic of some of the most damaging representations of Mexican Americans, and Guálinto's response to Harvey's speech indicates his utter rejection of these stereotypes. When Guálinto walks out of the auditorium, calling the principal a "sonofabitch" and avowing that he "never want[s] to see him or any of them again," he equates the state education system with the Anglos who have taken his family's land, abused his sister, cheated his uncle, and caused the death of his other uncle.[91] His rejection of state education is a rejection of state hegemony.

Yet this equation of state education with the hegemonic oppression of Mexican Americans causes a narrative impasse when Guálinto, having learned the truth about his father's death, promises his uncle to fulfill his father's last wish to become a "leader of his people." Without any knowledge of how his father died, Guálinto assumes that leadership requires a college education and official credentials, which, in turn, requires contacting the high school principal who will support his application. In effect, it requires turning around and metaphorically walking back into the auditorium still ringing with the words of K. Hank Harvey, the racist historian. Thus, according to the narrative structure of the novel, accepting college entails accepting the dominant view of U.S. history, the very one that a younger Guálinto has fought in the classroom. The irony of the novel is that through this acceptance, Guálinto necessarily loses the ability to become a true "leader of his people"; he has put himself on the path that leads to military enforcement of the hegemonic idea of the border as one that requires security against sedition. Oedipus-like, in trying to fulfill his father's dying wish, he has transformed himself into the very agent of his father's death, a national form of the Texas Ranger.

The enforced ignorance about the military occupation of the U.S. Southwest throughout the novel resonates with Bulosan's necessary suppression of military action in the Philippines in response to the requirements of the U.S. publishing industry. While Carlos reframes his resistance to this occupation as a generalized resistance against oppression, Guálinto is haunted by dreams and resurfacing memories that are opposed to his new, official identity. His most vivid dream is one in which he recreates the Battle of San Jacinto, routing both Santa Anna and Sam Houston and ensuring that "Texas and the Southwest will remain forever Mexican."[92] The text soon reveals that Guálinto's dream of becoming a Mexican American hero is actually the recreation of the daydreams he has suppressed in his everyday life; the dreams are in fact memories. Significantly, the desires he has suppressed are directly antithetical to his current existence. He dreams of building an arms factory that would defeat the U.S. military and "reconquer all the territory west of the Mississippi River and recover Florida as well," even as he works for the U.S. military to keep anything of the sort from happening. Similarly, he dreams of an "enormous, well-trained army that included Irishmen and escaped American Negro slaves" even as he officially changes his name to erase any possibly association with African Americans.[93] This is the power of literature: Guálinto cannot lead his people by conforming to the sanctions of the state education system, but Paredes *can* craft a novel in which even the hero (or antihero) is haunted by his betrayal.

EDUCATION, HISTORY, AND NATIONAL IDEOLOGIES

Both *America Is in the Heart* and *George Washington Gómez* demonstrate the ways in which the history of U.S. imperialism in Asia and Latin America has been largely erased from national consciousness. In the case of the Philippine-American War, this "collective amnesia" was a deliberate response of the U.S. government to a costly, controversial war and an attempt to downplay atrocities committed by U.S. troops in the Philippines. The authors of an exhibit and book of political cartoons of the time conclude that "Forgetting was officially sanctioned so that a war that was at least fifty times more costly in human lives than the Spanish-American War could be diminished in American textbooks, in the rare cases of its mention, as only an 'insurgency.' . . . Soon, Americans would only remember a ten-week war with Spain while a fifteen-year war in the Philippines would fall off the pages of history textbooks."[94] The invasion of the Philippines, accompanied by the deaths of up to one million Filipino people, has been relegated to a footnote in history, replaced by the more anti-imperialist narrative of the Spanish-American War as well as by the rhetoric of racial progress that naturalized American colonization of the Philippines through exhibits like the 1904 World's Fair in Saint Louis. Imperialism in Latin America has fared no better, despite the continuing jurisdiction of the U.S. federal government over Puerto Rico and the incorporation of formerly Mexican lands into the states of Texas, New Mexico, Arizona, California, and Colorado. In the case of Mexican

Americans of the border region, historical references too often omit any reference to U.S. imperialism, resistance, or institutional racism, dwelling instead on limited understandings of border history; thus, for almost two centuries, Santa Anna's actions at the Alamo have been used to justify discrimination and violence against Mexican Americans.

Asian American and Latina/o literary texts have the power to rewrite dominant historical narratives to insist on the importance of imperialism in shaping the United States ideologically, geographically, and demographically. In Filipino American literature, U.S. imperialism has become an increasingly evident theme, from Jessica Hagedorn's novel *Dogeaters* (1990), which juxtaposes imperialist historical records with stories of extreme corruption among the U.S. and Filipino elite, to Cecilia Manguerra Brainard's novel *When the Rainbow Goddess Wept* (1994), which portrays U.S. support of the Philippines in World War II as a continuation of earlier colonial policy.[95] Carlos Bulosan's *America Is in the Heart,* one of the first Filipino American texts and an integral part of the Asian American literary canon, is not openly critical of U.S. imperialism. Published in the fervently patriotic post-World War II years, it aims its political critique at the "fascism" evident in policies of land ownership in the Philippines and the anti-union laws in the United States. Yet Bulosan's description of his family's poverty and the dispossession of their land in the Philippines, along with his own disability and death from poverty-related disease, counter the rhetoric of civilizing uplift that accompanied U.S. invasion and administration of the islands. Composed within the framework of an American Jeremiad, and unable to articulate a direct resistance to U.S. imperialism, the text nevertheless draws attention to the hollowness of U.S. strategies of "benevolent assimilation." By identifying with Igorot resistance to the U.S. invasion of the Philippines and by documenting the structural violence that accompanied the legacy of imperialism, the narrator of *America Is in the Heart* emphasizes his own role as revolutionary writer, using English as his own weapon in a time when the prevailing idea was that books were weapons in the "war of ideas."

Latina/o literature, too, has seen an abundance of recent commentaries on U.S. imperialism in Latin America and the Commonwealth of Puerto Rico, from Esmeralda Santiago's pointed description of colonial "hygiene" lessons in *When I Was Puerto Rican* (1994) to Gloria Anzaldúa's influential exploration of United States-Mexico border violence in *Borderlands/La Frontera: The New Mestiza* (1987). Américo Paredes's *George Washington Gómez* was one of the first works of Latina/o literature to overtly question U.S. imperialism. Not only does it reinsert one of the nation's largest race riots, the rebellion of the Plan de San Diego, back into the narrative of U.S. history, but it emphasizes the ways in which misrepresentations of the Mexican-American War and preceding events like the Battle of the Alamo have been used to justify violence against Mexican Americans. Through the protagonist Guálinto, Paredes challenges the rhetoric of manifest destiny, even while he demonstrates the power it has over contemporary lives along the border. Like *America Is in the Heart,* Paredes's novel also indicts the United States for erasing the fact of imperialism from national consciousness. While Bulosan's protagonist evokes "faith in America" despite the author's imminent death from tuberculosis and alcoholic despair, Paredes's protagonist joins forces with U.S. military efforts in "border security" despite his father's death at the hands of Anglo "security" forces. Both texts critique the nationalist ideology displayed by a U.S. colonial education system.

Recent efforts in Texas and Arizona to erase imperialism from school curricula illustrate that the effort to forget the Philippine-American War, Mexico-United States border politics, and a history of imperial policies dating back over 150 years continues well into the twenty-first century. The juxtaposition of Asian American and Latina/o literary texts demonstrates that this erasure has been a concern of multi-ethnic literature since at least the Great Depression. If foundational works of the Asian American and Latina/o literary canon emphasize the limitations of the Western educational apparatus in the formation of "ethnic" subjects, then this comparison has something important to say about the role of state education in forging hegemonic structures of race in the United States. The fact that this hegemony is predicated on the deliberate forgetting of imperialism makes Asian American and Latina/o literature crucial to the project of questioning the politics of U.S. national memory.

2 • BATTLE ON THE HOMEFRONT: WORLD WAR II AND PATRIOTIC RACISM

To decide which is the "greatest generation" involves a double choice. One is the choice of a particular time period. The other is the choice of who will represent that time period, that generation. Neither is decided arbitrarily, but rather on the basis of one's political philosophy.

—Howard Zinn, "The Greatest Generation?"

In *The War Complex: World War II in Our Time*, cultural critic Marianna Torgovnick posits that the way we remember war intensifies cultural patterns of memory-work, emphasizing some events while distorting or omitting others even when the elided events are well-known to the public. Torgovnick refers to these ellipses as history "hiding in plain sight"; they are events that are documented but never register in public awareness because they contradict established patterns of cultural memory.[1] For World War II, cultural memory in the United States focuses on specific tropes, including D-Day, the fight against totalitarianism, and the Holocaust as a Nazi crime against humanity: "these events and ideas form part of America's image of itself, frequently cited in public discourse and often memorialized. They place Americans in virtuous, heroic roles—how we like to think of ourselves and present ourselves to the world, even at those times when the United States has been a belligerent and not-much-loved nation."[2] In contrast to the war in Vietnam or other military conflicts of questionable moral justification, World War II was the "good war"; it is remembered as an effort fought for a clear and just cause, to defeat the dangerous fascism of Nazi Germany and defend the nation against the military aggression of imperial

Japan.[3] This nationalist nostalgia has only deepened as the generation of World War II survivors reaches the end of their natural lifespan, and those who remember them hasten to pay homage to their wartime sacrifices. Dubbed the "Greatest Generation" by journalist Tom Brokaw, the men and women who lived through World War II have been the subject of best-selling nonfiction books, television miniseries like HBO's *Band of Brothers* (2001), and award-winning movies like *Saving Private Ryan* (1998). The term "Greatest Generation" has entered into the general lexicon in the United States, along with Brokaw's sweeping rhetoric about the "men and women whose everyday lives of duty, honor, achievement, and courage gave us the world we have today."[4] World War II has become a sacred part of our nation's past.

But what was the "good war" for those who were not generally considered Americans, despite their official citizenship? Who qualified as a member of the "Greatest Generation," and who qualifies even today in narrative accounts of the war? Journalists like Brokaw occasionally acknowledge the experiences of African Americans, Asian Americans, Latina/os, and Native Americans in separate chapters or episodes. In his book *The Greatest Generation,* Brokaw admits that "They [the Generation] weren't perfect" and that "They allowed McCarthyism and racism to go unchallenged for far too long."[5] However, such statements ironically recognize the injustice of racism while disallowing racial and ethnic minorities from constituting a part of the "they" of the "Greatest Generation." They draw upon a rhetoric, long-held in the United States, that relegates nonwhite characters to supporting roles that exist solely to teach, reflect, or demonstrate important characteristics of a white protagonist. Toni Morrison famously theorizes this phenomenon as "playing in the dark," when people of color narratively "ignite critical moments of discovery or change or emphasis in literature not written by them,"[6] and Sau-ling Cynthia Wong calls it the "psychospiritual plantation system" of narrative.[7] Certainly, in the wave of World War II nostalgia that has swept the United States in recent years, a psychospiritual plantation system is at work shaping how we remember the narrative of United States history.[8] Thus, even while Brokaw dedicates a section of his book to stories of citizens who suffered racism at home while fighting fascism abroad, he names the section "Shame," a term that either reflects the shame of the nation (if the nation is defined by its white leaders) or the shame of the actual people featured in the rest of the book—for example, the all-white cast of men and women in the "Heroes" section. Either way, the experiences of minorities in the war, however respectfully related, are relegated to a small and nondefining part of the overall story. Ultimately, in the grand historical narrative that constitutes popular understanding of World War II in the twenty-first century, the violation of the civil rights of African Americans, Asian Americans, Native Americans, Latina/os, and other ethnic minorities constitutes a heroic flaw, a shortcoming of the nation and the heroes who make up the "Greatest Generation."

Latina/o and Asian American literature challenges the default assumption that the so-called greatest generation is a (somewhat flawed, but still greatest) Anglo white generation. More importantly, it challenges the very nature of how we understand racism and injustice. As the works of writer-activists like Luis Valdez and Mitsuye Yamada demonstrate, the racism experienced by Asian Americans and Latina/os during World War II was not limited to the painful exclusion, lack of opportunity, and hostile environment suffered by all racialized minorities at the time. Rather, the wartime intensification of nationalistic fervor resulted in the emergence of what legal scholar Angelo Ancheta calls "patriotic racism," a focused hostility directed specifically at those considered "alien" to the nation. Ancheta defines patriotic racism as "a peculiar and especially deep-seated form of nativistic racism."[9] This racism is based on the association of an internal minority group with values, social ties, and biological connections to "foreign" elements. It is rooted in the fear of an enemy within, whether that be a literal enemy nation during a time of war, or a more figurative enemy during times of economic uncertainty. As Ancheta observes, nativistic or patriotic racism does not fit within the model of a "black-white framework" of understanding race; indeed, spokesmen for patriotic racism often use this framework in an attempt to forge black-white alliances against Latina/os or Asian Americans.[10] However, it is increasingly important to understand race in ways that encompass nationalistic, nativistic, or "patriotic" racializations of Latina/os, Asian Americans, and others (such as Muslim Americans during the extended War on Terror) as these characterizations become central to national debates about immigration, terrorism, and economic competition with China. Latina/o and Asian American literature about World War II helps us place patriotic racism within the framework of our understanding of racializations in the United States. It also helps reframe our national memory of World War II in ways that do not relegate minority experiences to a single chapter or a heroic "flaw" but question the very relationship between patriotism and injustice, between love of country and hatred of others, and between national ideas of belonging and exclusion.

Like Bulosan and Paredes before them, playwright Luis Valdez and poet Mitsuye Yamada are activists as well as scholars. The son of Chicano migrant farm workers in California, Valdez has become a legendary figure in Chicano studies as the founder of El Teatro Campesino (the Farmworker's Theatre), a group created in 1965 to raise awareness of social and political issues that affect Chicanos in the United States.[11] As part of the cultural movement associated with the civil rights era of the 1960s and 1970s, Valdez's plays were written to protest the exploitation of farm workers, inhumane working conditions, and violence against Chicanos.[12] *Zoot Suit*, which first opened in 1978, particularly examines the infamous "zoot suit riots" that began in Los Angeles in 1943. In contrast to outwardly-focused historical accounts, the World War II of *Zoot Suit* is represented from an internal perspective as a catalyst for violence against Latinos, and the patriotism of its

Latino protagonist is thwarted by the patriotic racism of the justice system, the newspapers, and white sailors intent on punishing the Latina/o characters for their "foreign" aspect. As a work of activism, *Zoot Suit* delves into the past to offer an alternative narrative of history for Latina/os during World War II.

Yamada's work is also associated with the literary and political activism of the civil rights era. Born in Japan and raised in Seattle, Washington, Yamada was incarcerated with her family in a "relocation camp" for Japanese Americans in southern Idaho during World War II.[13] Yamada's collection of poetry chronicling this experience, *Camp Notes and Other Poems*, appeared in 1976. As a scholar and activist, Yamada's work also appeared in the ground-breaking feminist book *This Bridge Called My Back* (1981). Like Valdez, Yamada and her works have reached the general public; aside from her work as a university professor, she has been the subject of a PBS documentary called "Mitsuye and Nellie: Two American Poets" (1981) and a member of the Board of Directors for Amnesty International. Like *Zoot Suit*, Yamada's *Camp Notes* is an important contribution to our understanding of World War II, particularly the governmental incarceration of Japanese Americans that was occurring at the same time as the zoot suit riots. Ancheta cites this incarceration as an example of "patriotic racism at its worst, as a formal governmental policy."[14] Narrated in spare, economical verse, *Camp Notes* turns inside-out the popular justifications for the Japanese American incarceration, revealing the euphemisms of "evacuation," "protection," and "relocation" to be words concealing the reality of Yamada's own experience of being forcibly transported, guarded, and imprisoned. As in Valdez's play, in *Camp Notes* the issue of national loyalty is a painful one, as Japanese Americans are forced to demonstrate their allegiance to a government that has used patriotic fervor to justify their imprisonment without cause.

Examining Valdez's and Yamada's work together yields several important points about the potential of literature to revise and intervene in dominant historical narratives. First, and perhaps most obviously, these two works illuminate episodes of U.S. history that otherwise tend to be footnoted in dominant accounts (or placed in isolation as in Brokaw's section "Shame"). They also serve as reminders that these events were happening simultaneously. Even as the U.S. government was incarcerating Japanese American civilians with no evidence of criminal activities, the justice system in Los Angeles was convicting Mexican American youths without evidence as part of an attempt to repress a supposed "crime wave." In popular discourse of the time, Japanese Americans and Latina/os were singled out as examples of civic irresponsibility; according to historian George J. Sanchez, in Los Angeles newspapers in 1943 "accounts of Mexican juvenile delinquency either replaced or were printed alongside stories of supposed disloyalty among interned Japanese Americans."[15] Racialized descriptions of both groups were spurred by feelings of nationalism that placed "alien" races in opposition to patriotic fervor.

By featuring characters who volunteer to fight in World War II, these works emphasize that this discrimination was occurring even while Mexican Americans and Japanese Americans constituted important aspects of the war effort. Half a million Mexican Americans served in World War II;[16] in fact, Mexican Americans were disproportionately represented in the military, comprising a higher percentage relative to their population than any other ethnic group.[17] Meanwhile, the 100th Infantry Battalion of Japanese Americans from Hawai'i and the 442nd Regimental Combat Team of Japanese Americans drawn from the incarceration camps became the most decorated units in the history of the United States military, while suffering extremely high rates of casualties.[18] The wartime economy on the home front also depended heavily on Latina/o and Asian American labor, to the extent that the nation tended to expel these groups with one hand while welcoming them back with the other. The deportation of 120,000 Japanese Americans from largely agricultural occupations on the west coast, combined with the expulsion of approximately one million Mexican Americans during a time of hostility towards immigrants in the 1930s, created a severe labor shortage in agriculture—one that was partially filled by Filipino labor such as that described by Bulosan, but was largely alleviated by the creation of the Mexican/American "bracero," or guest worker program.[19] The juxtaposition of these histories allows us to see that Latina/os and Asian Americans were subject to racism during World War II that hinged on questions of loyalty and belonging, even while they constituted important parts of the nation's war effort both abroad and at home.

A second reason for examining these works together is that aside from simply illuminating the existence of "patriotic" racism against Latinos and Japanese Americans, they take these events as central aspects of World War II history. Torgovnick's work on World War II and cultural memory suggests that the holes or ellipses in our histories of the war form patterns that emphasize social unity at the cost of "othering" certain populations. She explains, "by looking-away from [these] events, cultural memory in the United States effected social unity based on processes of othering. . . . Such forms of othering forestall what I will call . . . a more creative—if sometimes problematic and difficult—process toward an ethics of identification."[20] Torgovnick is interested primarily in the consequences of "looking-away" from the atomic bombing of Hiroshima and Nagasaki, the incendiary bombing of German and Japanese civilians, and the tremendous casualties suffered by Soviet soldiers during the war. Failing to acknowledge these aspects of the war as important to its remembrance—obscuring them in heroic tales of Allied victories—relegates this human suffering to a footnote in history, a regrettable but forgettable consequence of justifiable actions, and may pave the way for future suffering to be seen as collateral damage rather than actual death on a massive scale. Yamada's and Valdez's work reminds us that civil rights violations on the homefront also need to be understood as integral parts of the war experience, that so-called minority experiences may also be central to understanding how wartime nationalism operates. As discussed in the introduction, Yamada's poem "Looking Out" illustrates this point well in eight short lines, as she uses a shift in perspective to overturn dominant societal assumptions about who is a "minority" and what constitutes a minority perception of events. Within the context of a Japanese American concentration camp, the poem suggests the value of reversing dominant perspective, of telling a story from within the camps "looking out," so that what is called into question is not the exceptional experience of Japanese Americans but rather the power structures that place racialized minorities in a position of vulnerability.[21] Valdez's work, too, redefines the framework by which we understand World War II. A few minutes into *Zoot Suit*, when the narrator tells Henry Reyna, the play's protagonist, to "Forget the war overseas, carnal. Your war is on the homefront," his words signal to the audience that the Chicano experience of racism during World War II is not a small part of the story, it *is* the story.[22] Unlike dominant narratives that consider patriotic racism to be an unfortunate aside to the real story of World War II, these works define it as central to our understanding of war and patriotism.

This understanding of how patriotism works is especially important as World War II continues to be mobilized as a trope in justifying military action of all kinds. Torgovnick's book is deeply concerned with how the cultural memory of World War II was employed post-9/11 to justify the invasion of Iraq under the rubric of "liberation" rather than "occupation": as Torgovnick succinctly puts it, "World War II or, more precisely, different versions of World War II, can make things happen."[23] In this effort, the media plays a role so great that Torgovnick refers to the "military-industrial-*media* complex" as a nexus of institutionalized forces that can steer public perceptions towards certain political effects and away from multi-vocality or dissent.[24] Both *Zoot Suit* and *Camp Notes* demonstrate the power of the artist to counter patriotic racism and other insidious forms of nativism, as they both directly critique the media, especially newspaper reports and war propaganda, in their accounts of the war. In a striking signal of the importance of this theme to the play, *Zoot Suit* begins with a switchblade slicing through the enormous facsimile of a newspaper, the headline of which reads "ZOOT-SUITER HORDES INVADE LOS ANGELES."[25] This image literally cuts through the media's rhetoric of "invading hordes," a phrase that implies that Latina/os are barbaric, alien, and hostile, even as it plays on white fears of Mexican American zoot-suiters carrying switchblades. *Camp Notes* also opens with a scene featuring the news media. In her first poem, "Evacuation," Yamada presents the reader with a photographer from the *Seattle Times* urging Japanese Americans to "Smile!" as they are led away to the camps.[26] The newspaper's caption for this photograph, "Note smiling faces/ A lesson to Tokyo," is highly ambiguous in the context of the poem. Is the smile meant to imply the docility of Japanese Americans and thus the power of the United States, or the willingness of Japanese Americans to aid the United States through their own incarceration?

Neither reason is quite adequate to explain the photograph's caption; rather, Yamada's poem emphasizes the way that the media and wartime propaganda used the idea of "Tokyo"—and its association with the faces of Japanese Americans—as a rhetorical tool to justify the violation of the rights of U.S. residents and citizens.

Ultimately, both Valdez and Yamada provide a valuable lens through which to view World War II, not through the journalistic and governmental accounts of the time, but through the perspectives of those people "looking out" of the prisons, camps, and hostile situations created by patriotic zeal directed at racialized minorities within the United States. These works were written in the 1970s during the latter part of the civil rights era; they were groundbreaking at the time and constitute foundational texts in Latina/o and Asian American studies today. Looking at them together suggests ways that we can create a dialogue across these respective disciplines to discuss how domestic racialization can be directly linked to wartime hostilities, as well as how today's memories of the "good war" rely on perspectives that elide the experiences of nonwhite men, women, and children in the United States in a way that ultimately perpetuates militarism at home and abroad.

LUIS VALDEZ'S *ZOOT SUIT* AND WARTIME PROPAGANDA

Luis Valdez once described his work with El Teatro Campesino as "somewhere between Brecht and Cantinflas," invoking both European leftist political theater—including the socialist traditions of "agitprop" or propaganda theater—and the folk humor of one of Mexico's most famous comic actors of the early twentieth century.[27] Indeed, Valdez's plays combine political messages with an exploration of Chicano roots, and they are remarkable for their success in widely disparate locations and among very different kinds of audiences. As critic Jorge Huerta succinctly puts it, in approximately fifteen years Valdez and El Teatro Campesino moved "from flatbed trucks to Hollywood sound stages," experiencing a meteoric rise in popular exposure.[28] El Teatro Campesino was originally formed in 1965 under the umbrella of the United Farm Workers Association, performing sketches for striking farm workers on stages rigged on the flatbeds of trucks in Delano, California.[29] From these localized beginnings, the group quickly attracted the attention of the general public as it performed on picket lines, at rallies and marches, and on college campuses throughout California. Within less than five years, Valdez's plays had found success off-Broadway and internationally.[30] *Zoot Suit*, Valdez's most well-known work, was commissioned by the Mark Taper Forum through a grant funded by the Rockefeller Foundation. It played to sold-out houses in Los Angeles for a record-breaking 46 weeks in 1978, and the following year, it became the first Chicano play to be performed on Broadway.[31] In 1981, Valdez adapted and directed the play as a Hollywood film.

The wide dissemination of *Zoot Suit* as a written play, performance piece, Hollywood film, DVD, and streaming video illustrates the power of drama to reach a large number of people and potentially change their view of historical events. Of course, each genre reaches a different audience and has a different visceral impact. While a written text is not limited by time and location, in its written form a play is unlikely to reach people outside of an academic setting. A live performance may reach a more varied audience and have the most visceral impact—there is nothing quite so immediate as a live production—but its audience is also restricted either by time and location (as with performances from flatbed trucks) or by the cost of tickets at the Mark Taper Forum or Broadway. Because of these limitations, the film adaptation probably has the farthest reach, joining a number of other dramatic productions about World War II in their attempt to (re)write history. As a note preceding the film reminds viewers, "The following film is based upon a true incident." By basing the drama on real events, Valdez signals its place within the genre of theater he calls *actos*; essentially, he adapts this genre for film. In their original form, *actos* were sketches that were collectively conceived by performers along with members of the audience in order to reflect the reality of social conditions among Chicanos. Obviously, a film cannot involve members of the audience in the same way. Yet Valdez retains the intent of these short pieces in both play and film, an intent he clarifies in the following definition: "Actos: Inspire the audience to social action. Illuminate specific points about social problems. Satirize the opposition. Show or hint at a solution. Express what people are feeling."[32] *Actos* use archetypal characters, often labeled with signs around their necks (e.g., "Patroncito," "Migra," "La Chicana") to demonstrate an existing situation and inspire political action among audience members.

Most scholars agree that *Zoot Suit* contains elements of the *acto,* despite a much longer form and a basis in historical, rather than contemporary, events. In its symbolism and extensive use of music, the play and film also combine aspects of other dramatic forms developed by Valdez, specifically the *mito* and *corrido,* or myth and ballad forms of Chicano theater.[33] To Valdez, the development of the *mito,* a mystical exploration of Aztec and Mayan mythologies, was as important as the *acto* to the cultural development of the Chicano movement. El Teatro Campesino might have existed somewhere between Brecht and Cantinflas, but it is important to note that even in its beginnings, Valdez did not characterize his work as belonging exactly to either tradition. Rather, in an influential essay titled "Notes on Chicano Theater," Valdez emphasized the need for Chicano theater to be revolutionary in form as well as content, to reject and reinvent European theater traditions. Comparing Chicano theater to a Chicano car—a General Motors product completely transformed into a "low-rider" or "particularly Raza" vehicle—Valdez described the need for a "revolutionary turn in the arts as well as in society," for theater to be "revolutionary in technique as well as content. It must be popular, subject to no other critics except the pueblo itself; but it must also educate the pueblo toward an appreciation of *social change*, on and off the stage."[34] The reinvention of European street theater into Chicano *actos*, the transformation of indigenous Mexican myths into Chicano *mitos*, and the dramatic incorporation of resistant music in Valdez's *corridos* illustrate his extraordinary effort to locate the "between" of the Chicano experience as a place of potential social change. By extending this effort to the genre of film, he effectively widens both the audience and the potential for change.

The historical basis for *Zoot Suit* centers on the Sleepy Lagoon murder trial that took place in Los Angeles in 1942, an event that led to violence later that year as white U.S. naval servicemen sought out, stripped, and attacked "zoot-suiters," most of whom were Mexican American. The facts of the trial are an illustration in racial profiling and miscarriage of justice and have been widely considered a catalyst for the Chicano movement that sprang up after World War II. When a young man named José Díaz was found murdered in August 1942 at a watering hole and romantic spot called the "Sleepy Lagoon" after a popular song of the time, police rounded up hundreds of young Mexican Americans and arrested twenty-two of them for the murder. The trial was noted for its legal irregularities: the sheriff's department submitted a report that declared "Mexicans inherently criminal and biologically prone to violence," and the judge refused to allow the defendants to change their clothes or cut their hair, deeming their increasingly bedraggled appearance relevant to the trial. Despite a lack of evidence explicitly connecting them to Díaz's murder, seventeen young men were found guilty of the crime and sentenced to jail time in the largest mass conviction in the history of California.[35] Inflammatory newspaper accounts accompanied the trial, particularly in the Los Angeles newspapers owned by William Randolph Hearst; activists of the time accused Hearst of deliberately stirring up anti-Mexican sentiments in his newspapers in order to incite racial animosity and increase his real-estate holdings by driving out Mexican Americans from Los Angeles neighborhoods. Historian Eduardo Obregón Pagán maintains that such accusations were probably exaggerated and that the press more accurately reflected a contested imagery and political struggle over the role of Mexican American youth in wartime Los Angeles.[36] However, it is certain that the press did much to perpetuate the image of Mexican Americans as "zoot-suiters," in reference to the highly stylized long-jacketed suit with tapered pants that was popular among young Mexican Americans, African Americans, Asian Americans, and white Americans who identified with jazz culture.[37] For this reason, the violence that occurred in the summer of 1943 became known as the "zoot suit riots" even though, as historian Griswold del Castillo observes, the events did not actually consist of riots caused by Mexican Americans wearing zoot suits, but rather consisted of a two-week attack by hundreds of U.S. military personnel on Mexican Americans in Los Angeles.[38] These attacks were random, and often entailed large numbers of naval servicemen setting out in search of Mexican American men and boys, tearing off their clothing, and brutally beating them while policemen witnessed the events in tacit approval.[39] At the time, the "zoot suit" or "Pachuco" riots were the largest race riot that had ever involved Mexican Americans, and the events made headlines across the United States and in Latin America.[40]

Valdez's play *Zoot Suit* follows the struggles of Henry Reyna, a fictionalized character based on the real-life Henry Leyvas, the leader of the 38th Street Social Club and chief defendant in the Sleepy Lagoon murder trials. The play also features the archetypal characters of the *acto* genre, most notably El Pachuco, a zoot-suit wearing Chicano figure described in the play as "the very image of the pachuco myth, from his pork-pie hat to the very tip of his four-foot watch chain."[41] The figure of El Pachuco, played on Broadway and in the film by actor Edward James Olmos, has become an iconic representation of the play, the time period, and Chicano resistance. *Pachuco* was a common term for Mexican American youths in the early twentieth-century, a term that had a contested meaning at the time and continues to be defined and redefined today by Chicano activists, historians, and artists like Valdez. Perhaps the most famous—and controversial—early characterization of the *pachuco* was written by Nobel Prize-winning Mexican writer Octavio Paz, who began his collection *Labyrinth of Solitude* with an essay titled "The Pachuco and Other Extremes." Based on his observations during a two-year stay in Los Angeles, Paz described the *pachuco* as the embodiment of negativity. In Paz's view, the *pachuco* was neither Mexican nor "North American," and he was resistant because he "has lost his whole inheritance: language, religion, customs, beliefs."[42] Paz considered the sartorial choices of the *pachuco*—e.g., the zoot suit—to be equally nihilistic, imitating the style of the Anglo culture that had rejected him.[43]

While Chicano activists of the 1960s and 1970s agreed that the *pachuco* was a resistant figure, many were outraged at Paz's negative characterization of the *pachuco* in terms of loss. Historians today emphasize the multiracial character of the zoot suit, its affiliations with jazz culture, and the ways in which zoot suiters "practiced their own cultural politics" in order to "craft their own identities and claim dignity."[44] In *Zoot Suit,* Luis Valdez uses the figure of El Pachuco as an allegory for Chicano resistance in which the cultural politics of the Mexican American zoot suiter are directly opposed to popular narratives, represented by the archetypal character of the Press. As an allegory for cultural resistance, El Pachuco is a complex mixture of masculinity, pride, and cynicism. Valdez also sets up the character in strongly positive terms, as a redefinition of victimhood into something far more powerful. As the play opens, El Pachuco declares that "It was the secret fantasy of every bato / in or out of the Chicanada / to put on a Zoot Suit and play the Myth / más chucote que la chingada."[45] Here, the *pachuco* becomes the stuff of legend, and the characteristic of *chucote* (from the word *pachuco*) replaces the trope of conquest represented by the mythical figure of the *chingada*, the violated mother of the Mexican people. As critic Chon A. Noriega interprets this statement, "with the right clothes, and consequently being *chucote* rather than *chingada*, even conquest could be overcome."[46] El Pachuco thus becomes a defining moment in masculine Chicano expression. As an archetype, he accomplishes the political aim Valdez sets out for his *actos,* and as the embodiment of a myth, he also incorporates elements of Valdez's *mitos.* Broyles-González has observed that El Pachuco's colors, red and black, as well as his association with smoke and mirrors in the play link him to the Aztec figure Tezcatlipoca.[47] Through El Pachuco, Valdez creates an archetypal figure of Mexican American resistance, one associated with both the zoot suit and indigenous Mexican mythology. Rather than exhibiting a nihilistic destructivism based on loss of "authentic" Mexican culture, El Pachuco in Valdez's play illustrates a resistance that draws on Mexican cultural roots as well as U.S. American jazz style.

El Pachuco's function as the narrator and master of ceremonies of the play highlights the ways in which *Zoot Suit* is particularly constructed to counter dominant narratives about Mexican Americans during World War II. The Press in the play has a role, often taking on the part of the prosecution during the scene depicting the Sleepy Lagoon murder trial; however, its role is not allowed to frame the story. Instead, El Pachuco frames the narrative. His are the first and the last words of the play, and his action—literally slicing through a newspaper montage with a switchblade—opens the narrative and sets the stage for the events to follow. Critics usually trace Valdez's drama genealogically either to the four hundred year old Mexican tradition of religious drama or to the agitprop theater of the European left;[48] Valdez himself traces Chicano theater to pre-Columbian human sacrifice in Mexico.[49] However, there is also more than a hint of Shakespearean drama in El Pachuco's performance. In his opening scene, El Pachuco begins with a hybrid language—"¿Que le watcha . . . ?"—mixing English and Spanish with street slang to emphasize the unique linguistic identity of the Mexican American, but then "breaks character and addresses the audience in perfect English."[50] These English lines consist of rhymed verse ("the play you are about to see / is a construct of fact and fantasy") recalling Shakespearean characters such as Puck in *A Midsummer Night's Dream,* who also directly addresses the audience in rhymed couplets. When theater historian Jorge Huerta asked Valdez what the Chicano Theater Movement could gain from having a play on Broadway, Valdez reportedly replied, "They won't take us seriously until we succeed on their turf, on their terms."[51] Through El Pachuco's ability to switch effortlessly between the hybrid language of the streets and "perfect," Shakespearean rhymed couplets, Valdez demonstrates his intention of subverting "perfect" English, of beating the Western dramatic form at its own game by giving the role of Puck, the trickster, to a Chicano *pachuco.* The press may refer to "zoot-suited goons" and "Mexican baby gangsters," but El Pachuco has the first and last word in this narrative.[52]

El Pachuco's message is threefold: first, to redirect the popular rhetoric of war and justice to civil rights issues on the home front; second, to express solidarity with other minorities experiencing racial oppression, especially Asian Americans and African Americans; and third, to remind the audience of the importance of this history today, of the contemporaneity of the issues that are depicted in the play. The first of these aims Valdez accomplishes through El Pachuco's role as a foil, an alter-ego to Henry Reyna and a voice of opposition to the Press. When a character expresses any kind of war propaganda, El Pachuco cuts through the sentiment as cleanly as he cuts through the newspaper headlines with his knife, reminding the characters and the audience that Mexican Americans have no place within a nationalistic narrative—or even more strongly, that the existence of Mexican Americans actually contradicts the narratives of U.S. nationalism. Thus, when the Press delivers headlines describing the Sleepy Lagoon murder case, repeatedly naming its location as the "City of the Angels," El Pachuco interrupts "sharply" to correct him: "El Pueblo de Nuestra Señora la Reina de los Ángeles de Porciúncula, pendejo."[53] With this comment, El Pachuco reminds the audience of the Mexican origins of Los Angeles, that before it was the "City of the Angels," it consisted of Mexican ranches and lands. El Pachuco's sharp correction recalls California's long history as a Spanish colony and then as "Alta California," a remote province of Mexico, a history that is actually written into the names of cities, place names, and natural features in a way that cannot easily be translated. As El Pachuco says, what the reporters call the "City of the Angels" is a shortening of the "Town of Our Lady the Queen of the Angels of the Porciúncula River"; it is a town that was named by Mexican settlers for the Virgin Mary. The rhetoric of invasion that paints Chicanos as youths coming up from Mexico to take over a U.S. city ignores the Mexican origins of Los Angeles, a history old enough to beg the question of who is actually doing the invading.

El Pachuco also questions Henry Reyna's desire to defend "his" country by joining the Navy, telling him it is a "stupid move, carnal," and mocking him as "muy patriotic, eh?"[54] Henry confesses that his desire was to "come back a hero," but El Pachuco observes that by repeatedly jailing him on trivial charges, the police will already have marked him as "unfit for military duty" because of his record. To the idea that Henry could go off to fight for his country, El Pachuco is even more scathing, observing that "this ain't your country. Look what's happening all around you. The Japs have sewed up the Pacific. Rommel is kicking ass in Egypt but the Mayor of L.A. has declared all-out war on Chicanos. On you! ¿Te curas?"[55] As Henry's inner voice, El Pachuco forces him to face the fact that he can never be a war hero because the dominant society does not consider him truly American. Moreover, as an archetype in opposition to the archetypal Press, El Pachuco forces the audience to question what being American actually means, if the Anglo residents of Los Angeles are occupying what once was Mexican land. When El Pachuco advises Henry to "forget the war overseas" and observes "your war is on the homefront,"[56] he effectively reframes the action of World War II to another theater, the war at home. Just as Henry Reyna's fate is redirected, from Navy recruit to prison inmate, the narrative of the war is redirected, as patriotism is revealed to be a privilege restricted to the white majority.

In addition to cutting through the rhetoric of wartime propaganda, El Pachuco functions as the play's most vocal expression of racial solidarity with other minorities fighting civil rights battles on the home front. From the beginning of the play, Valdez indicates the presence of other racialized minorities by showing the "zoot-suit" dance scene to be comprised of a diverse group of young people. Historian Luis Alvarez has demonstrated that in fact, the zoot was worn by disenfranchised youth of all races and both genders; Alvarez begins his account of World War II zoot-suit culture with a passage about the importance of this clothing to the resistance of the young Malcolm X.[57] The film version of *Zoot Suit* highlights the historical presence of African Americans as part of the zoot-suit culture of resistance; African American dancers play a prominent role in the first dance scene. In the play, however, Valdez makes a different choice: the inclusion of the character Manchuka, a Japanese American dancer. Manchuka is given a name in the play, but no lines. The notes to Scene 1 simply specify that "a SAILOR called SWABBIE dances with his girlfriend MANCHUKA among the couples."[58] When the police arrive to round up the dancers, Swabbie and Manchuka are among them until the sergeant sees Swabbie and orders him to go. Swabbie says, "What about my girl?" and the sergeant says "Take her with you." When Henry asks "What about my girl?" he is told, "No dice."[59] Manchuka exits with Swabbie and is never seen on stage again.

The brief inclusion of Manchuka in this scene resonates with the episode in Paredes's *George Washington Gómez* in which a pair of Japanese American students are allowed in a restaurant, but the darker-skinned Mexican Americans are not. At first glance, both episodes seem to reinforce dominant stereotypes of Japanese Americans as foreigners; the scenes seem to suggest that even though the United States is at war with Japan, Japanese Americans are treated better than Mexican Americans. However, in neither scene do Japanese Americans possess racial privilege. Rather, in both cases they are subject to the same kind of scrutiny as the Mexican American protagonists. The fact that they do not receive the same penalties as Guálinto or Henry Reyna is not due to racial privilege but to other factors; in the case of the Japanese American brothers in Paredes's novel, the boys are the son of a prominent businessman, and their wealth serves to mitigate the racial stigma attached to them. In the case of Manchuka, it is only her association with the Anglo Swabbie that allows her to leave unmolested by the police. It is Swabbie who is singled out for special treatment, not Manchuka, and her exit is a sign of his masculine, white privilege; he can protect "his girl" in a way that Henry Reyna cannot.

In fact, the character of Manchuka is less remarkable for her status than for her presence in the play at all. She is silent, existing only as a name in the program and the description "Japanese-American dancer."[60] However, her presence contrasts sharply with the dance scene later in the play, when Swabbie reappears without Manchuka as a serviceman during the attacks on zoot-suiters. Manchuka's absence during this scene is significant, because it reflects the reality of Japanese American incarceration during that time; while she could have been dancing in 1942, she would not have been present in 1943 for the "riots." Her relative powerlessness in the first scene, combined with her absence in the second, is a quiet reminder that Japanese Americans, too, were encountering the war on the home front. The link between the oppression experienced by Japanese Americans and Mexican Americans is later expressed verbally by Alice Bloomfield, a progressive reporter who repeats allegations made by the "regular press" when she asks Henry, "What about the American Japanese? Is it true they are directing the subversive activities of the pachucos from inside the relocation camps?"[61] By placing this line in the play, Valdez directs the audience to the simultaneity of the camps and the murder trial, as well as the outlandish nature of the allegations being made in the press at the time, allegations that demonstrated the ways in which internally directed racism masqueraded as wartime security measures.

The character of Alice Bloomfield is another deliberate choice on the part of Valdez to bring the theater of the war to the home front. Broyles-González criticizes this choice, considering that it takes away the agency of Chicano/as in the narrative; in historical fact, she observes, the woman named Alice McGrath on whom Valdez based the character was a paid employee of the Sleepy Lagoon Defense Committee, and the role attributed to her in Valdez's play was "occupied by Chicanas, namely Josefina Fierro and Luisa Moreno."[62] In truth, the SLDC was headed by activist Carey McWilliams and administered by Alice McGrath along with Chicanas such as Moreno; it drew supporters among noted celebrities and involved activists from Jewish, Mexican American, African American, communist party, and labor community leaders.[63] However, Broyles-González's observation emphasizes the fact that among a diverse range of supporters, Valdez chose Alice McGrath, a Jewish woman, to develop as a central character in the play. In part, this choice provides the play with an interesting dramatic tension, as a cross-racial, cross-class romance develops between Alice, a "square paddy chick," and Henry, who is heavily invested in a masculine *pachuco* image.[64] But this choice also allows Valdez to draw a parallel between the oppression of the Jews and of Mexican Americans. When Alice tells Henry that she is fighting for him "because I'm a Jew, goddammit!" and tells him, "If you lose, I lose," the war in Europe is truly brought to the home front. Alice clarifies this further by saying that "only Hitler and the Second World War could have accomplished" the "love and hate it's taken to get us together in this lousy prison room."[65] The atrocities perpetrated by Hitler have motivated Alice, a Jew, to fight for the rights of other oppressed minorities. The fact that these minorities are being oppressed by the U.S. justice system brings home the irony of a "good war" in which both sides ascribe to racial hierarchies.

El Pachuco articulates crossracial alliances in the text further when he tells the Press that the words "pachuco" and "zoot suiter" are coded terms that refer to that racial hierarchy. When the Press says the zoot suit violates good taste, El Pachuco retorts, "like the Mexicans, Filipinos and blacks who wear them."[66] Taunting the Press and the sailors into dropping their racially coded language, El Pachuco is finally attacked by a mob who accuses him of being "half monkey—just like the Filipinos and Niggers that wear them."[67] El Pachuco's words and the reactions he elicits unite Mexican Americans with the discrimination experienced by Filipino Americans and African Americans. Even as the presence/absence of Manchuka, the Japanese American dancer, reminds the audience of the incarceration of Japanese Americans during World War II, and the Jewish identity of Alice explicitly compares European and American racial hierarchies, the words spoken by El Pachuco express racial solidarity with Filipino and African Americans. World War II, for these characters, is certainly being fought on the home front.

El Pachuco's final function, in the play, is to demonstrate the relevance of history for the present day. When Henry and his friends are released on appeal, and he concludes happily that "we won this one," El Pachuco sarcastically agrees, announcing a "happy ending y todo" and cutting the lights with a sweep of his arm. He then turns them back on, stating:

> But life ain't that way, Hank.
> The barrio's still out there, waiting and wanting.
> The cops are still tracking us down like dogs.
> The gangs are still killing each other,
> Families are barely surviving,
> And there in your own backyard . . . life goes on.[68]

As master of ceremonies, El Pachuco refuses to allow the Sleepy Lagoon murder trial and the "zoot suit riots" to fade into history. The issues at stake—the poverty, discrimination, and violence—are relevant to 1978; as an ongoing performance, *Zoot Suit* states that they are relevant to any time in which the play is performed. Moreover, the memory of these events is key to understanding issues of racial justice in history. The ambiguous ending of the play highlights the power of history as narrative. According to the Press, Henry Reyna's life ends in prison; according to his brother, he dies a war hero in Korea; according to Alice, he becomes the father of a politically active family of Chicanos. Each character in the play has a different interpretation of Henry's life as narrative: "the born leader . . . the social victim . . . the street corner warrior . . . el carnal de aquellas . . .

the zoot suiter." However, in Valdez's narrative, it is not the Press, but El Pachuco who has the last word on what this story means. According to El Pachuco, Henry Reyna as *pachuco*, both man and myth, "still lives."[69]

In *Zoot Suit*, the announcement that Henry Reyna and other Mexican Americans have won their appeal is drowned out by the cheers of people celebrating victory over the Germans and Japanese during World War II. The Sleepy Lagoon murder trial and the "zoot suit riots" have become a footnote in history, too insignificant to merit repetition in the Press. Valdez's *Zoot Suit* is a full-length *acto* that revives this history. Through the mythical character of El Pachuco, Valdez cuts through the racially coded, biased language of dominant discourses represented by the Press, the prosecution in the trial, and the naval servicemen looking for "zoot suiters" to attack. He carefully frames the issues facing Mexican Americans within the civil rights discourse of all oppressed minorities; the figures of Manchuka and Alice, as well as the naming of Filipinos and African Americans along with Mexican Americans, express Valdez's desire for racial solidarity among groups. They also bring the war home to Los Angeles, changing the way the story of World War II is told. Here, El Pachuco shapes the narrative, and the war is an ongoing one for justice on the home front.

"LOOKING OUT" FROM MITSUYE YAMADA'S *CAMP NOTES*

If *Zoot Suit* demonstrates the power of drama to bring Chicano politics to a national stage, Mitsuye Yamada's work illustrates the revolutionary potential of poetry. Poetry by people of color, and particularly by women of color, has been and continues to be an important part of the civil rights movement. Audre Lorde famously expressed the urgency of this writing in the title of her essay "Poetry Is Not a Luxury."[70] As Lorde explains, in its essence poetry is a project of reimagining, of willing into being new kinds of social change. "Poetry is not only dream and vision," Lorde writes, "it is the skeleton architecture of our lives. It lays the foundations for a future of change, a bridge across our fears of what has never been before."[71] Poetry, too, is economical; it does not need to meet Virginia Woolf's oft-cited requirements of a room of one's own and an independent income, but can "be done between shifts, in the hospital pantry, on the subway, and on scraps of surplus paper."[72] Recalling the months that Carlos Bulosan spent lying in a county hospital, remembering that the time he spent writing *America Is in the Heart* was purchased at the cost of several ribs and large portions of his tubercular lungs, one can readily appreciate the advantages of spare, "economical" writing. Like performing on the flatbed of a truck, writing poetry is a revolutionary art form that historically has been well-suited to those with limited access to typewriters, reams of paper, and private spaces.

As Lorde states, poetry can also be an important tool for envisioning social change. Asian American studies scholar Juliana Chang suggests that throughout the twentieth century, poetry played a critical role in Asian American racial discourse. Following theorists Michael Omi and Howard Winant, Chang considers Asian American poetry written during the civil rights period to constitute a "racial project," in that it does the work of linking cultural representations with structural situations of both racial inequality and empowerment.[73] As a genre in which every word has meaning—and sometimes multiple meanings—poetry can also highlight the importance of language in enabling and reflecting structures of power, even while it disrupts this power by bringing words and ideas into sharp focus for the reader. Mitsuye Yamada's poetry constitutes a racial project because it does this critical work. In the poem cited previously, "Looking Out," Yamada questions the very concept of "minority," drawing attention to the irony of a racial discourse that uses a numerically based terminology—a minority, by definition, is a group comprised of fewer members than a majority—but in reality draws on the peculiarly racialized logic of a power structure that has little to do with numbers. Yamada's poem "Mirror Mirror" also illustrates her commitment to poetry as a racial project. "Mirror Mirror" consists of a seven-line exchange between a mother and son. The son, disturbed that "people keep asking where I come from," states that his "trouble" is that he is "american on the inside / and oriental on the outside." To this, the mother insists that he "turn that outside in / THIS is what American looks like."[74] In these lines, the mother's wisdom suggests that nationality cannot be based on outside appearances; rather, "American" can look "oriental," just as on the inside, America historically and demographically encompasses people of all races, including Asian Americans. Moreover, the poem's title calls attention to the politics of the question itself, as "Mirror Mirror," echoes the French fairy tale's question, "Who is the fairest of them all?" In the fairy tale, the wicked queen's question is intended to reinforce her own status as the most beautiful in the land, but the query inadvertently hails her rival, Snow White. Similarly, the question of "where I come from" overtly reinforces the white (or non-Asian American) status as the true American, but on another level reveals America itself to be an illusory construction, its real people as diverse as its history. The mirror hails Snow White as the fairest and the "oriental" as "American," reversing the questioners' assumptions about beauty and race. Through poems like these, Yamada accomplishes the racial project of culturally representing the inequalities experienced by Asian Americans in the United States, even while her words work to undermine the basis for this racial hierarchy by constantly shifting perspective, turning words and phrases inside out and "outside in" to reveal the violence of the rhetoric on which this hierarchy is founded.

As a racial project, the poems in Yamada's collection *Camp Notes* are particularly concerned with the rhetoric used to justify the incarceration of Japanese Americans during World War II. This slim volume of poetry breaks through the popular rhetoric surrounding the incarceration by serving as a record of the lived experience of the 120,000 Japanese Americans who were forcibly interned during the war. Recent decades have seen a significant increase in historical accounts, education, and recognition of this experience.[75] However, this awareness has been hard won, the result of extraordinary efforts of Asian Americans in the late twentieth century to obtain legal redress and bring Japanese American history into the national consciousness. It took more than forty years of writing letters, circulating petitions, and testifying before members of Congress before Japanese American citizens' groups and other activists achieved the passage of the Civil Liberties Act of 1988, which contained a national apology and $20,000 in monetary remuneration to each survivor of the camps.[76] In order to achieve this recognition, their campaign first had to break through years of governmental insistence on the military necessity of the incarceration. For decades, the U.S. government officially maintained that the imprisonment of Japanese Americans during the war was critical for reasons of national security, despite the fact that no Japanese American was ever found guilty of espionage, and Japanese Americans from Hawai'i, who were geographically closer to Japan but vital to the state's economy, were not evacuated.

The government also maintained that the incarceration was necessary (and even beneficial) for the protection of Japanese Americans from racial harassment by the general public. Thus, after the war, President Harry S. Truman awarded a medal to the director of the War Relocation Authority, the agency responsible for carrying out the incarceration, for his program of "progressive relocation, reintegration and rehabilitation of this racial minority" through camps that supposedly served as "an affirmation of American faith in the validity of democratic processes."[77] The 1988 reparation of $20,000 to each survivor hardly mitigated the (conservatively) estimated $400 million lost by the Japanese American community during the war,[78] and it could never make up for the loss of freedom, generational fragmentation, and personal hardships experienced by survivors of the camps, but the Act was still a major victory for civil rights activists; it acknowledged the injustice of the incarceration in a way that the U.S. government and the War Relocation Authority never had.

Appearing in 1976, Mitsuye Yamada's poetry was among the first published works to document and interpret the camp experience during World War II from a Japanese American perspective. The relative silence of the Japanese American literary community during the period immediately following the war was in part due to the psychological trauma of their wartime experiences. Critic Stan Yogi explains that "in an effort to rebuild their lives, many sought to merge into the American mainstream, to forget about the traumas of internment, and in some cases to escape from nikkei [Japanese-ancestry] communities and heritage."[79] However, this silence was also due to a public lack of support, often amounting to an actual hostility, for historical counternarratives, especially by people who were conflated in popular imaginations with Japanese nationals. John Okada's novel *No-No Boy*, for example, which depicts the devastating consequences of the incarceration for members of the Japanese American community, appeared in 1957 but went "practically unnoticed" until activist Jeffery Chan "discovered it" in a bookstore in 1970 and began disseminating it across the country as part of the Combined Asian-American Resources Project.[80] Hisaye Yamamoto's short stories, which depicted prewar life as well as wartime experiences of Japanese Americans, were not collected for publication until 1988. Even Toshio Mori, who has been described as an "optimistic" writer, in that he urged Japanese Americans to put aside their bitterness and cooperate with the government during the war, was unable to get his volume of stories published during the war. Scheduled for publication in 1941, Mori's *Yohohama, California* did not actually appear in print until nine years later.[81] According to critic Susan Schweik, the fact that Yamada's poetry was written during the war but did not appear in print for thirty more years is central to understanding both its importance and its themes. Books by Japanese Americans, like Yamada's or Mori's, "constituted double threats, both in their subject matter and in their very existence."[82] They rendered visible what was meant to remain invisible, the existence of a group of Americans who contradicted the myth of a nation united in the war effort.

Indeed, Yamada's poetry testifies to the harsh experience of Japanese Americans during the war. The narrative arc of the poems that constitute *Camp Notes* begins with "Evacuation," in which the narrator boards a bus for a "vacation / lasting forever"[83] and ends with "Cincinnati," a chronicle of the narrator's experience of racial hostility upon her release from the camps. In between, the collection of poems parallels Yamada's own experience of incarceration in Mindoka, Idaho. Emphasizing the collection's function as a historical record, Yamada also includes two poems written by her father, accompanied by a footnote explaining "Jakki was the penname of my father, Jack Yasutake, formerly an interpreter for the Immigration Service, who was interned by the FBI during the years 1941–1944."[84] This blending of historical fact with poetic form reveals the collection's intention of offering a particular interpretation of the historical period that encompassed World War II. This interpretation is highly ironic, juxtaposing phrases like "vacation" with "lasting forever," in order to demonstrate the political import of the author's personal experiences. Even the footnote mentioning Yamada's father illustrates an irony, that of an employee of the U.S. Immigration Service himself being held as an enemy alien. Her father imprisoned and unable to perform his job as a linguistic interpreter, Yamada took on his role by poetically interpreting the history unfolding around her.

Like *Zoot Suit*, *Camp Notes* achieves this reinterpretation of history by exploding the rhetoric used by the popular media, citizens' groups, and U.S. government during World War II. Critic Anita Haya Patterson has compared Yamada's poetry to Ansel Adams's photographic critique of the Japanese American incarceration. The restrictions placed on Adams in creating his photographic essay of the camp at Manzanar illustrate the government's attempt to rhetorically shape the event: like other photographers and journalists, Adams was forbidden to record images of guards, guard towers, or barbed wire.[85] Suppressing images that suggested imprisonment, official photographs instead attempted to depict willing cooperation, a cheerful atmosphere, and the overall happiness of the Japanese American people. Government photographs released in 1942 portrayed well-dressed, smiling girls on their way to "Assembly Centers"; men and women smiling as they are escorted onto a train, their final destination a "Relocation Center for evacuees"; and happy residents staging amateur theatricals, a picture of jovial camp life.[86] Both the language used to describe the incarceration and the images released at the time were carefully constructed to tell a particular story about the incarceration. Adams's photographs critiqued this story by disobeying some injunctions and subverting others: by photographing barbed wire as part of a landscape, by including the perspective if not the image of a guard tower, and by showing unsmiling people experiencing tedium, military regulation, and anxiety.[87] Yamada's poetry, too, constitutes a powerful critique of the imagery of the camps that was released to the public during the war.

What *Zoot Suit* accomplishes with archetypal characters, *Camp Notes* achieves with carefully placed incongruities; even as El Pachuco forms a critical counterbalance to lines spoken by the Press, the poems in *Camp Notes* critically juxtapose governmental euphemisms with the historical experience of incarceration. As with the images released by the government, official terms like "evacuation," "relocation," "assembly centers," and even "camps" minimized the impact of forcible removal and indefinite detention on Japanese Americans. During the war, the War Relocation Authority ordered all personnel to use these euphemisms to describe the situation, forbidding the use of words such as "internees" and "prisoners," and even devising new euphemisms as the old ones took on undesirable associations.[88] Yamada's poetry highlights the jarring incongruity of these terms with her experiences in the camps. For example, in "Desert Storm," the people take shelter from a twister, slamming shut windows and doors in their barracks. The poem opens with military imagery, reminding readers that this chaotic storm is occurring in a highly regimented environment; it takes place "Near the mess hall / along the latrines / by the laundry / between the rows of black tar papered barracks."[89] Yet in this military setting, the people in the poem have no weapons to shield themselves from the storm. They use butter knives to stuff "newspapers and rags / between the cracks," but are caught as the "Idaho dust / persistent and seeping / found us crouched / under the covers." Rather than protection, the camp offers exposure to the elements; the people huddle in fear even as their lives are regimented by a military environment. The poem ends with the broken lines:

This was not
im
prison
ment.
This was
re
location.[90]

These final lines of the poem contain unusual line breaks, a technique that emphasizes the words "prison" and "location." For what else can it be but a prison, if the people are surrounded by the apparatus of the military but themselves wield only butter knives and rags? Even the term "location" begs the question of where Yamada and others were placed, drawing attention to the fact that the camps were located in some of the harshest natural environments in the continental United States. The line breaks also disrupt the euphemistic language by literally taking it apart. A narrow column on the page, the words form a twister that breaks apart the language of internment and necessitates a readerly reconstruction of the words "imprisonment" and "relocation." Yamada denaturalizes the words, forcing readers to adopt a critical distance in which the language of the camps is no longer automatic but must be considered anew, reassembled or rejected according to its ability to describe prisoners during a desert storm.

Camp Notes also counters the logic of military necessity by depicting the innocuous nature of everyday life in the camps. In "The Watchtower," the guard is the one who is "in solitary / confined" by the tower, while the people below engage in their ordinary social activities. The narrator walks to her midnight shift at the hospital, and in the "rec hall" teenagers dance while a live band plays popular music of the day. The poem's final lines reveal that this evening is a typical record of daily activities in the camps: "This is what we did with our days. / We loved and we lived / just like people."[91] Here, the jarring phrase is the last; there is a bitterness in the fact that the poem does not state "we *were* people," but instead observes that the Japanese Americans were "just like" people. Given the prevalent use of racial imagery of the time period that metaphorically compared the Japanese and Japanese Americans to rats or other vermin, this statement must be read as a reversal of dominant imagery. In the poem, the military apparatus of the camp is a "centipede / with barracks for legs," while the Japanese Americans are equated to people, living and loving with entirely human emotions.[92] A similar reversal can be found in "The Trick Was," in which the narrator is denied acceptance by one hundred thirty-three colleges in the United States, noting the irony that "THEY were afraid of ME."[93] In this poem, the narrator relates the myriad ways she tried to "keep the body busy" in order to avoid mentally succumbing to the psychologically traumatic experience of intense racism and hostility. As she relates her attempts to keep busy—"be a teacher/ be a nurse/

be a typist/ read some write some/ poems/ write Papa in prison"—the logic of military necessity evaporates in the face of the ordinary nature of the activities, which simply illustrate the mind-numbing tedium of imprisonment.

Finally, as in *Zoot Suit,* Yamada's poetry critiques the very idea of national loyalty during times of war. El Pachuco tells Henry Reyna that "this ain't your country," and indeed Chicanos during the "zoot suit riots" were placed in a catch-22 position: targeted by police for alleged gang activity, which rendered them ineligible to serve in the military, and then attacked by naval servicemen for supposedly unpatriotic behavior.[94] Japanese Americans in the camps were confronted daily with the fact that the United States wasn't "their country," even as they were formally being asked to declare that it was. In his book *American Inquisition: The Hunt for Japanese American Disloyalty in World War II,* legal historian Eric L. Muller delves into the "multi-agency apparatus" that judged the loyalty of Japanese American citizens during World War II, calling it the most burdensome and suspicious of all government loyalty tests ever administered by the United States, including the infamous McCarthy trials.[95] In 1943, all Japanese Americans in the camps over the age of seventeen were required to complete questionnaires to assess their "loyalty." Question 27 of this questionnaire asked Japanese American men whether they were willing to serve in the U.S. armed forces; Question 28 asked all individuals to "swear unqualified allegiance to the United States of America and forswear any form of allegiance or obedience to the Japanese emperor, or any other foreign government, power or organization."[96] Administered to a people imprisoned by their own government, the questionnaire placed Japanese Americans in the impossible position of having to prove their loyalty to a nation that had already categorized them as enemy aliens, or be judged "disloyal." In its original form, Question 28 was phrased in a way that left first-generation Japanese Americans stateless if they signed the oath.[97] Furthermore, it denied the possibility that first-generation immigrants could feel national allegiance to more than one country. In Yamada's poem "The Question of Loyalty," a mother protests "I am doubly loyal / to my American children / also to my own people. / How can double mean nothing? / I wish no one to lose this war."[98] The mathematical impossibility of the equation, that double can mean nothing, illustrates the complicated nature of national allegiance. It also demonstrates the ways in which wartime obscured and worked to negate the very existence of Japanese Americans, people whose citizenship, cultural ties, and family networks often crossed international lines. Poet and activist Lawson Inada described the situation succinctly: "It was as if the term 'Japanese-American' no longer signified a viable whole but denoted an either/or situation, a double bind."[99] Here, Yamada's poem inverts the same negativity that Octavio Paz attributed to the *pachuco*; while Paz claimed that Mexican Americans possessed neither Mexican nor U.S. national heritage, El Pachuco transformed the "nothing" of this equation into a unique identity, a Chicano figure who draws on the cultural identity of both nations to forge something new. Similarly, Yamada's poem takes the "nothing" of the loyalty oath and makes it "double"; the equation works by addition rather than subtraction, subversively wishing for peace rather than destruction.

In questioning the issue of national loyalty, *Camp Notes* ultimately takes a position elided in the rhetoric of patriotism: an anti-war position that subtly undermines the very idea of a "good war." The loyalty questionnaire administered to Japanese Americans equated national allegiance with willingness to fight. There was no place for a mother's sentiment that she wished "no one to lose this war." Other poems in *Camp Notes* illustrate the irony of a patriotic rhetoric that figures wartime "duty" as privilege. In "Recruiting Team," for example, Yamada ends the poem on a note that is almost humorous in the incongruity of its language: a man's voice insisting to the recruiting officials, "Why should I volunteer! / I'm an American / I have a right to be / drafted."[100] Here, the irony of the fact that those in a prison camp are the only American men of eligible age *not* being drafted demonstrates the false nature of the "choice" presented by the recruitment team; in reality, the men must submit to the military either by "volunteering" or by remaining in the camp. The inversion of the imagery also works to counter the rhetoric of the war itself through the very illogic of the idea that compulsory military service could be considered a right instead of the catastrophic upheaval that it was for most Americans in World War II. In this poem, Yamada associates national identity with forced military service; "American" means the right to be drafted, a prospect that must have resonated strongly for her 1976 readers. If "The Question of Loyalty" suggests the existence of loyalties that transcend national boundaries and conflicts, "Recruiting Team" critiques the desirability of national identity itself.

As a racial project, *Camp Notes* thus works on several different levels. The poems in this collection break through the official governmental discourse that euphemistically described internment as anything other than imprisonment. They render absurd the justification of the process on the grounds of military necessity, and they call into question the singularity and desirability of national loyalty. Published thirty years later, these poems express racial solidarity with the oppression experienced by other minorities in the United States. The inclusion of the poems "Thirty Years Under" and "Cincinnati" at the end of the collection serves as an example of this solidarity. In these poems, presumably written or revised years after the composition of the others in the collection, the narrator has packed up her "wounds in a cast / iron box / sealed it / labeled it / do not open . . . / ever . . . " The impetus for opening the box, publishing the poems, comes from an incident in which one day she hears "a black man with huge bulbous eyes / say / there is nothing more / humiliating / more than beatings / more than curses / than being spat on / like a dog."[101] The narrator then relates her own experience being spat upon by a stranger in the street, in which a voice hissing "dirty jap" illustrates the racial nature of the act.[102] The fact that this incident occurs after she leaves the camps for Cincinnati widens the scope of the collection, bringing it outward in geographical range and forward in time. The central contradiction of this final poem is that even though the narrator thinks she is "in a real city / where / no one knew me," she finds in the end, "everyone knew me."[103] Her anonymity is compromised by a racial hierarchy in which anonymity is the privilege of the white majority. What "everyone" knows is that society hails her as a "dirty jap"; her wartime experience cannot be left behind because patriotism, nationalism, and race are still conflated in the minds of the general public. By comparing her experience to that of a black man, Yamada generalizes her critique of a racialized society. Like Valdez, she gestures towards the possibility of racial solidarity between peoples of color based on common experiences of white oppression.

Although the poems in *Camp Notes* were composed during the war and published in 1976, the perspective they express ensures their continuing relevance for how we understand the war, civil rights, and the construction of historical narrative. In an essay written after the publication of her poetry, Yamada states that "political views held by women of color are often misconstrued as being personal rather than ideological."[104] Openly defying this misinterpretation, Yamada's poems express a continuing political message, a racial project detailing what it means when an "outgroup" takes the brunt of a nation's fear and hostility during times of war. Yamada explains that when she hears her students in the late 1970s discussing their political positions against "ungrateful" Iranian Americans who dare protest government actions, "I know they speak about me."[105] *Camp Notes* not only provides a historical record of the experience of Japanese Americans during World War II; it serves as an anti-war statement and a detailed look at how national loyalty and patriotic racism can occupy different sides of the same coin.

REMEMBERING THE "GOOD WAR": MEMORY, HISTORY, AND ART

Perhaps no document from the war so aptly illustrates the parallel between public perceptions of Latina/os and Asian Americans as the sheriff's report filed during the Sleepy Lagoon murder trial in 1942. In this report, Lieutenant Edward Duran Ayres of the Los Angeles County Sheriff's Department stated that Mexicans were Indian by race, and the Indian "is evidently Oriental in background—at least he shows many of the Oriental characteristics, especially so in his utter disregard for the value of life." He continued:

> Although a wild cat and a domestic cat are of the same family, they have certain biological characteristics so different that while one may be domesticated, the other would have to be caged to be kept in captivity, and there is practically

> as much difference between the races of man as so aptly recognized by Rudyard Kipling when he said when writing of the Oriental: "East is East and West is West, and never the twain shall meet," which gives us insight into the present problem.[106]

This rhetoric is part of a long tradition of Anglo representations of all things Spanish as orientalized, typing the Spanish through orientalist tropes as backwards, cruel, and decadent; the orientalizing of Spain was also "mapped onto" Latina/o populations of the U.S. Southwest in the nineteenth and twentieth centuries.[107] During World War II, the United States was at war with the East, and both Mexican Americans and Japanese Americans, despite their efforts in that war, served as orientalized representatives of non-Western peoples.

The literary works of Luis Valdez and Mitsuye Yamada delve deep into the racialized scapegoating, fear-mongering, and legal injustices that were happening on the home front during the war. They counter government and newspaper rhetoric about "zoot-suiter hordes" and Japanese vermin with the perspective of Americans caught in unexpected battles on U.S. soil. For Henry Reyna, El Pachuco, and the Japanese Americans incarcerated during the war, the experience of patriotic racism was central to understanding the logic of wartime nationalism. For those who were Americans by citizenship and self-identification, their exclusion from the nation during a time of war was not only painful, it was dangerous. Japanese Americans were left imprisoned and stateless, while Mexican Americans were assaulted by the very servicemen who were assigned to protect the coast. Valdez's and Yamada's art brings these experiences to the forefront of our understanding of World War II. After encountering *Zoot Suit* and *Camp Notes,* it is impossible to refer to the "good war" without placing the term in quotation marks to highlight its irony. As historian Howard Zinn maintains, World War II was certainly a war against "an enemy of unspeakable evil," as Hitler's Germany was expanding fascism, totalitarianism, and racial genocide throughout Europe; yet to paint the policies of England, the United States, and the Soviet Union as entirely free and democratic would be inaccurate.[108]

Patriotic racism is not the only aspect of World War II that has been lost—or, as Torgovnick calls it, "hidden in plain sight"—in popular representations of the war. Torgovnick also points to the failure to adequately consider the costs of Allied incendiary bombing of Germany and Japan, the dropping of the atomic bomb on Japan, and the tremendous losses suffered by the Soviet Union in the war against Nazi Germany.[109] Considering these aspects of World War II complicates national rhetoric about the war and is key to producing what philosopher Paul Ricoeur calls a healthy *dissensus* about historical events. Both Torgovnick and Ricoeur are ultimately interested not in the past, but in the present and the future. As Torgovnick says, "the truth is that certain activities and choices . . . might not take place if governments and populations could not count in advance on protective future elisions within the work of memory. We frequently iterate the cliché that memory prevents history from repeating itself. . . . But the holes in memory guarantee that the past will have a place to loop back into the present."[110]

In the end, it is possible and even crucial to honor the courage and sacrifice of a generation of men and women while deploring the necessity of war and emphasizing the injustices that accompanied it. Literary artists like Valdez and Yamada enable us to revise U.S. history so that the narratives we tell about World War II no longer engage in the rhetorical practice of "playing in the dark" or enable new injustices in the name of patriotism. Rather, they confront head-on the ways in which racial groups considered alien to the nation can become patriotic targets during times of national stress.

3 • COLD WAR EPISTEMOLOGIES

> The enemy becomes abstract. The relationship becomes abstract. The nation the enemy the name becomes larger than its own identity. Larger than its own measure. Larger than its own properties. Larger than its own signification.
>
> —Theresa Hak Kyung Cha, *Dictee*

> How do we live with the past? How do we tailor it so that we can go about living our daily lives?
>
> —Cristina García, "A Conversation"

In Susan Choi's novel *The Foreign Student* (1998), Korean American Chang Ahn (known in the United States as "Chuck") confronts the impossibility of explaining the war in Korea to a group of white Americans in 1950s Tennessee. Chang's slide show presentations about Korean culture and history are a condition of his scholarship as the eponymous "foreign student" at the University of the South at Sewanee. Yet speaking in churches throughout the South, Chang encounters the difficulty of translating the complexity of Cold War politics to audiences who understand Korea as a timeless, exotic place liberated from communism by American generosity. As the text of the novel gradually reveals, Chang's experience of the war has been brutal, a painful story of oppression and betrayal, torture, starvation, and terror at the hands of both the North Korean communist forces and the Republic of Korea's American-led military government. However, he is unable to reconcile this experience with the audiences' Cold War ideology; finally, he is reduced to comparing the shape of Korea to Florida and "groundlessly" equating the thirty-eighth parallel to the Mason-Dixon line.[1] This simplified and inaccurate narrative satisfies his audiences' understanding of the world in terms of two opposing forces, although notably it complicates ideas of justice by equating South Korea with the antebellum South.[2] As Chang discovers, however, complications are not welcome ideas to his American audiences; "the particularities of the UN force never interested anyone," even though these very particularities were key to his own fate and those of millions of Korean civilians during the war.[3] Trying and failing to bridge the gap between his own experience and his audiences' limited understanding, Chang focuses on the single ostensibly successful American military action in Korea: General MacArthur's landing at Inchon. Again and again, Chang explains to white American audiences, "I'm not here, if this doesn't happen."[4]

Chang's statement is deliberately framed to satisfy a Cold War epistemology that interprets the war as Korean liberation by American military action; if the "here" is understood to be a place of freedom, then MacArthur and the U.S. forces have enabled Chang's passage from a Korea menaced by communism to freedom in America. The paternalism that underlies this ideology is evident in many instances in the novel, as when a white American man jovially asks Chang, "How did you people like that war we had for you?"[5] However, the text necessitates that Chang's explanation also be read ironically, as a testament to the massive displacement and violence that occurred along with U.S. military intervention in Korea. Chang's "I" in the statement, incorporating the physical and emotional scars of the war, is "here" in a church in the U.S. South because he has cast his lot with the U.S. military as a strategy of survival, much as his father survived the Japanese imperial occupation of Korea by choosing to study in Japan. By drawing structural parallels between Chang's situation and that of his father, the novel forces a comparison between Japanese and American occupations of Korea. Thus, Chang's statement "I'm not here, if this doesn't happen" satisfies his audiences' desire for an American liberation narrative, but it also resonates with the postcolonial slogan: "We are here because you were there."[6] It traces a genealogy that emphasizes the continuities of imperialism and Cold War military interventions overseas to explain the development of new racial and ethnic demographics in the United States during the second half of the twentieth century.

The emergence of Korean American, Vietnamese American, Hmong, and Laotian American literature in the second half of the twentieth century, as well as the establishment of a significant body of Cuban American literature since 1959, unevenly reflects the large numbers of communities and individuals within the United States whose presence is directly tied to Cold War military operations.[7] More generally, Asian American and Latina/o cultural productions since the last decades of the twentieth century have served as important counternarratives to the Cold War rhetoric of containment, insurgency, and dualism that shaped twentieth-century politics and continues to inform U.S. policy in the age of "wars on terror." At the most basic level, Asian American and Latina/o writers and artists document and bear witness to suppressed histories of military intervention in Asia and Latin America during the Cold War, insisting that we remember not only the wars in Vietnam and Korea but also the "secret wars" that were fought in Laos and Cambodia in the twentieth century—forcing us to acknowledge not only the Cuban American communities shaped by Cold War politics but also the U.S. military presence in the Dominican Republic and throughout Central and South America. For civilians, these wars constituted some of the bloodiest, brutal, and deadly conflicts in recent history. The "Forgotten War" in Korea left a staggering three million civilians dead from violence and starvation and forced survivors into underground caves to escape relentless aerial bombing and the implementation of new chemical weapons such as napalm.[8] During the same years in Latin America, a CIA-led coup in 1951 initiated a period of violence in Guatemala that lasted four decades and included the torture and massacre of up to two hundred thousand civilians, mostly indigenous villagers, in a genocidal reign of terror.[9] Histories of U.S. involvement in East and Southeast Asia, Central America, South America, and the Caribbean belie the simple explanation of Cold War politics that audiences like Chang's have been led to believe. If the dominant historical narrative of the Cold War is a triumphalist one, celebrating the fall of the Berlin Wall in 1989 as the victory of freedom and democracy over Soviet oppression, Asian American and Latina/o writers offer an alternative frame of reference. Underneath Chang's statement "I'm not here, if this doesn't happen" is a narrative that painfully documents the physical and psychological costs of the Cold War for peoples in the Third World.

Asian American and Latina/o literature can also interrogate the politics of the national amnesia that follows the Cold War into the present day. This amnesia is encapsulated and reinscribed in names like "The Forgotten War" and "The Secret War"; declassification of military documents has revealed military operations with obscure code names like Operation *Limpieza* and Operation Mongoose, which describe actions in Guatemala and Cuba, respectively. By defining war in Korea as forgotten, conflict in Laos as secret, and operations in Guatemala and Cuba with names not only ominous but obfuscating, standard histories continue to define these operations as existing outside of the kind of history that is worthy of remembrance or acknowledgement. In this chapter, I consider two literary works that not only write back in the history of U.S. military involvement in Asia and Latin America but also take on the task of deconstructing the Cold War as an ideological project, one that exceeds its official dates during the middle decades of the twentieth century as well as its official, bilateral axis as a U.S.-Soviet conflict. Both Choi's *The Foreign Student* and Cuban American writer Achy Obejas's *Memory Mambo* (1996) trace the ways in which Cold War ideology in the United States was (and is) complicit with internal racism, earlier imperial practices, and gendered violence.

Writing at the turn of the twenty-first century, both Choi and Obejas engage the Cold War from the perspective of a critical historical reconstruction that has personal as well as artistic and political implications. The daughter of a Korean father and a Russian Jewish mother, Susan Choi was born in 1969 in Indiana and raised in Texas; *The Foreign Student* is based on her father's experiences in Korea and the U.S. South during the 1950s.[10] Her novel is thus a historical reconstruction, one that critic Daniel Y. Kim convincingly analyzes within the larger category of "postmemorial" art. Kim borrows from Marianne Hirsch's definition of postmemory to describe Choi's complex relationship to her novel's subject as a second-generation Korean American writer. According to Hirsch, postmemory is a phenomenon in which the children of trauma survivors are haunted by stories so powerful that these stories come to constitute memories in and of themselves.[11] Postmemory is different from survivor memory; its emotional impact derives from the fact that "its connection to its object or source is mediated not through recollection but through projection, investment, and creation."[12] Like her protagonist Chang Ahn, Choi's father (also named Chang) lived through the events of the Korean War and then attended the University of the South at Sewanee in the 1950s. However, as a postmemorial text, the novel adds a layer of interpretation to Chang's story that stretches far beyond the literal experiences of Choi's father, both in Korea and the United States. Chang's story is an act of translation and creation, more a meditation on memory than an eyewitness account. Most strikingly, the novel incorporates the completely fictional story of Katherine Monroe, Chang's white American love interest, whose experiences of Southern patriarchy and sexual exploitation serve as reminders of the race and gender hierarchies on which Cold War ideologies were founded. Indeed, ultimately the novel is both a historical reconstruction *and* an interrogation of U.S. politics and society during the Cold War, in which its true object is to highlight the transnational ties between that war and domestic structures of power. In this project, memory is self-consciously unstable. Of writing the novel, Choi has said: "It's not simply that the book is a huge departure from his life . . . but that I'll never really know how things went. Memory was compromised."[13] Thus, as Kim observes, the novel is less a reconstruction of facts than a theorization of memory through the trope of translation, a "postmemory that marks the vanishing point of an original that is nonetheless 'actually there.'"[14] It is an act of deferred translation, in which, as in Chang's slide presentation, memories of the Korean War can never quite be translated in the context of a nation that has chosen to name the war "forgotten."[15]

Memory Mambo may also be read as a postmemorial text, one that explicitly reflects on the slippage between personal and cultural memories. Achy Obejas was born in Cuba in 1956; like her protagonist Juani, her family came to the United States illegally by boat when she was six years old and settled in the Midwest. Yet Juani's story is set twenty years later than Obejas's own life, and the issues she faces are not Obejas's own: in an interview, Obejas has described the book's events as "something that could have happened to me but didn't."[16] Indeed, like Choi's novel, *Memory Mambo* is less concerned with documenting a particular experience than with exploring the ways in which Cuban/American experiences are shaped by Cold War politics. For Juani, these experiences are deeply personal; the central plot of the novel revolves around her obsessive desire to remember both her family's journey to the United States and her own violent confrontation with an ex-girlfriend: her insatiable need to know "what *really* happened."[17] Juani's two obsessions are intertwined, as the violence between the two women is both political and sexual: it pits Puerto Rican independence activism against Cuban American complicity with U.S. Cold War ideology, even while it centers on the inability of some race-based activists to acknowledge gay, lesbian, and other nonheteronormative rights. In *Memory Mambo*, as in *The Foreign Student*, memory is unstable; it also extends beyond the individual. Juani explains: "sometimes other lives lived right alongside mine interrupt, barge in on my senses, and I no longer know if I really lived through an experience or just heard about it so many times, or so convincingly, that I believed it for myself—became the lens through which it was captured, retold, and reshaped."[18] Like Chang, Juani struggles to translate experiences that contradict the Cold War ideology that interpellates her as a Cuban American success story, a refugee from a communist regime and an unquestioned supporter of U.S. containment policies. Through the trope of memory, the text of *Memory Mambo* pieces together a critique of both Cuban communism and U.S. Cold War policies, especially demonstrating the ways in which the latter is commensurate with imperialist and domestic racial ideologies and gendered violence.

For both Choi and Obejas, the Cold War is a problem primarily of memory. As postmemorial texts, these novels position Asian American and Latina/o literature as a way of highlighting the disconnect between experience and ideology, between the Asian American and Cuban "immigrant success story" and the lived reality of grappling with a traumatic past that is globally connected to the webs of race, class, and gendered power that immigrants from Asia and Latin America must negotiate in the United States. The unstable memories of these novels' protagonists signal the difficulties of subject formation for Asian American and Latina/o immigrants to the United States. However, they also demonstrate the power of Asian American and Latina/o literature to deconstruct and interrogate national memory. First-generation testimonial texts like Bulosan's *America Is in the Heart* or Yamada's *Camp Notes* are important because they contradict and subvert dominant narratives; they insist that the structural violence of imperialism or nativistic racism must not be forgotten. Postmemorial texts question how family and national memories are formed in dialogue with political ideologies. Strikingly, both *The Foreign Student* and *Memory Mambo* link Cold War ideology to patriarchal, gendered oppression; military violence abroad complements sexual violence at home in which both men and women become active agents of their own destruction. It is a commonplace in feminist and other civil rights discourses to insist that the personal is political. Asian American and Latina/o literature about the Cold War demonstrates the ways in which the political is also personal, as domestic spaces come to reflect the power and the contradictions of Cold War epistemologies.

"TRANSLATION'S UNNATURAL BYPRODUCT": SUSAN CHOI'S *THE FOREIGN STUDENT*

Nearly sixty years after the war that is known in the United States as the "Korean War," an article by the Associated Press demonstrates the continued importance of Cold War political ideologies in U.S.-Korean relations. Titled "In North Korea, Learning to Hate US Starts Early," the article describes four-year-olds in twenty-first century North Korea who are being taught in state kindergartens to seek vengeance against their worst enemies, the "Yankee imperialists."[19] The posters depicting this message comprise the crudest kind of propaganda, featuring U.S. soldiers as "cruel, ghoulish barbarians with big noses and fiendish eyes," engaging in graphically violent acts such as branding prisoners, wrenching out children's teeth with pliers, and crushing a girl with an army boot, "blood pouring from her mouth, her eyes wild with fear and pain." The article explains how these violent pictures are used to foment anti-American sentiment in children from an early age:

> North Korean students learn that their country has had two main enemies: the Japanese, who colonized Korea from 1910 to 1945, and the U.S., which fought against North Korea during the 1950–53 Korean War. They are told that North Korea's defense against outside forces—particularly the U.S., which has more than 28,000 soldiers stationed in South Korea—remains the backbone of the country's foreign policy. And they are bred to seek revenge . . . [20]

In North Korea's official version of history, the "American imperialists" started the Korean War, and North Korea must not only continue to endure the pain of being a divided country, but also develop and stockpile nuclear weapons against future attacks by U.S. forces.

In contrast to this narrative, the AP article explains that "outside North Korea, history books tell a different story." The author elaborates:

> Western textbooks say that two years after North and South Korea declared themselves separate republics, North Korean troops marched into South Korean [sic] capital, Seoul, on the morning of June 25, 1950. U.S.-led United Nations and South Korean forces fought communist North Korean troops backed by Chinese soldiers in a three-year battle for control of the peninsula. The U.S. and North Korea finally called a truce in 1953, and Korea remains divided to this day.[21]

The differences between these two twenty-first century narratives are striking. In the first narrative, the United States plays the role of an imperialist occupying force, invading Korea much like Japan did decades earlier, and continuing to threaten Korean sovereignty in the present day with its military presence in South Korea. In the second, the war of 1950–1953 is attributed entirely to North Korean aggression against a sovereign republic; the United States was involved, but the true oppositional "forces" were South Korean and that of an international governing body, the United Nations. Yet while an American reader is clearly meant to dismiss North Korean allegations accompanied by shockingly violent images hung in kindergarten classrooms (and situated alongside heroic and obviously apocryphal stories of the nation's dictator), it is worth noting that neither version of history adequately explains the events of 1950–1953. If North Korean propaganda omits any mention of North Korean military aggression or alliance with China, Western textbooks omit the fact that it was a Soviet-U.S. agreement, not a Korean-led endeavor, that divided the country at the 38th parallel in 1945. Neither history mentions the tremendous number of casualties—100,000 Koreans dead even before the "official" start of the war in 1950[22]—as the result of a conflict that was both a civil war *and* a global war, a failed project of decolonization and the event that came to define Cold War ideology.[23]

The fact that these opposing narratives still circulate well into the next century, justifying nuclear proliferation and military actions in the United States and North Korea, illustrates the power that Cold War narratives still hold in international politics. Susan Choi's *The Foreign Student* addresses the ongoing relevance of these narratives by providing a counter-narrative to historical accounts of the Cold War for contemporary readers. The novel uses postmodern techniques, especially the self-reflexive trope of translation, to create this counter-narrative. As a number of critics have noted, the trope of translation is central both to the story and to the intention of the text itself; in other words, even as various characters struggle to translate their words and experiences from Korean to English, Japanese to Korean, and English to Korean, the novel engages in a meditation on what it means to translate the lived experience of a Korean civilian during the war into language that an American audience can understand—whether this audience is sitting in a church hall listening to Chang's lecture or reading Choi's novel more than fifty years later. Moreover, the novel's extended meditations on the impossibility of perfect translation draw attention to the ways in which language, particularly the language of Cold War-era paternalism and patriarchy, creates categories that are not only restrictive, but also complicit with racial, political, and gendered power.

The trope of translation runs throughout the novel, from Korea to the United States, and from Chang's story to Katherine's. For Chang, the act of translation begins as a literal job, first working for John Hodge, the real-life U.S. military governor of South Korea from 1945–1948, and later for the United States Information Service (USIS), "overseas purveyor of American news and American culture, Gershwin and *Time* and democracy."[24] At first, Chang worries about the Americans' disdain for nuance. Working for Hodge, he struggles with the impossibility of doing his job well: "Chang had done enough translation already to know that there weren't ever even exchanges. You wanted one thing to equal another, to slide neatly into its place, but somehow this very desire made the project impossible. In the end there was always a third thing, that hadn't existed before."[25] Chang's inability to connect Korean experience with American terminology results in humorous literal translations, as Korean army members run around yelling "Grab your mechanical-gun-that-shoots-fast and get into the car-with-no-top!"[26] However, as time progresses and Chang moves to the USIS, the rupture becomes more severe, until Chang describes his work within a "zone of intentional misinformation."[27] Determined to establish that "they were not an occupation government at all, but a facilitating presence," the Americans adjust battle figures, maps, and refugee stories.[28] Indeed, the very event defining U.S. success in Korea, MacArthur's landing at Inchon, involves the literal destruction of information, as U.S. troops intentionally torch the National Library in order "to make a dramatic backdrop for MacArthur's ceremony of restoring to [South Korean President] Rhee the city keys."[29] In this novel, the zone of intentional misinformation involves not only mistranslation but also the literal annihilation of knowledge in a quest for rhetorical power.

Eventually, what Chang describes as the "third thing," the excess of meaning that is produced by the intersection of two competing worldviews, comes to define Chang himself. As the son of a Japanese-educated Korean living after the Japanese withdrawal from Korea, and as the Korean employee of an American agency representing neither the Northern PRK (People's Republic of Korea) nor the Southern ROK (Republic of Korea), Chang senses that he has "no real place in South Korea. He was the third thing, that people like Hodge both despised and required. Translation's unnatural byproduct."[30] As translation's unnatural byproduct, Chang embodies the failure of either side's rhetoric to define the situations of millions of Koreans. Abandoned by his American employers, Chang nearly starves to death in his hiding place during the invasion of Seoul by the PRK army; his capture by the PRK would result in certain execution. Yet ultimately, the novel's most graphic scenes of torture occur at the hands of the Republic of Korea Army (ROKA), who jail and nearly kill him as a suspected spy. While it is true that Chang's experience of the war exceeds both communist and Western Cold War ideologies, the majority of the novel's criticism is aimed at the United States and ROKA, for the primary narrative that Chang's story works against is the one his church audiences in the U.S. South expect to hear: the triumph of democracy through U.S. intervention. Daniel Kim explains that Chang's experiences in Korea show that the United States, "rather than being exceptional, has simply been the most recent of a succession of foreign powers that have shaped events on the peninsula to suit their interests."[31] For Hodge and the American men at USIS, their unwillingness to confront the nuances of their situation—to look beyond the black-and-white rhetoric of the Cold War—is a betrayal not only of linguistic accuracy but of the "third thing" that is Chang himself.

The theme of translation, established in Korea, takes on additional meaning in the scenes of the novel that take place in the U.S. South. Here, Chang's identity as a Korean subject who exceeds Cold War categories is intimately linked to his racially ambiguous position as the "foreign student," nicknamed Chuck, at the University of the South at Sewanee. Literary critic Leslie Bow has described this link as a "conceptual parallel" in which both locations—South Korea and the U.S. South—"are invested in the imaginary lines that define, in a visceral way, inclusion and exclusion."[32] A key example of this conceptual parallel is Chang's American moniker, Chuck, which is bestowed on him not in the United States but in Korea by his employer at USIS, a man named Peterfield who "had decided that he couldn't deal with Korean names."[33] A British reporter comments on the irony of replacing an easily pronounced, one-syllable name with a nickname of equal length; according to him, the uselessness of such an endeavor is matched by the useless propaganda the USIS produces to convince a country of people already clamoring to go to America: "American imperialism is nothing if not redundant."[34] The reporter's analogy may not be entirely accurate, as most Northern Koreans were obviously not clamoring to immigrate to America, but it does highlight the redundancy of power operating through American imperialism. Just as the USIS supplemented U.S. economic and military power in Korea with the power of the media and exported popular culture, by giving Chang the nickname Chuck his USIS employers supplement their economic and military power over an individual with the power of the English language. Furthermore, the name "Chuck" is not arbitrary, for the full name, Charles, is equally monosyllabic, American, and similar to the Korean Chang. The fact that Peterfield chooses "Chuck" rather than "Charles" indicates Chang's social position among his American employers; it is a name that connotes either familiarity or social inferiority, much like the generic "Charlie" that was later used to refer to Viet Cong soldiers. Since Chang is later betrayed by these same employers, left to die during the invasion of Seoul by the PRK army, it can be inferred that the nickname is not given with the familiarity of affection, but rather with the presumptive familiarity of power.

The force of this power follows Chang to the University of the South at Sewanee, where institutional privilege is vested in a man named Charles—*not* Chuck—Addison, a professor of English and the longtime lover of Katherine Monroe. As many critics have observed, Chang does not fit easily into the racial hierarchy of the 1950s South, where racial lines were clearly drawn along a black-white axis. Bow observes, "once in the South, Chang/Chuck's status as an unnatural 'third thing' describes his racial standing, which rests in inexact measure somewhere within Jim Crow's embedded continuum."[35] The actions and attitudes of characters in the South make it clear that Chang does not fit along this axis. His attempts to shake hands with an African American table servant at a formal dinner meet with disapproval by his roommate Crane, the son of a Grand Dragon of the Ku Klux Klan. Crane's admonishment—"you can't be casual with them"—along with his insistence that Chang come home with him at Thanksgiving and meet his family, demonstrate the extent to which Chang cannot be categorized as black in the South.[36] This point is further driven home when Chang attempts to join the African American servants for dinner during a break between terms. Attempting to serve himself, Chang is firmly stopped by Louis, one of the servants, who calls him "Mister Chuck" and insists, "Let me make you a plate."[37] Miserably, Chang realizes that to Louis and his friends, "Mister Chuck" interrupts the between-term camaraderie of the African American wait staff and "embodied the force of observation from which they'd expected a reprieve."[38]

Yet if Chang/Chuck cannot be considered black in the South, he is not entirely "white" either. At a gas station outside Sewanee with Katherine, a white woman, ten or twelve people gather to watch him—"to watch her and Chuck, standing there."[39] The moment is not curious but sinister, as both Katherine and Chang feel threatened and try not to show their fear. Crane's insistence that Chang is outside the gaze of the Klan is likewise less comforting than disconcerting, as he follows the phrase "They don't hang Orientals" with the qualification "There aren't any down there to hang. I don't think they'd know one if they saw him. I wonder if they would hang him."[40] Neither black nor white, Chang's racial coding in the South is ambiguous, and it is certainly significant that over the course of the novel, he moves along the black-white axis from "honorary white" to "honorary black," as he is falsely accused of stealing from an employer and forced to give up his scholarship. In the novel's final chapter, Chang is working in the kitchen crew with Louis and has gained a measure of acceptance among the African American men, though it is an acceptance based on a distancing of intimacy; "they never peered into his thoughtful silences, but they accepted him with humor, and their company sheltered him."[41] Ultimately, however, it is Chang's very mobility along this axis, his racial ambiguity with respect to the Jim Crow lines of the South, that suggest that Chang's race is actually being coded along another axis, the axis of American imperialism.

The operation of American Cold War imperialism within U.S. borders is most evident in Chang's scenes outside of Sewanee, as when a young boy on a bus condescendingly offers Chang gum because his soldier brother has told him that "gooks are nuts about gum."[42] The boy's obsession with the vice to be found in the big city is paralleled by his excitement over comic books in which enemy Chinese soldiers threaten Americans with bayonets and a wordless, Orientalized cry, "Aiee!"[43] Chang's identification as an enemy alien is even more evident later in the narrative when he is detained in New Orleans by authorities as a possible communist spy. However, as Bow has observed, even Chang's preferential treatment in Sewanee is marked by "racist love," a term she borrows from Asian American activists Frank Chin and Jeffery Paul Chan to describe the phenomenon by which "others cultivate their superiority through condescension, in this case, the projection of Oriental docility."[44] Whether the Asian (male) figure is an alien to be feared or a guest to be patronized, he is interpellated in the South as an outsider subject to white paternalism; here, the paternalism stands for both the action of the state in protecting the world from a communist menace and the action of the individual in welcoming a guest from afar in ways that mark him as a social inferior. When Katherine finds a book in the library that describes "the average Korean man" in terms of his "not unhandsome Mongoloid features," a book that contains statements such as "Korean ideas of hygiene are almost as negligible as those of a Hottentot," the novel reveals the link between ideas of racial superiority and imperialism.[45] Even if twentieth century American rhetoric may condescendingly complement the Korean subject as "not unhandsome," it equates Koreans with a South African people long considered by Western colonial powers to exemplify the "primitive" beginnings of human evolution. It marks them as "other," off-limits to white women like Katherine.

The name "Chuck" reminds the reader that the American imperialism at work in the renaming of Chang in Korea is still in operation when Chang comes to the United States as a scholarship recipient. Indeed, the paternalism is most evident in the dynamic between Charles Addison, the privileged white Southern man, and the student now known as Chuck (a linguistic diminutive of Charles). The darling of Sewanee society, Addison is described as "famously brilliant, academically careless, slight, unathletic, pseudo-aristocratic, and strangely devastating to the girls."[46] He is a man who fails to make a mark in his profession but wields considerable power in the closed society of Sewanee. For Chang/Chuck, he embodies the Southern paternalism of "racist love" as he seeks the student out to take long walks during which he tries to teach Chang to pronounce "the letter 'V' and the fricative 'th.'"[47] Much as Addison possesses the power to have the "eccentricity" of being "friendly with the colored help," a friendliness that always reminds others of his superiority, his relationship with Chang/Chuck exemplifies his power to patronize a foreign student with unasked-for lessons in English pronunciation.[48] If the USIS in Korea cannot "deal" with foreign names, then Addison cannot deal with foreign accents; in playing "Charles" to Chang's "Chuck," Addison not only asserts his social superiority as an older man and a professor, he asserts his racial superiority as a white man accustomed to patronizing those of other races.

The character of Charles Addison also links Chang to Katherine and thus racial power to gendered power. Here, the setting of the novel in the South is once again key to Choi's themes, for it allows her to loosely parallel Chang's story with that of Katherine, another "unnatural byproduct" of translation. In the white American literary tradition of Faulkner and Styron, the Southern gothic novel is marked by themes of race and sex and especially by the transgression of racial and sexual boundaries through miscegenation and incest. By adding the voice of Katherine to the novel, Choi sets her novel within this Southern gothic tradition, reworking it to include the figure of the Asian American. Katherine's story is overtly one of near-pedophilia and emergent adolescent sexuality; having begun an affair with the adult Addison at the age of fourteen, Katherine's unconventional sexuality has placed her (but not him) outside of societal acceptance. More than one scholar has described Katherine as the "Hester Prynne" of Sewanee in reference to her isolation as a result of her sexual behavior.[49] But while Bow reads Katherine's situation as one that mirrors Chang's—because both "occupy interstitial places within mirrored racial and sexual caste systems"—I am more interested in the ways in which Katherine's relationship with Charles furthers Choi's critique of patriarchy/paternalism.[50] If the adolescent Katherine transgresses sexual boundaries by desiring Addison, he transgresses them with the knowledge and power of an adult. And while Katherine is shocked by her mother's threat to call their sexual relations "rape," Choi's description of their sex is violent and not entirely consensual. When Addison comes upon the sleeping Katherine, the reader is told that he "forced himself into her . . . thrust at her viciously, and rubbed his chest back and forth over her small breasts as if he wanted to erase them; her eyes had flown open and she gasped raggedly."[51] Far from granting Katherine the power to make decisions in their relationship, he keeps her in a state of dependence, constantly accusing her of being "babyish" or "a sniveling baby"; they have sex "whatever way that he wanted, in adherence to his dictates," and he thinks of her as his possession and his creation, claiming that her value lies in the fact that "he had carved her out and no one had followed to alter his work."[52] As her father's friend and a man who engages in sexual banter with Katherine's mother, Addison's constant reminders of the difference in their ages make their relationship not only near-pedophilic, but also incestuous. Yet in this society, his power over her cannot be critiqued; instead, it is she who is "Addison's whore," she who is "ruined."[53] When Katherine's mother accuses her years later—"the fault was yours"[54]—both women truly believe that Katherine has acted as an equal (or rather, more culpable) partner in the affair, despite her lasting psychological dependence on an adult man who reciprocated her adolescent sexual advances with the full force of his social position as a white, male professor and friend of her father.

The juxtaposition of Chang/Chuck's and Katherine's stories serves at least two main purposes. First, it links Southern white patriarchy with the paternalism that has accompanied American imperialism in Asia. The "racist love" that Bow identifies as key to understanding white attitudes towards Chang—Peterfield's casual, presumptuous bestowal of the name "Chuck" and Addison's later demonstrations that he is the superior Charles to Chang's Chuck—parallels, to some extent, the extremely damaging patriarchal "love" that Addison shows for Katherine. In both cases, Chang and Katherine are placed in positions of dependence to those in power, and their emotional attachment to others is betrayed by the racial and gendered hierarchy of white, imperial male privilege. When Peterfield abandons Chang to die, Chang feels a loss "as powerfu[l] as heartbreak. Sometimes his stomach would seem to drop away and there in the void was the realization he had been discarded."[55] When the adult Katherine meditates on her lifelong despair, she wonders at her own belief that "the power to withhold her happiness lay outside herself."[56] As such, the narrative is a meditation on the power and privilege of men such as Charles Addison.

The second effect of combining these very different stories is to rewrite the ending of the Southern gothic novel, to insert an Asian American epistemology into a tale of incestuous love and miscegenation. For if the incest and racial mixing in Faulkner's *Absalom! Absalom!* result in murder, fire, and the demise of the Sutpen family, and the incestuous relationship in William Styron's *Lie Down in Darkness* ends in suicide and despair, Choi's novel bestows a more hopeful ending to the novel's critique of racial and gendered hierarchies. It is no accident that the relationship between Chang and Katherine is consummated at the Charles Hotel in New Orleans, as their connection severs and supplants their dependence on Charles Addison; by disregarding Addison's claim to Katherine, Chang/Chuck and Katherine reclaim their agency through racial miscegenation. The move is not without cost for either character, but it does enable the novel to end, not with the violent torture of Chang by ROKA U.S.-allied forces, or with the disturbing sex between Addison and the child-Katherine, but with Chang's declaration of independence from "shame and uncertainty" and his assertion that "this war would never define him. . . . He was already free."[57] Ultimately, both Chang and Katherine exceed the narratives that claim to define them. Neither communist spy nor third world recipient of American benevolence, Chang cannot be defined by Cold War ideology, nor can Katherine be defined as Addison's whore. Instead, Choi's novel casts them as translation's unnatural byproducts, people and ideas that have no official existence in Cold War-era ideas of race, empire, and gender roles. By setting the story in Korea and in the U.S. South, Choi not only reworks the Southern gothic novel but also sets up a powerful critique of Cold War ideology that crosses through space and time to question, subvert, and redefine U.S. memories of the Korean War.

"WHAT REALLY HAPPENED": ACHY OBEJAS'S *MEMORY MAMBO*

In defining Asian American cultural politics, theorist Lisa Lowe has observed: "the material legacy of the repressed history of U.S. imperialism in Asia is borne out in the 'return' of Asian immigrants to the imperial center. In this sense, these

Asian Americans are determined by the history of U.S. imperialism in Asia *and* the historical racialization of Asians in the United States."[58] Certainly, Chang's identity in *The Foreign Student* is determined both by the United States' military presence in Korea and his racialization in the U.S. South. A similar statement may be made for Cuban Americans, whose identities are as determined by U.S.-Cuban relations as they are by their ambiguous racialization in the United States. In fact, among Latina/o populations in the United States, Cuban Americans occupy a unique position that is directly tied to the political relationship between Cuba and the United States during the Cold War and during earlier periods of paternalistic U.S. foreign policy in Latin America (e.g., the 1903 Platt Amendment, which gave the United States extensive economic and land rights in Cuba). As Suzanne Oboler states, unlike other immigrants from Latin America, Cuban Americans have been able to create a strong and politically powerful "ethnic enclave" in Miami based on the simultaneous arrival of a large wave of upper- and middle-class white Cubans in the early 1960s. The majority of these Cuban Americans were comprised of a light-skinned elite who benefited from the political and economic ties between the United States and Cuba: they were the "bankers and professionals, often highly educated and literate in English," many of whom "had previously visited the United States, owned real estate properties, had long established business and financial ties in Florida."[59] It was this elite, "returning" to an imperial center, who left their country for political reasons after Fidel Castro came to power and who received what Oboler calls a "financially supportive welcome" from the U.S. government.[60] Although later waves of Cuban immigrants were more racially and economically diverse, most notably the 125,000 "Marielitos" from nonwhite and working class backgrounds who arrived in 1980, the Cuban American community has largely managed to retain the political strength and image associated with that first wave of immigrants. In fact, the politics of older Cuban American groups, politically right-wing and fiercely anticommunist, are somewhat of an anomaly in Latina/o studies, as they contradict the popular and critical construction of Latina/os in the United States as a resistant and oppositional group. Latina/o studies scholar Marta Caminero-Santangelo explores the pervasive "notion of the Cuban enclave as a population separate indeed from other Latinos," a notion that persists not just among political pundits and presidential candidates vying for Latina/o votes, but also in literary and critical scholarship on "latinidad."[61] For Caminero-Santangelo, the task of Cuban American writers such as Achy Obejas and Cristina García is to bridge the gap between Cuban American issues and a larger body of Latina/o literature. She explores the ways in which these writers "imagine the possibilities of a pan-ethnic Latina/o (or Latin American) identity that might conceivably include Cuban Americans."[62]

While Caminero-Santangelo's work explores the relationship between Cuban American literature and a larger body of Latina/o literature, I am interested in examining its connection to other literatures of the Cold War. Structurally, by the very nature of their political reception within the United States, Cuban American groups have much in common with other ethnic groups shaped by Cold War divisions, such as South Vietnamese refugee communities in Southern California.[63] Of course, the analogy cannot be stretched too far, as each ethnic group has faced unique historical and sociological challenges. Nevertheless, an examination of Achy Obejas's novel *Memory Mambo* reveals that the novel can be understood productively *across* ethnic affiliations as well as within them, as a response to civil conflicts that split communities during the Cold War and bound ethnic statuses within the United States to a political ideology complicit with racial and gendered hierarchies. In this sense, the critical question is not why Cuban American literature is politically different from other Latina/o literatures, but what are the ways in which Cuban American literature is shaped by its reaction to Cold War ideologies at work across the world? What can we learn by studying Cuban American literature along with Southeast Asian American literature, or with Korean American literature like Choi's *The Foreign Student*? Certainly, like Choi, Obejas has written a novel that takes a critical look at the ways in which Cold War ideologies continue to resonate decades later, affecting not only people's lives, but how we in the present day remember U.S. history.

Like Choi in *The Foreign Student*, Achy Obejas's 1996 novel *Memory Mambo* takes on Cold War ideology as a deconstructive project. Whereas Choi's novel can be understood as a response to Chang's church audience, who desire a particular narrative of U.S. heroism against communist aggression in Korea, *Memory Mambo* can be read as a response to the Cold War mythology of Cuban refugees fleeing communism to achieve a miraculous economic success within the United States. Political scientist Sheila Croucher has identified this narrative as the "Cuban American success story," an idea that is only partly a product of statistics and empirical facts. While the idea of Cuban American exceptionalism among Latina/o immigrant groups has its roots in the first wave of elite immigrants that Oboler describes, Croucher demonstrates that in fact, Cuban Americans have not uniformly achieved the economic miracle that this idea perpetuates; rather, the Cuban American success story is a myth that "has functioned to protect and promote the power and privilege of certain individuals and groups—whether North American capitalists, U.S. politicians, or Cuban elites."[64] According to Croucher, this protection of privilege has occurred through the elision (or denial) of the political, racial, and class diversity of Cuban Americans in the United States from the very first wave of immigration in the early 1960s. And while certainly, the myth has operated to the benefit of Cuban American elites, Croucher reveals that many of these claims about Cuban immigration were originally issued by the U.S. federal government:

> The Cuban revolution dealt a serious blow to the US in its ideological struggle with the Soviet Union, and having "lost" Cuba to communism, the exodus of Cuban refugees from the island provided the US with potent material for an ideological counter-attack. Widely publicized accounts of Cubans risking their lives to escape tyranny served to discredit the revolution and the ideological principles upon which it was founded, and photographs of Cubans kneeling to kiss the ground in Miami portrayed the US, and the principles for which it professed to stand, as an option superior to that of Communism. The discourse on Cubans as victims of tyranny also helped to restore US national honor after the severe loss of prestige suffered during the failed Bay of Pigs invasion.[65]

The U.S. investment in the Cuban American success story was not only ideological; it had important financial ramifications. The Cuban Refugee Program, established by the Kennedy administration in 1961, provided Cuban exiles with food, clothing, health care, housing, and job placement assistance. It also provided a monthly stipend and federal loans for education or businesses. In all, the program cost the U.S. government more than $2 billion. Not only was the program unique among Latin American immigrants, but it was also one of the most costly and longest running refugee programs in U.S. history.[66] Thus, the Cuban American success story can be understood as a Cold War narrative that has strategically positioned Cuban immigrants as ideological weapons in the war against communism: their economic success is proof of the success of the American Dream, discursively created through financial investment in addition to public proclamations.

Memory Mambo provides a counternarrative to the Cuban American success story through the characters of Juani Casas and her family. Arriving in the United States in 1978, far too late to constitute part of the "first wave" of Cuban exiles, they settle in Chicago rather than Miami, over a thousand miles away from the site of the purported Cuban American economic miracle. Her family is working class with no economic advancement in sight; Juani, her parents, aunts, uncles, and cousins work at the family laundromat—the Wash-N-Dry Laundry/Lavanderia Wash-N-Dry—a place where the main attraction is a wall of video arcade games and a pay phone frequented by gang members. Originally a Polish and Latino neighborhood, the area has changed to incorporate upscale "Anglo artists" and "new Hispanics" who have "moved in, driving German compact cars and recording English-only messages on their voice-mail."[67] However, Juani's family is not considered "new Hispanics" but rather members of the "original Latinos," only able to refuse the ethnic hostility of the Polish American store owners by buying at Sears, not by moving out of the neighborhood or joining in the area's gentrification. Indeed, the Cuban American men Juani knows are almost all part of a blue-collar existence; they play the lottery every week and "drea[m] of winning—of being delivered from [their] life's drudgery with one magical combination."[68] In this narrative, the only member of the family who has found material success is Juani's estranged uncle Raúl, a communist fighter during the Cuban revolution.

Yet the novel does not simply provide examples contradicting the Cuban American success story; ironically, despite their lack of economic success, Juani's family is deeply invested in the very narrative their existence disproves. According to Juani's father, the family was destined for prosperity because back in Cuba, he invented duct tape, or as he calls it, "duck tape—*cinta pata, cinta maricona*," employing the Spanish double meaning of "pato" as duck or homosexual.[69] According to Juani's father, if his formula had not been stolen by the CIA, the family would have been rich and "much happier."[70] Juani's family believes in the myth of Cuban American exceptionalism, but they believe that they have been tricked out of their success by the American government. The fact that much of this myth was manufactured by the government as an ideological weapon during the Cold War highlights the contradictory nature of the narrative. This contradiction is more than just ironic or humorous; rather, it enables Obejas to interrogate Cold War ideology on a number of levels, to question not only its objective reality, but also its relationship to sexual politics, race, and gender hierarchies in the United States.

The centrality of the duct tape story as an organizing theme in *Memory Mambo*—as one that brings together Cold War mythologies, narratives of exile, and the politics of sexuality—has been unexplored by literary critics, who tend to focus instead on the novel's depiction of Juani's relationship and conflict with her Puerto Rican girlfriend Gina.[71] What Juani wants so badly to remember, her insistence on knowing "what *really* happened," refers both to her family's immigration journey to the United States and to the brutal fight that ends her relationship with Gina.[72] Unable to bear the political differences between them—Gina's dismissal of Juani as a *gusana* ("worm"), a pejorative term for an émigré who has betrayed the Cuban revolution, and Juani's failure to stand up for Gina when her family tells racist Puerto Rican jokes—the women attack each other with a violence that lands them in the hospital and leaves them permanently scarred. Juani's anguished lie to her family, her claim that the attack was the work of an outside assailant, grows out of proportion until she can neither tell it nor write it, even in her private journal. Instead, she finds herself writing about the invented assailant: "But I knew that wasn't what happened! *Or was it?*"[73] "What really happened" is thus a dual reference to Juani's immigration story and to her own capacity for violence. Linking the two together is the trope of duct tape, which refers directly back to Cold War politics and provides the novel with its organizing theme of memory instability and sexual oppression.

The fact that Juani's father calls his invention "duck tape—*cinta pata, cinta maricona*" overtly links his narrative to the idea of queer sexuality.[74] As author and critic Lawrence La Fountain-Stokes explains, in the Hispanic Caribbean and other parts of Latin America, pato (male duck) "is a synonym or popular variant for 'homosexual,' or at least for an effeminate man (a *maricón*)" and pata (female duck) is a referent to lesbians.[75] While the violent and homophobic Jimmy softly corrects him, "duct tape," Juani's father's insistence on calling the tape "duck tape" is not actually incorrect.[76] According to the Oxford English Dictionary, the term "duck tape" predates "duct tape" by over half a century and refers either to the tape's ability to repel water (like a duck) or to the fact that it was originally manufactured from duck cloth.[77] Today's "duck tape" was developed during World War II as a way to bind ammunition and equipment securely to military vessels and planes, and it was only in the 1950s and 1960s, when the tape became widely used for ductwork, that it became known as "duct tape."[78]

As a symbol, duck or duct tape has the power to hurt Juani by simultaneously invoking homophobia and the American Dream. As "*cinta pata, cinta maricona*," her father's words associate his own idealized past with a way of life that could never accept Juani as a lesbian. La Fountain-Stokes quotes his elderly mother to demonstrate the pain associated with the word: "Pato is a very ugly word," she says. "I do not like it at all, and it has been used as far back as I can remember." He concludes, "Many are the traumas and bitter memories that we have from hearing this word used against us in childhood."[79] Yet "duck tape" is not just Juani's father's lost dream; it is a potent symbol of the American Dream itself. In the United States, duct tape has an almost cult-like following as a positive example of the American "can-do" mentality; urban legends claim that duct tape can fix anything, from sinking boats to removing unsightly warts. Duck Tape brand duct tape even sponsors an annual design contest to see who can make the best prom dress entirely out of duct tape. About the hermeneutics of duct tape, American studies scholar Joe Barrett states, "duct tape isn't simply practical anymore; it has come to *mean* a certain practicality. Unlike computers, fax machines, and cellular phones, duct tape is a democratic, equal access technology—anybody can use it, anybody can understand it. . . . A person who uses duct tape is making a fundamental statement about his or her values. He or she is throwing in with a long line of American pragmatists."[80] Duct tape also has a "dark side," however—it is not infrequently used in rapes and murders to bind and suffocate victims.[81] The history of duct tape, therefore, is a multilayered symbol in the novel. As a peculiar example of linguistic hypercorrection, the true story of the tape is one in which the "duct" has replaced the "duck" as a symbol of can-do attitude rather than military necessity. Yet duct tape is inextricable from both its past and present manifestations; whether used to bind weaponry or to bind rape and murder victims, the tape is associated not just with practicality, but also with violence. As a symbol, it links key parts of the American Dream—the idea that there can be a democratic, equal access technology, and that an individual can fix anything with the right attitude—to military and sexual violence. And through the

Spanish association of "duck" with the words *pata* and *maricona*, it links this American Dream to homophobia as well.

The political significance of duct tape within the novel is underscored by the fact that Juani tells the story of her father's invention—and loss—of a recipe for duct tape through the reactions of the novel's most polarized characters, the ultra-right-wing Jimmy and the Puerto Rican *independentista* Gina, as they listen to the oft-repeated narrative. Jimmy, the abusive husband of Juani's cousin, arrived in the United States through the Mariel boatlift and is vehemently anti-Castro. He believes that Juani's father was a "prosperous businessman" who not only invented duct tape but was later recruited by the CIA after the revolution for his ability to procure boats to get people off the island.[82] According to this version of the story, Juani's father was from one of Havana's oldest families and therefore knew everyone at the Miramar Boat Club; he had access to boats for purchase by the CIA and even helped the old dictator Fulgencio Batista to flee. When things started getting "hot" for him, he asked the CIA to get him out of Cuba "before the communists killed me in front of my wife and children."[83] The CIA refused to help, and he managed to procure one last boat for the family. However, in the family's haste to leave, the mother forgot or lost the formula for duct tape. For Jimmy, this story is entirely "reasonable" and "sensible"; it emphasizes a Cuban past lost to Castro and the inferiority of women.[84] As critic María de los Angeles Torres explains, "the first group of postrevolution emigres turned nostalgia into a principle of constructing community," and this narrative is nostalgic in the extreme.[85] The fact that Jimmy was not a member of that first group, that he arrived along with the mixed-race, lower class "Marielitos," does not obviate his need to identify with the Cuban American success story.

The story gets more complicated, however, when the family arrives in the United States. According to Juani's father, the first thing they saw in a hardware store window was duct tape, the formula stolen and the product manufactured and distributed by the CIA. While Jimmy sympathizes with the family's loss of stature due to the Cuban revolution, he cannot understand a government conspiracy to steal a duct tape formula. He tells his wife later that he thinks duct tape had already existed in the United States prior to the family's arrival, but his objection to the story is more than factual: "It offended all his sensibilities" (30). Jimmy cannot believe in the fallability of the U.S. government and keeps peace only by returning to the narrative he can identify with: "If only Fidel hadn't come . . . things might have been different."[86] Surprisingly, it is Gina, Juani's leftist Puerto Rican girlfriend, who thinks that the government theft of the family duct tape formula "wasn't all that far-fetched."[87] Although she politely nods and remains silent through the first part of the story, her hostility towards the CIA makes her sympathetic to the possibility of a conspiracy. Juani explains, "That she didn't believe my father had a damn thing to do with the development of duct tape didn't stop her for one minute from thinking Uncle Sam could have ripped him off." After hearing the end of the story, Gina promises "in solidarity" with the family never to use duct tape again.[88]

Juani's growing obsession with finding out the truth about her father's invention of duct tape reflects her divided political loyalties and comes to shape her desires and relationships in harmful ways. The fact that the story is shot through with impossibilities does not lessen its desirability; other family members question her father's high-class position, his age (he was too young to have helped Fulgencio Batista out of Cuba), and the facts of his story, yet Juani increasingly finds her own memory invaded by her father's stories. Just as her private journal is invaded by false memories of her fight with Gina, her own childhood memories are invaded by images of "buckets of bubbling mystery soup."[89] Memory is unstable in this novel, precisely because different versions of history represent a different set of alliances. As a version of the Cuban American success story, the duct tape story gives meaning to Juani's existence in the United States. It allows her family to claim the position of exiles from their homeland. Most confusingly for Juani, the position of exile is also valuable to her identity as an out lesbian, for Juani identifies her freedom to exist openly as a lesbian with her escape from a more repressive society. In an interview, Obejas has described her fascination with how, "in Cuba, a lot of the discussion about homosexuality is extremely complicated because of the terrible history in Cuba during the '60s, that is during the revolutionary times, when there were labor camps set up for homosexuals."[90] In the novel, this fascination takes the form of Juani's obsession with her cousin Titi in Cuba, whom she is convinced is an unhappily closeted lesbian. While other members of the family attribute Titi's attempts to escape to "a great craving for a near mystical freedom and democracy," Juani believes "that Titi's addiction to the notion of escape, her desire to come to the United States, has nothing whatsoever to do with any of that patriotic crap, but with a whole other, perhaps even crazier idea—that once here, she might be free to be queer."[91] Thus, when Juani's lover Gina rejects her family's position as exiles from a communist regime, calling them *gusanos* or "worms," she devalues not only Juani's family, but also Juani's personal investment in the Cuban American success story, her belief that it is only in the United States that she can exist as an out lesbian.

While Gina obviously does not advocate labor camps for homosexuals, her leftist politics mirror the politics of the Cuban revolution in considering all other concerns secondary to nationalist goals:

> Look, I'm not interested in being a *lesbian*, in separating politically from my people," she'd say to me, her face hard and dark. "What are we talking about? Issues of *sexual identity*? While Puerto Rico is a colony? While Puerto Rican apologists are trying to ram statehood down our throats with legislative tricks and sleights of hand? You think I'm going to sit around and discuss *sexual identity*? Nah, Juani, you can do that—you can have that navel-gazing discussion.[92]

Gina identifies Castro as a political hero and the United States as a colonialist and capitalist enemy of third world peoples. Yet she lacks understanding of two key aspects of Juani's life: first, that Juani's family has not benefited from their ideological alliance with U.S. Cold War politics: while Gina considers Juani's family privileged because of the tremendous money poured into the Cuban Refugee Program, Juani describes her own family as "trying desperately to stay afloat."[93] And second, Gina fails to understand that Juani's identity as a lesbian is intimately tied to her identity as a Cuban American exile.

Yet the real horror in this narrative does not lie in Gina's misunderstanding of Juani, but in Juani's inadvertent alliance with Jimmy, her racist, homophobic, physically and sexually abusive cousin-in-law. In attacking Gina, Juani has invested her identity in her family's (failed version of the) Cuban American success story, and the novel gradually peels away layer after layer of Cold War ideology to reveal the ways in which this story is itself invested in violent racial and sexual hierarchies. Most immediately, the duct tape story only thinly masks Juani's mother's narrative, which complements the family's claims to Cuba's upper class. Described as a "*café con leche mulata,*" Juani's mother Xiomara's life goal is to "deny her real lineage" and whiten the family by producing children who are "colorless and beautiful."[94] To Juani's mother, the real problem of the Cuban revolution was the opportunity that it afforded people of color. Having witnessed black Cubans riding tanks triumphantly after the revolution, "her immediate goal became to get us out of Cuba, out of Latin America, out of any country where we might couple with anybody even a shade darker than us: We had to get to the United States, which was close by and chock full of frog-eyed white people such as Joe Namath and President Ford."[95] Juani's mother is attracted to her father for his ancestry; supposedly, he is the direct descendant of the Spaniard Bartolomé de Las Casas, "The Apostle to the Indies."[96] However, even this history is subject to dispute and interpretation. The narrative alternately describes Las Casas as either a protector to the Indians or the originator of slavery in Cuba; furthermore, neither parent has an adequate explanation for how the family is descended from a celibate priest, at least without polluting the family's supposed whiteness. Structurally, Xiomara's story of Las Casas parallels her husband's duct tape story: both stories are seeming impossibilities. Both require extraordinary suspensions of disbelief, which means that each parent must have extraordinarily powerful reasons for believing in them. The fact that her parents fervently believe both stories—that they are presented as different, but complementary perspectives on the same set of events—links the Cuban American success story to racial hierarchies both in Cuba and in the United States; it depicts the compatibility of Cold War ideology and racism. This idea, articulated by Gina's claim that the family are "racists and classists," is further validated by Jimmy's joke, "What's the difference between a Cuban and a Puerto Rican? A Cuban's a Puerto Rican *with a job.*"[97] Even though Gina points out that they make fun of Puerto Ricans because most of them are "poorer and darker" than Cubans, Juani actually thinks the joke is "kind of funny." Despite her love for Gina, Juani's allegiance to the Cuban American success story makes her identify racism as a "Cuban cultural thing."[98]

More seriously for Juani, her allegiance to this manifestation of "Cuban culture" also allies her to Jimmy sexually. After Juani's fight with Gina, Jimmy creates the false story of an unidentified assailant and convinces Juani that she is grateful to him for doing so. She finds herself identifying with Jimmy. When her cousin comments, "you two react to things the same way . . . you talk alike, you even stand alike, okay?"[99] Juani does not dismiss the comparison as the delusion of an abuse victim who insists on staying with her abuser; instead, she consciously tries to change the way she stands and talks. On some deep level, Juani believes that her fight with Gina has actually turned her into Jimmy. Although she hates him, she thinks he is the only one who understands her: "Our communication is instant, silent, totally natural."[100] Juani's identification with Jimmy is a part of her fear and self-loathing after discovering that she is capable of extreme violence; the brutality of the fight between the women strips away the illusion that patriarchal violence is only enacted by men. Instead, the novel channels the homophobia of the communist revolution in Cuba and the violence associated with duct tape, American militarism, and the Cuban American success story into the conflict between the two women. As critic Kate McCullough has shown, the novel proves that erotic and romantic desire, "so often fondly held as the most private and autonomous of forces," is actually politically and publicly determined.[101] The fact that Juani becomes sexually aroused by Jimmy, despite her repugnance for his violent tendencies, demonstrates that even her erotic desires are politically determined by her allegiance to the Cuban American success story. However, it is the flip side of McCullough's statement that creates the novel's true horror: that the Cold War politics of militarism, racism, homophobia (on both sides), and violence can manifest themselves in the actions of two Latinas, despite those women's apparent love for one another and desire for a pan-Latina solidarity.

It is because of this horror that Juani displaces her need to know "what really happened" with Gina onto her father's story about duct tape. Unable to tell her sister the truth about Gina, Juani researches the chemical composition of duct tape on the internet, calling her mother repeatedly and screaming her need to know into the phone. "I was obsessed," she explains. "I wanted to know what my father really knew about duct tape, I wanted to test him, I wanted him to fail that test, and to nail him. I wanted to throw myself on the floor and kick and scream and cry."[102] The novel describes the conversation itself as violent, as Juani finds herself hearing her accusations "like bullets piercing" her mother, and it leaves Juani herself feverishly collapsed on the floor.[103] Yet the truth about duct tape remains elusive, because its importance does not lie in historically verifiable facts, but in the way it binds together narratives of class, race, the American

Dream, the Cold War, and military and sexual violence. Essentially, Juani is trapped within choices carved out by Cold War ideologies: binary choices of capitalism or communism, of Jimmy or Gina, of sexual violence or sexual repression. The final scene offers scant hope for its protagonist. After witnessing Jimmy's sexual molestation of her infant niece, Juani joins her family in violently rejecting him. Afterwards, in a coffee shop, when she asks herself, "*What really happened?*" she is finally able to recover her own "authentic memory" of hurting Gina. However, at the same time, she articulates "another memory," her sexual attraction to Jimmy, whom she has witnessed sexually violating her niece.[104] The last scenes of the novel cut between Juani's conversation with a sympathetic cousin and a fly struggling to escape from a puddle of water on the table. As Juani exits the coffee shop, she flicks her finger at the fly, but "it crawls a bit, then takes off, making an aimless loop in the air, then smashes itself against the window pane."[105] It is a bleak end to a narrative that suggests no escape for the fly or for Juani. Her identity, her desires, and even her memory are entirely shaped by Cold War ideologies, and like the fly, she can never be free.

NATIONAL MEMORIES, NATIONAL AMNESIA

Ultimately, both *The Foreign Student* and *Memory Mambo* demonstrate how Asian American and Latina/o literature can uncover, question, and deconstruct Cold War epistemologies. By their very existence, these literatures link together ethnic communities within the United States and histories of Cold War military intervention. Because so many of these interventions were secret, or were wrapped in obfuscating ideologies of heroism and freedom, Asian American and Latina/o literatures must engage in narrative acts of reconstruction, rewriting dominant historical narratives to include military operations in Asia and Latin America. Often based on real-life histories, like that of Susan Choi's father in Korea and the U.S. South, or Achy Obejas's own immigration from Cuba to Chicago, these narratives also question the bilateral framework of the Cold War. They tell the stories of individuals caught in the violent turmoil of war, emphasizing the disconnect between Asian/American and Latin/American subjects' experiences and the ideological justifications that have been put forth for U.S. intervention in these wars.

It is significant that both Choi and Obejas present memory as unstable, even on an individual, personal level, because this instability emphasizes the difficulty of seeing past Cold War ideologies that have dictated political and public rhetoric for more than half a century. As Korean and Cuban American, Chang and Juani find their own personal memories affected by trying to translate a period of rapid decolonization into the bilateral framework of the Cold War. In some senses, Chang and Juani both struggle to establish themselves as nonaligned individuals, unaffected by either side of the Cold War argument.

Desperate to survive in Korea, Chang declares that "he would be loyal to nobody but himself," and Juani simply wants for herself, like Titi, to be "free to be queer."[106] Yet what *A Foreign Student* and *Memory Mambo* illustrate, above all, is the extreme difficulty of nonalignment given that Cold War rhetoric encompasses nonalignment within its ideology. It is illuminating to compare Chang's and Juani's dilemmas with President Truman's 1947 announcement of what was to become the guiding principle of the Cold War, the idea that the nonaligned nations of the world depended on the United States to intervene on their behalf to win for them their "freedom":

> At the present moment in world history *nearly every nation must choose* between alternative ways of life. . . . One way of life is based upon the will of the majority, and is distinguished by free institutions, representative government, free elections, guarantees of individual liberty, freedom of speech and religion, and freedom from political oppression. The second way of life is based upon the will of a minority forcibly imposed upon the majority. It relies upon terror and oppression, a controlled press and radio, fixed elections, and the suppression of personal freedoms.[107]

Truman's stirring rhetoric emphasizes freedom to the point of redundancy—"The free peoples of the world look to us for support in maintaining their freedoms"[108]—yet a maintenance of freedom that depends on military violence is, for Chang, one that curtails his own personal liberty. On a national level, Truman's speech also fails to acknowledge the fact that in 1947, many nations throughout the world were engaged in revolutionary struggles to attain a different kind of freedom, the freedom from colonial occupation. This was certainly the case in Korea, Vietnam, and Cuba, and one achievement of Asian American and Latina/o cultural productions has been to interrogate the connections between the freedom referred to in Cold War rhetoric and imperial or colonial occupation.

The Foreign Student and *Memory Mambo* make these connections. Chang's own attempt at political nonalignment in Korea fails because Truman's doctrine of military intervention defines nonalignment as a position of dependency; Chang is renamed "Chuck" in an expression of U.S. paternalistic policy even before he arrives in the United States as a dependent of the Episcopal church. Similarly, Juani's attempt to break free from the Cuban American success story fails because it is more a Cold War-era ideological weapon than a reality. It comes to define her in terms that echo the racial ideology of prerevolutionary Cuba. In fact, both Choi and Obejas not only demonstrate the failure of Cold War bilateralism to account for the politics of decolonization, they also reveal the ways in which Cold War ideology within the United States is complicit with racial, gendered, and sexual oppression. In *The Foreign Student,* the white, Southern

Addison both patronizes Chang/Chuck and places Katherine in a position of sexual dependency. Imperialism is linked to colonial paternalism, which in turn is linked to racial hierarchies and sexual violence. In *Memory Mambo*, the anti-Castro Jimmy tells racist jokes, beats his wife, and molests an infant girl; furthermore, the trope of duct tape links the Cuban American success story to military and sexual violence. If communist North Korea and Cuba are sites of oppression and danger in these novels, the United States as expressed through Cold War containment ideologies is equally as dangerous.

The Cold War has much to tell us about U.S. history, from the 1940s to the present day. Both Choi and Obejas wrote their novels forty years after the high point of the Cold War and nearly a decade after the fall of the Berlin Wall officially marked the war's "end." Yet since the publication of their novels, North Korea was named one of George W. Bush's three nations comprising an "Axis of Evil" during the twenty-first century's War on Terror, and Cuba was later included in an expansion of that list.[109] Cold War terminology and ideas about containment continue to affect the ways in which the United States and other Western nations think about terrorism and state-sponsored terror. Asian American and Latina/o literatures about the Cold War help us remember the dangers of bilateral thinking; they help us rewrite a history shaped by politics in order to interrogate racial and sexual violence that occurs across national boundaries but may be deeply inscribed in national ideologies.

4 • GLOBALIZATION AND MILITARY VIOLENCE IN THE LATINASIAN CONTACT ZONE

> When I visit Los Angeles or San Francisco, I am at the same time in Latin America and Asia. Los Angeles, like Mexico City, Tijuana, Miami, Chicago, and New York, is practically a hybrid nation/city in itself. Mysterious underground railroads connect all these places—syncretic art forms, polyglot poetry and music, and transnational pop cultures function as meridians of thought and axes of communication.
>
> Here/there, the indigenous and the immigrant share the same space but are foreigners to each other. Here/there we are all potential border-crossers and cultural exiles.... Here/there, homelessness, border culture, and deterritorialization are the dominant experience, not just fancy academic theories.
>
> —Guillermo Gómez-Peña, *The New World Border*

Exactly halfway through Karen Tei Yamashita's *Tropic of Orange* (1997), one of the novel's seven main characters loudly proclaims, "Cultural diversity is bullshit."[1] The speaker, Japanese American Emi, is sitting at a sushi bar in Los Angeles with her Chicano boyfriend Gabriel, and her statement seems to jar with the fact that she is part of a markedly diverse cast of characters. From Rafaela, an indigenous Mexican immigrant, to Manzanar Murakami, a homeless Japanese American man, and from Buzzworm, an African American self-styled social worker, to Bobby Ngu, who is "Chinese from Singapore with a Vietnam name speaking like a Mexican living in Koreatown,"[2] the novel's seven protagonists reflect much of the ethnic, racial, and socioeconomic diversity of the late twentieth-century United States. Indeed, the only racial category that is conspicuously absent from the group is the dominant one; none of the main characters is white. Why, then, is Emi so insistent that "it's all bullshit" and that she "hate[s] being multicultural?"[3]

Yamashita's point becomes clear as Emi's provocative statements on cultural diversity escalate into a confrontation with the white woman sitting next to her, an unnamed character wearing chopsticks in her hair. Turning not to Emi, who has just offended her, but to the chef, whom she pointedly addresses as "Hiro-san," the white woman voices her own ideas about multiculturalism:

> I happen to adore the Japanese culture. What can I say? I adore different cultures. I've traveled all over the world. I love living in L.A. *because I can find anything in the world to eat, right here.* It's such a meeting place for all sorts of people. A true celebration of an international world.[4]

For this woman, "cultural diversity" is about consumption and more particularly about food; she considers ethnicity, race, and culture primarily in terms of a variety of restaurants that she can enjoy. Indeed, her self-professed adoration of Japanese culture seems to rely entirely on a decontextualized consumption of Japanese cultural markers, symbolized by her love of sushi and the chopsticks in her hair (a fashion choice that provokes Emi into threatening to stick forks into her own hair). Emi summarizes the ways in which such consumption is tied to the commodification of ethnicity when she addresses the chef herself: "See what I mean, Hiro? You're invisible. I'm invisible. We're all invisible. It's just tea, ginger, raw fish, and a credit card."[5]

One pressing concern of contemporary Asian American and Latina/o studies is to address precisely this invisibility, along with the "tea, ginger, raw fish, and a credit card" version of ethnicity that critical race theorists call the liberal discourse of multiculturalism. The unnamed woman in the story voices a late twentieth- and twenty-first century trend that links ethnicity with domestic consumption of difference and the commodification of culture for white tourists.[6] The liberal discourse of multiculturalism, prevalent not only in popular and public spheres, but also in academic arenas, is essentially a celebratory rhetoric that flattens race and ethnicity into a horizontal field of equal nodes of difference without drawing attention to asymmetries of power. While a celebration of diversity may be more progressive than ideologies of white supremacy, such a discourse can also function to contain politicized debate about inequalities of race, gender, and class in First World societies by unmooring "culture" from its historical and political context. According to the discourse of multiculturalism, culture must be appreciated in terms of cooperation, coexistence, and equality, regardless of whether those aims have actually been achieved. The unnamed woman in Yamashita's novel does not know (and might not care) about the World War II incarceration of Japanese Americans that has profoundly affected

Emi's family. To her, this is not what "Japanese culture" is about; rather, she considers Emi's disruptive behavior to be reprehensible, saying "It just makes me sick to hear people speak so cynically about something so positive and to make assumptions about people based on their color."[7]

In his introduction to *The Ethnic Canon,* Asian American theorist David Palumbo-Liu describes the ways in which the discourse of multiculturalism can act against the very groups it purports to celebrate: "To put it plainly, the sentiment that 'no one likes to argue' has effectively been validated by a particular revision of history and deployed to silence contestatory voices in the present, whose continued protest is then regarded as 'uncooperative complaining,' 'special interest lobbying,' or 'manipulative identity politics.'"[8] Certainly, the unnamed woman in Yamashita's novel attributes Emi's protest about her invisibility to a bad attitude and a so-called reverse racism in which it is Emi who is discriminating against the white woman for refusing to recognize multiculturalism as a positive force. Yet in the world of the novel, Yamashita gives Emi the last laugh; the woman "blanches" when Emi threatens to stick forks in her hair. Instead of being silenced, Emi's contestatory voice trumps in this scene and exemplifies her more general role as the novel's trickster figure, a character who critiques dominant culture from a hybrid, crossroads, or outsider perspective.[9]

Like *Tropic of Orange,* many Latina/o and Asian American cultural productions of the late twentieth and early twenty-first century reject the liberal discourse of multiculturalism, engaging instead in what Palumbo-Liu calls "*critical* multiculturalism," an exercise that involves "a critique of the ideological apparatuses that distribute power and resources unevenly among the different constituencies of a multicultural society."[10] According to Palumbo-Liu, ethnic American literary works are particularly well equipped to make this kind of critique, one that locates culture within specific histories of engagement with the dominant society. In this chapter, I look at how Latina/o and Asian American literature of the past few decades engages in critical multiculturalism by reconceptualizing U.S. geography in the age of globalization. Instead of an urban terrain characterized by an endless stretch of ethnic restaurants, the national geography that emerges from this literature is more akin to Mary Louise Pratt's concept of the "contact zone," a space in which people with distinct histories and identities "come into contact with each other and establish ongoing relations, usually involving conditions of coercion, radical inequality, and intractable conflict."[11] The difference between understanding the United States according to the liberal discourse of multiculturalism and understanding it as a contact zone is profound. While the first implies consent and containment, the second allows for protest of unequal social and economic conditions; while the former implies a Euro-American center, a white consumer who "celebrates" the ethnicity of others, the latter shifts the point of view to the relationship between people from previously disparate cultures, acknowledging the asymmetry that often characterizes that relationship. As Pratt explains, the contact zone "invokes the space and time where subjects previously separated by geography and history are co-present, the point at which their trajectories now intersect."[12] It questions large-scale power structures such as colonialism and imperialism and sees the current age of globalization as a continuation of earlier power struggles rather than a total disruption of previous repressive regimes.

More specifically, Latina/o and Asian American cultural productions of the past few decades can be understood as reconceptualizing the geography of the Americas as a *LatinAsian* contact zone, a space in which people of Latin American and Asian descent do not always constitute distinct groups, but are co-present in ways that reflect migrations of labor across multiple borders. As discussed in the introduction to this book, María DeGuzmán has coined the term "Latinasia" to describe the transnational convergence of Asians and Latin Americans or Latinos over the course of the last three centuries: "that is, the enormous influx of Asian immigrants and the movement of Latina/o peoples across the Americas, south to north and west to east."[13] To conceptualize the Americas as a LatinAsian contact zone is to redefine American geography in a way that acknowledges the coexistence of Latina/o and Asian populations in North and South America. It is another way of rethinking the border, opening up the idea of borderlands to encompass not only the United States-Mexico border but also the East-West border that separates the Americas from Asia. Gloria Anzaldúa has famously theorized border zones as conceptual spaces of possibility as well as physical spaces of violence: "The U.S.-Mexico border *es una herida abierta* [an open wound] where the Third World grates against the first and bleeds. And before a scab forms it hemorrhages again, the lifeblood of two worlds merging to form a third country—a border culture."[14] The image of a border formed of an open wound is one that fully incorporates the conflict, dispossession, and violence that have historically characterized the United States-Mexico border. Wars in Asia that have sent refugees fleeing across the Pacific, along with American hostility towards Asian immigrants (as recorded, for example, in Chinese poetry scrawled on the walls of Angel Island detention facilities), render it not unreasonable to stretch the metaphor of the open wound to encompass the East-West border of the Pacific Ocean. At the same time, Anzaldúa's theorization of the borderlands as a conceptual space, as a place where the mixing of races and cultures opens up possibilities for new modes of consciousness, may also apply to the understanding of the Americas as a LatinAsian contact zone, a space that enables new alliances between people of Latina/o and Asian descent.

Anzaldúa relies on the symbolism and the lived experience of the *mestiza* to theorize the borderlands; LatinAsia also encompasses people and communities of mixed race and mixed ethnic descent. Because Latina/o is not a racial category *per se*, it is possible to be of both Latin American and Asian descent, and the LatinAsian contact zone contains people and communities such as the

Chinese populations found throughout Latin America in *barrios chinos* (Chinatowns) or mixed with Latina/os of Spanish, Indian, or African ancestry. As part of the plantation era of colonialism, nations like Cuba and Peru imported tens of thousands of Chinese laborers during the nineteenth and twentieth centuries. Asian populations have also been present since the mid-nineteenth century in Mexico along the United States-Mexico border, in response to U.S. exclusion laws.[15] Historian Evelyn Hu-DeHart describes the way notions of race in Latin America necessarily "come with a Latin twist," as colonial Latin America recognized 14 different *castas*, or racially mixed groups, aside from whiteness.[16] According to Hu-DeHart, an "Asian admixture was hinted at in some of these *castas*, as their presence in Spanish America was well-known by the seventeenth century" in places like the Philippines, where Spanish colonists intermarried (or intermixed) not only with native Filipinos, but also with a sizable Chinese population.[17] Asians of Chinese, Japanese, and Filipino descent have been present in Spanish America for centuries.

The idea of contact zone may also be used to describe Latina/o and Asian American populations living in the same communities as neighbors, classmates, coworkers, and partners. In Los Angeles, for example, Latino/s and Asian Americans constitute the largest so-called minority groups at 48.5 percent and 11.3 percent of the city's population, respectively.[18] Meanwhile, historian Rudy Guevarra, Jr., reports that nearly a quarter million people identified as both Asian and Latino in San Diego in the 2000 census, including a significant "Mexipino" community of both Mexican and Filipino ancestry.[19] This population diversity can be attributed at least partly to urbanization. Anthropologists James Holston and Arjun Appadurai describe cities as especially complex and volatile spaces in the global economy, as "the transnationalization of labor generates a new global network of cities through which capital and labor pass."[20] Whether labor is "passing through" cities or reconstituting them, cities can act as sites of intensification of globalized forces. Performance artist Guillermo Gómez-Peña claims that when he visits the major cities of California, Los Angeles and San Francisco, "I am at the same time in Latin America and Asia."[21]

However, the convergence of Asian and Latina/o populations is not limited to major cities. A recent editorial in suburban North Carolina noted "dramatic increases in Latino/Hispanic and Asian populations" in the decade between 2000 and 2010.[22] Not surprisingly, the conservative commentator celebrated Orange County, North Carolina's "becoming a 'darker' shade of Orange" by discussing increased food options for white consumers: "These numbers confirm a change one can see, smell, and taste with the terrific restaurants Orange County hosts, including the best Mexican, Chinese, and Indian restaurants anywhere in the state."[23] This writer's opinion, that the relatively high cost of living in his area is not detrimental to "diversity" because he can eat Asian and Mexican food in his community, reveals a profound ignorance of the local Latina/o and Asian/

American populations, which include not only professional and entrepreneurial classes but also Latina/o immigrants and Southeast Asian refugee populations living in conditions of poverty. Like the scene in the sushi restaurant in *Tropic of Orange*, the commentary demonstrates a nationwide need to push beyond the idea of cuisine to theorize new forms of diversity.

Conceiving of the United States as part of a LatinAsian contact zone may serve as a corrective both to culinary-oriented discourses of multiculturalism and to overly celebratory conceptualizations of globalization, because the very idea of the contact zone emphasizes the discontinuities and the difficulties of migration. In a revised version of her well-known volume *Imperial Eyes: Travel Writing and Transculturation*, Pratt directly applies the concept of the contact zone to the accelerated transnationalism of the present moment. She notes that instead of the metaphor of "flow" that is so often used to characterize globalization—flows of people, goods, and capital across borders—the contact zone emphasizes the opposite of flow: that is, disruption and violence. There is nothing fluid, Pratt argues, about migrants dying in the backs of trucks or walking across a desert. Neither does capital flow; rather, it is sent by migrants at great expense to their families and themselves. According to Pratt, the metaphor of flow disguises the violence of a world "whose forces are not horizontal but vertical."[24] In contrast, the idea of the contact zone can act as a countermodel to globalization theories that celebrate the heightened mobility and freedom of globalization, yet fail to acknowledge that the state still has the power to confer or withhold citizenship and rights, as well as the power to deport noncitizens.

Finally, to consider the United States to be part of a LatinAsian contact zone is to decenter Eurocentric models of globalization. Like Françoise Lionnet's and Shu-mei Shih's concept of "minor transnationalism," it allows for the consideration of interethnic solidarities between Asian Americans and Latina/os despite their different historical relationships to the dominant society. Lionnet and Shih build on Gilles Deleuze and Félix Guattari's theorization of global relations as a rhizome, or more specifically, "an uncontainable, invisible symbolic geography of relations that become the creative terrain on which minority subjects act and interact in fruitful, lateral ways."[25] Lionnet and Shih use the idea of the rhizome in part to critique theories of transnationalism that privilege dominant forces: the "major" globalizing forces of media, capital, and political might. In these theories, minority cultures can play just two roles, assimilating to the major or resisting it through adhering to local practices. In reality, Lionnet and Shih observe, minority cultures play a far more complex part in the present transnational moment: "the minor and the major participate in one shared transnational moment and space structured by uneven power relations."[26] For Lionnet and Shih, theorizing a minor transnationalism is key to establishing dialogue between different disciplines that may otherwise occupy minority positions within major disciplines. As examples, they cite Lionnet's position working on postcolonial and ethnic studies from within the discipline of French and Shih's position working on Asian and Asian American studies from within the discipline of Chinese. The idea of minor transnationalism establishes the existence of minor-to-minor networks; it recognizes common interests between peoples with distinct historical trajectories.

Karen Tei Yamashita and Cuban American author Cristina García write from within the LatinAsian contact zone. Born in 1951, Yamashita is a third-generation Japanese American with extensive experience of South America.[27] After graduating from a U.S. college with a degree in English and Japanese literature, Yamashita went to Brazil in 1975 on a fellowship to conduct anthropological research on Japanese immigration to Brazil.[28] According to Yamashita, "all of a sudden, a world opened up to me, that there were Japanese communities in South America, particularly in Peru and in Brazil."[29] As with Chinese communities on the Mexican side of the United States-Mexico border, the Japanese communities in South America date to historical periods in which Asian immigration to the United States was heavily restricted. As Yamashita grappled with the most effective means to convey the Japanese Brazilian experience, her research project became a creative writing project. Yamashita lived in Brazil for nine years, during which time she married a Brazilian architect, raised a family, and began writing her two "Brazilian" novels: *Through the Arc of the Rain Forest* (1990) and *Brazil-Maru* (1992). When she returned to Los Angeles, the city in which she grew up, she found "a city that was very different, filled with people from all over the globe." Her own Japanese-Brazilian-American family was part of a great migration of people to Los Angeles, a migration that was changing the city in ways that she felt no one was yet writing about. According to Yamashita, the purpose of *Tropic of Orange* was "to bring in those who have been invisible in the literature of Los Angeles."[30] In the novel, Los Angeles is transformed by migration from Asia and Latin America; the novel also contains representatives of Asian Americans and Latinos from earlier migrations, as well as African American characters. Yamashita has observed that a friend of hers read the book and commented that "there are no white characters in it," to which Yamashita herself replied, "Well, someone else gets to tell the story for a change."[31] *Tropic of Orange* renders visible the demographic shift that has given cities like Los Angeles a significant Latina/o and Asian American presence. At the same time, it critiques aspects of globalization that create radical asymmetries of wealth and privilege. Organized into a grid that Yamashita calls a "hypercontext," the people, time, and places of the book rework the geography of globalization to emphasize the discontinuities and disruptions that characterize a contact zone.

Writer Cristina García also evokes a LatinAsian contact zone in her most recent works, including the novel *The Lady Matador's Hotel* (2010). Born in 1958 in Havana, Cuba, García grew up in New York City, where she moved with her parents at the age of two after Fidel Castro came to power.[32] She is perhaps best known for her 1992 novel *Dreaming in Cuban,* which tells the story of three generations of women divided by time, illness, and the politics of the Cuban Revolution. In recent years, however, García's novels have grown increasingly international—and ethnically hybrid—in scope. Her novel *Monkey Hunting* (2003) is particularly LatinAsian in theme, as it explores the history of the Chinese in Cuba, tracing four generations of a family from China to Cuba to the United States (and on to Vietnam during the war). In an interview at the conclusion of this novel, García discusses her interest in "compounded identities," ethnic backgrounds that complicate the idea of Americans living with a single hyphenated identity. Her own daughter has such a background, one that García describes as "part Japanese, part Cuban, part Guatemalan, and part Russian Jew."[33] Although *Monkey Hunting* focuses on the nineteenth century story of Chen Pan and his journey from Chinese laborer (or more accurately, slave) to prosperous Cuban merchant, it also tells the story of ethnic and racial mixture across generations. The most contemporary character in the novel, Domingo Chen, describes himself as part of a "whole new race—brown children with Chinese eyes who spoke Spanish and a smattering of Abakuá."[34] He is a Cuban national of Chinese descent who has immigrated to New York, living in Vietnam as an American soldier during the war. In García's words, Domingo is a "twenty-first century man in the twentieth century," a character whose issues concerning identity are pertinent to both time periods; in writing the novel, García says, "I had to ask myself what identity meant when it's such a mix. And are the ways in which we discuss identity still meaningful or are they becoming obsolete?"[35]

The Lady Matador's Hotel (2010) brings these concerns into the twenty-first century with another LatinAsian protagonist, Suki Palacios. The eponymous matador of the novel's title, Suki is a Japanese-Mexican American from California who travels to a fictionalized Guatemala for an epic bullfighting match.[36] The hotel where she is staying is inhabited by a former revolutionary turned waitress, a right-wing general, a Korean businessman, his Latina mistress, and several U.S. couples hoping to adopt Latina/o children. The hotel is in essence a microcosmic contact zone, a place in which characters identify with each other with passive-aggressive lines like, "I've always thought of Koreans as the Cubans of Asia."[37] At the same time, like *Tropic of Orange,* García's novel takes a critical stance towards globalization policies of the twentieth and twenty-first centuries. Specifically, *The Lady Matador's Hotel* critiques U.S. involvement in military atrocities in Latin America and the availability of Central American "orphans" for international adoption. In the novel, arms and military support move from the United States to Central America, while babies move from Central America to a waiting U.S. market. Here, the literary depiction of the U.S. consumption of third world children symbolizes the racial politics of the United States as a global presence.

Both Yamashita and García evoke the image of the Americas as a LatinAsian contact zone in ways that move far beyond the liberal discourse of multiculturalism. In these novels, the Latina/o and Asian presence is not represented by a landscape of ethnic restaurants or attractions for white tourists, but rather by people within distinct historical, social, and political contexts. The novels address movement across borders—both North/South and East/West—in ways that are critical of aspects of globalization. In discussing minor transnationalism, Lionnet and Shih claim, "Globalization has brought many others home but also sent many abroad, producing alternate circuits of transnationality that have been largely undertheorized."[38] Yamashita and García lay the groundwork for this theorization through their literary depiction of alternate circuits of transnationalism: through the movements of nonwhite protagonists across borders as tourists and migrants, and through darker circuits of transnationalism including drug and arms smuggling and human trafficking. The end result is a picture of LatinAsia that invokes a highly critical multiculturalism, to use Palumbo-Liu's terminology. It redefines the border as a place of both violence and possibility for Latina/o and Asian Americans, and it redefines the United States as part of a global meeting place of people, places, and histories. From the viewpoint of this border zone, *Tropic of Orange* and *The Lady Matador's Hotel* invite readers to look critically at aspects of globalization that create highly asymmetrical allocations of power and resources.

TEXT, CONTEXT, AND HYPERCONTEXT: KAREN TEI YAMASHITA'S *TROPIC OF ORANGE*

Karen Tei Yamashita's novel *Tropic of Orange* begins with a two-page grid titled "HyperContexts," a chart that crosses the major characters in the novel with the days of the week, indicating the place of each chapter in a larger pattern. In an interview, Yamashita compares this grid of information to a Los Angeles road map: "The hypercontext at the beginning is sort of the map of the book. You have your map, you're in LA, and you have to drive."[39] Traffic is an important trope in this novel, and Los Angeles traffic in particular acts as a metaphor for the fast-paced migration of an increasingly globalized world. On the freeways of Los Angeles, people hurtle through space at great speeds (or get stuck in great traffic jams), moving back and forth across the city even as migrants, goods, and media move in new ways across the globe. And on the periphery, but still integral to the cityscape and Yamashita's hypercontext, are the dispossessed, the homeless crossing over and around the freeways, living under overpasses and on embankments. *Tropic of Orange* is a postmodern tale of globalization, an ethically complex story that brings Latin American magical realism to a U.S. context. Through the fantastical path of an orange, the story highlights the beauty and hope of migration across borders as well as the incredible damage wrought by neoliberal economic policies such as the North American Free Trade Agreement (NAFTA).

Given the importance of freeways and driving to everyday life in Los Angeles, it is perhaps not surprising that traffic is a major trope of *Tropic of Orange*. Yet the concept of "hypercontext," a conflation of the words "hypertext" and "context," maps the city in ways that emphasize unexpected connections and discontinuities rather than flow. According to the Oxford English Dictionary, *hypertext* is:

> Text which does not form a single sequence and which may be read in various orders; *spec.* text and graphics . . . which are interconnected in such a way that a reader of the material (as displayed at a computer terminal, etc.) can discontinue reading one document at certain points in order to consult other related matter.[40]

As a way to theorize the effects of globalization, the cybernetic metaphor of the hypertext suggests that people and places may be linked in unexpected ways; it highlights the need to rethink geographically fixed nation-states as primary modes of organization. The idea of hypertext also captures the high-speed nature of transnational movement in the age of globalization and the fragmentation that characterizes the postmodern condition. If the *hyper* in hypercontext suggests cybernetic structure, it also literally implies excess, an overabundance of speed or of reference. Political economist David Harvey has theorized the condition of postmodernity as one of built-in acceleration; it is the cultural experience of the economic system of late capitalism.[41] While earlier literature may have reflected the fragmentation, acceleration, and "imploding centralization" of urban life, postmodernity responds to an even more intense acceleration of production and consumption, a so-called time-space compression.[42] The postmodern condition is one in which flexible regimes of capital accumulation spur new forms of transportation and communication, making the world a "smaller" place; it is also a condition in which rapid turnover time in the production and consumption of commodities accelerates our temporal experience. As a postmodern novel, *Tropic of Orange* builds in a good deal of this time-space compression. In the (warped) time of seven days, it contains a freeway disaster of epic proportions, the disappearance of oranges from U.S. markets, and the collapse of the United States-Mexico border.

Yet the novel does not only reflect the experience of postmodernism; it is also a critique of the system of late capitalism. If a *hypertext* suggests new links between people with previously disparate histories, the notion of *context* insists on the ongoing importance of these histories, which may include imperial conquest, colonization, and racial oppression. The idea of the hypercontext is similar in this way to the idea of the contact zone, in that both concepts map multiculturalism within frameworks that emphasize unevenness and historical inequalities. In *Tropic of Orange,* the hypercontext maps traffic discontinuously, as Yamashita uses the metaphor of traffic and its antithesis (the pedestrian occupation of the freeway) to expose social injustice across national borders. As seen in Emi's strong statements about cultural diversity, the novel rejects discourses of multiculturalism that define race, ethnicity, and globalization through food or cultural commodification. Instead, these concepts are explored through the idea of traffic: the symphony of human movement, the heterogeneity produced by migration, the unpredictability of unregulated flows of goods and capital, and the exploitation of human capital symbolized by organ trafficking. In this novel, Los Angeles is a center of global traffic, even as its literal traffic is stopped to reveal the social stratification at the heart of the city. The novel writes LatinAsia as hypercontext; race, space, and borders are linked in new ways as Yamashita maps the ethical complexity of globalization onto the freeways of Los Angeles.

The importance of traffic to the novel is demonstrated in a number of ways, not least through the eccentric character of Manzanar Murakami, a homeless man who conducts a symphony of cars and trucks while overlooking the Harbor Freeway in Los Angeles. The homeless conductor is Emi's long-lost grandfather and the embarrassment of the Japanese American community, which considers him mentally ill and keeps trying to remove him to a less prominent location. If Manzanar's surname recalls the postmodern Japanese author Haruki Murakami, his first name is a reminder of the incarceration camp in which he was born during World War II and suggests his disenfranchisement. Even now, he lives on the periphery of society despite a former career as a highly skilled surgeon. Yet his gift in this novel is to hear the musical grandeur of the city in its freeway system. For Manzanar, Los Angeles traffic is a symphony marked by weather and disasters, fires and earthquakes. In his mind, he is a contemporary composer, conducting pieces in epic proportions: "The freeway was a great root system, an organic living entity. It was nothing more than a great writhing concrete dinosaur and nothing less than the greatest orchestra on earth."[43] Manzanar's vision is at once inspiring and hopeless as it captures the beauty and the insanity of human connections. He conducts traffic from within his own head; he makes music that no other person can hear. His name, too, is a symbol of national dysfunction, a reminder of the racism that resulted in the incarceration of Japanese Americans during World War II. Yet Manzanar's visions also reveal something positive in the "commerce of dense humanity" that makes up the city: on the freeways, people of all races, genders, and nationalities come together.[44] When a drug-laced orange causes a freeway accident of epic proportions, shutting down traffic entirely and resulting in the occupation of abandoned cars by the homeless population, the space truly represents a cross-section of Los Angeles: the freeways become a microcosmic contact zone.

The metaphor of traffic also characterizes the United States as a border zone, the site of migration and movement of people, money, and goods across national borders. Critics generally regard *Tropic of Orange* as a "border novel," as many of its themes explore the physical and conceptual space of the United States-Mexico border.[45] In fact, the novel looks not only south to Latin America, but also west across the Pacific to Asia. Claudia Sadowski-Smith observes that *Tropic of Orange* "focuses on important similarities between Asian Americans and Latinos," particularly with respect to undocumented border crossings.[46] These similarities are exemplified by the characters Rafaela Cortes and Bobby Ngu, a married couple situated politically, ethnically, linguistically, and socially in the borderlands. Rafaela is a Mexican migrant working herself through community college, and Bobby is a "pan-Asian" character with claims to Chinese, Singaporean, Vietnamese, and Korean identities; Bobby's socialization in Latino communities and his use of Latino slang also identify him as an "Asian Latino."[47] The similarities between Rafaela's and Bobby's situations are telling, as both Latino and Asian communities have been affected by neoliberal economic policies. While media reports in the United States generally focus on undocumented Mexicans crossing the border to find jobs, the first economic border crossers in *Tropic of Orange* are Asian: Bobby and his brother migrate to the United States from Singapore because an American company has driven their family's bicycle factory out of business. In addition, the illegal border crossing that takes place in the novel is that of Bobby's teenage cousin, a young Chinese girl smuggled on a ship from Asia and then across the United States-Mexico border to Los Angeles. If this is a "border novel," it is one that works on two fronts: the U.S. border with Mexico and its western border with Asia.

The fact that the novel contains two LatinAsian couples, Rafaela/Bobby and Gabriel/Emi, emphasizes the text's commitment to crossethnic solidarities that withstand transnational border crossings. Lionnet and Shih note that new immigrants have often been "placed in a paradoxical position with regard to the claims of authenticity and cultural nationalism that have fueled the development of ethnic studies."[48] In other words, ethnic studies has been framed primarily within U.S. domestic space as a struggle for the recognition that minority populations have always been a part of U.S. history and are constitutive of the very fabric of the nation. Transnational media and increased migration in the era of globalization challenge this paradigm. Notably, *Tropic of Orange* incorporates both new and older immigrants in its framework: if Emi and Manzanar represent older Asian American populations, Bobby Ngu is newly arrived from Singapore. Likewise, Emi's boyfriend Gabriel Balboa is a Chicano reporter inspired by the civil rights era; newer migrant Rafaela Cortes, Bobby's wife, is a Mexican American woman who works on both sides of the United States-Mexico border. While Emi and Gabriel employ the discourse of U.S. ethnic studies, Bobby and Rafaela stretch this paradigm across borders to Asia and Latin America. They define the city as LatinAsian not only because of the historical presence of Asian Americans and Latina/os, but also because of its transnational ties through ongoing migration from Asia and Latin America.

The trope of traffic, exemplified by these border crossings, forms the core of the novel's central conceit: the magical movement of the entire North-South border through the transport of an orange. As the title of the novel suggests, the plot of *Tropic of Orange* centers on an orange that mysteriously contains the Tropic of Cancer, which the text describes as a thin, nearly invisible line running through Gabriel's vacation property near Mazatlán, Mexico. When the orange is picked up and transported north on a bus, the Tropic of Cancer travels with it: the orange simultaneously symbolizes and disrupts traffic across the United States-Mexico border. The effect of the orange's movement is to denaturalize the political border, to highlight the arbitrary placement of the "line" that divides the United States from Latin America. As the orange moves northward to Los Angeles, it causes the dislocation of the United States-Mexico border along with the collapse of natural boundaries of space and time. In the world of magical realism, a world in which fantastic events are granted realistic and logical consequences, the movement of the Tropic of Cancer has an enormous impact on time, the movement of the sun, and the summer solstice. By making this natural border tangible, Yamashita emphasizes the imaginary, constructed quality of the political border. Her use of an orange also emphasizes the shared ecological history of the continent. The orange falls from a navel orange tree that Gabriel has transplanted from Riverside, California, "maybe the descendent of the original trees first brought to California from Brazil in 1873."[49] The orange and its ancestors have travelled from Brazil to the United States, from the United States to Mexico, and from Mexico back to the United States. Through this border-crossing orange, Yamashita reminds readers that one of the staple crops of Southern California is itself a product of exchange across borders. U.S. immigration myths rarely highlight the transformation of the host country by traffic across borders. In contrast, Yamashita's "Tropic of Orange," carried northward, constantly reminds the reader of the history and culture transformed and blended through the process of migration: a history as natural as the movement of an orange.

Of course, the magical realism of the border-containing orange also associates this Asian American novel with Latin American literary forms. Yamashita has stated, "I was always reading Marquez and love his work,"[50] and her character Arcangel, the mythical being who carries the Tropic-containing orange, may best be described as Guillermo Gómez-Peña torn from the pages of Gabriel García Marquez. Like Gómez-Peña, a writer and provocative performance artist whose "toast to a borderless future" is quoted in the pages that preface the novel, Arcangel is an "actor and prankster, mimic and comic, freak, and one man circus act."[51] He also happens to be a very old man with enormous wings, a characterization that recalls García Marquez's short story of the same name.[52] In a nod to this story, a scene in Yamashita's novel describes one of Arcangel's installations in which "Gabriel García Marquez himself came to the opening, drank martinis and tasted ceviche on little toasts in the society of society."[53] As a South American figure appearing in a North American literary text, Arcangel embodies the common history of the Western hemisphere. He remembers the entire history of the Mexican, Central, and South American people from pre-Colombian times to the age of NAFTA. In the hypercontextual grid that maps the novel, Arcangel's chapter titles consist of simple verbs describing basic human actions: "To Wake," "To Wash," "To Eat," "To Labor," "To Dream," "To Perform," and "To Die." If the orange serves as a reminder of the shared ecology of the Americas, Arcangel reminds the reader of the common humanity of border crossers throughout history. To this end, midway through his journey north to Los Angeles, he takes on the identity of "El Gran Mojado"—the great wetback—a pejorative term for undocumented Mexican migrants transformed into a colorful caped superhero.

The term *mojado*, or wetback, demonstrates the novel's commitment to the historical context of United States-Mexico border relations. The word wetback is not only a racial slur; it also recalls official policies like the 1954–1955 Operation Wetback, a massive deportation of Mexican workers by the U.S. Immigration and Naturalization Service (INS). During this operation, more than a million Mexicans who presumably had entered the United States illegally were deported, even while the United States doubled participation in the Bracero Program.[54] Legal scholar and activist Bill Ong Hing describes Operation Wetback as beginning what was to become standard U.S. policy for the next half-century: "a familiar dichotomy of stiff enforcement, on the one hand, and enticing and exploiting Mexican laborers, on the other."[55] Such a dichotomy was not without dire consequences to the people who were deported. Historian Mae M. Ngai reports that Mexican migrants were "returned" with little attention to their place of origin, on ships that a congressional investigation likened to an "eighteenth century slave ship," or dumped in the desert just miles from the border.[56] After 88 men died in Mexicali of sunstroke in 1954, the Red Cross intervened to prevent further deaths from so-called repatriation efforts.[57] The fact that Arcangel becomes El Gran Mojado thus has a double meaning in the text. On the one hand, it reclaims a pejorative term by making the "mojado," the illegal border-crosser, into a superhero. With "ski mask in camouflage nylon, blue cape with the magic image of Guadalupe in an aura of gold feathers and blood roses, leopard bicycle tights, and blue boots," El Gran Mojado is a champion preparing to fight for his people.[58] On the other hand, this "man going north" dismantles the border altogether. By traveling with the orange, he brings Mexico into the United States, rendering his very name meaningless. If the border now exists within the space of Southern California, then El Gran Mojado's presence within the United States can no longer be illegal. He disrupts the dichotomy of simultaneous deportation and enticement of Mexican workers evident in policies from Operation Wetback to the present day.

El Gran Mojado also voices the novel's strong critique of NAFTA for its false promises that mask a great structural inequality. Arcangel becomes El Gran Mojado, but his arch-nemesis is SUPERNAFTA, an embodiment of the North American Free Trade Agreement as a social and economic construct. As an economic policy, NAFTA has been disastrous for the majority of Mexico's people. Enacted in 1994, the pact agreed to eliminate tariffs and quotas between Canada, the United States, and Mexico in order to facilitate trade between the three countries. As Hing explains, the idea behind the agreement is the economic theory of "comparative advantage"; that is, in a free market each country theoretically mutually benefits from such an agreement because it allows each country to specialize in the products or activities in which it has an advantage.[59] In reality, NAFTA was put into effect without considering the devastating effects of flooding Mexico's market with heavily subsidized U.S. products. By 2010 U.S. corn was sold in Mexico at prices that were 30 percent below the cost of production, driving Mexican farmers and farm workers out of business.[60] Ironically, a policy that ostensibly aimed to improve the Mexican economy has led to widespread joblessness, a decrease in manufacturing wages, and a widening of the gap between rich and poor.[61] Not surprisingly, it also led to significant increases in migration among Mexican workers, both from rural to urban areas in Mexico and to the United States. This increase in traffic across the United States-Mexico border has been met with hostility by lawmakers and many members of the general public in the United States, who do not understand that several of the most significant "push" and "pull" factors driving this migration can be traced back to neoliberal economic policies, and particularly to NAFTA.

Although *Tropic of Orange* was published just three years after NAFTA took effect, the text demonstrates a full awareness of the consequences of the pact for Mexican workers. Before his great showdown, Arcangel stops in a café named La Cantina de Miseria y Hambre, or the Cantina of Misery and Hunger. Arcangel brings with him a bag of nopales, or cactus leaves, and asks the waiter to prepare this local, indigenous food for him. However, indigenous food is not on the menu; instead, the other customers are "all eating hamburgers, Fritos, catsup, and drinking American beers."[62] As one Mexican customer puts it, SUPERNAFTA is "kicking ass" at the cantina and "saying we are North, too!"[63] The implication is that the omnipresence of U.S. American products is part of a general condition of deprivation because local products are no longer available. The implication becomes even clearer when El Gran Mojado actually takes on SUPERNAFTA in an Ultimate Wrestling Championship at the Pacific Rim Auditorium "at the very Borders."[64] As an embodiment of neoliberal economic theory, the titanium-suited SUPERNAFTA promises freedom, progress, and a twelve-percent cut of the profits for the "multicultural rainbow of kids out there."[65] Given the novel's earlier discussion of multiculturalism through the character of Emi, it is not surprising that the villain of the novel describes "multicultural" children as a "rainbow," an uncritical image much like the urban terrain of ethnic restaurants that must be viewed in terms of complementarity and not inequality. In response, El Gran Mojado demolishes both this discourse and the neoliberal economic policies that fail to acknowledge inequalities of wealth, saying:

The myth of the first world is that
Development is wealth and technology progress.
It is all rubbish.
It means that you are no longer human beings
but only labor.
It means that the land you live on is not earth
but only property.
It means that what you produce with your own hands
Is not yours to eat or wear or shelter you
If you cannot buy it . . .
How will ninety-five percent of us
Divide twelve percent?[66]

El Gran Mojado foresees the decline of subsistence farming, and he rhetorically sets up the dichotomies of human beings/labor and earth/property. The distinction between human beings and labor, made by the Great Wetback, recalls policies like Operation Wetback that failed to acknowledge the fluidity between wetbacks (illegal labor) and braceros (legal labor), who were often coworkers, members of the same family, and at different times the same people.[67] Through this dichotomy, the text criticizes the contradictory hiring and deporting of Mexican workers that has characterized U.S.-Mexican labor relations for decades and the inhumane treatment of deportees, left stranded in desert towns far from their homes. Likewise, the distinction between earth and property draws attention to the increasing alienation from the land that has occurred in the Americas since NAFTA. U.S. agricultural policies that favor corporate agribusiness have driven small farmers on both sides of the border out of business, dividing up what was once "earth" or "land" into "property." Finally, through their use of numbers and percentages, both superheroes parody the deceptive inequality of neoliberal economic policies. When SUPERNAFTA promises a twelve-percent cut to "multicultural" children, he emphasizes the gain in terms of dollar value: "What's twelve percent of a billion dollars? One hundred twenty million! That's multimillions."[68] What he does not mention is the radical inequality inherent in such a promise. El Gran Mojado's question—"How will ninety-five percent of us / Divide twelve percent?"—reveals the truth behind the numbers, that far from the mutual benefits promised to each country, policies like NAFTA favor the richest five percent of people through concentrating wealth into multinational corporations. In evaluating the actual effects of NAFTA, Hing reports that despite officials' claim that NAFTA would raise the wages and standard of living of all Mexicans, the opposite has in fact occurred. During the first ten years after its implementation, real wages in Mexico were lower, the gap between U.S. and Mexican wages had widened, and the gap between the rich and poor in Mexico had widened as well, with 90 percent of Mexicans having lost or experienced no change in their income in a decade under NAFTA. Only the richest 10 percent saw their income rise.[69]

Yamashita's novel frames the United States-Mexico border as a contact zone in which neoliberal economic policies have led to the increasing coexistence of white, Latino, Asian, and African American populations within significant structural inequalities. The personification of NAFTA as a supervillain allows the text to voice the rationale behind neoliberalism while simultaneously exposing the flaws in its logic. However, perhaps the most striking critique of neoliberalism in the novel is its enactment in the form of "rotten trade," especially an illegal organ trade that endangers Rafaela's and Bobby's child, Sol. Anthropologist Nancy Scheper-Hughes uses the economic concept of rotten trade to describe a "trade in 'bads'—arms, drugs, stolen goods, hazardous and toxic products as well as traffic in babies, bodies and slave labor—as opposed to ordinary and normative trade in 'goods.'"[70] Scheper-Hughes's own work on organ trafficking is a salient reminder of the very real flow of organs from impoverished nations to First World recipients, as well as the importance of organ-theft rumors in expressing the anxiety felt by Third World residents about the economic, political, and military power of the United States and Europe. In *Tropic of Orange*, rotten trade is first encountered as a shipment of oranges goes awry: "Rainforest Russian roulette oranges," which contain a highly concentrated form of cocaine smuggled over the United States-Mexico border.[71] A Salvadorean street vendor and a street youth die instantly from consuming the narcotic-laced oranges, as do two young men on the Harbor Freeway whose Porsche collides with a "monstrous semi pulling 40,000 pounds of liquid propane under pressure," causing a traffic snarl of enormous proportions.[72] The resulting explosion stalls cars for a mile and blows apart the homeless camp under Manzanar's overpass, sending homeless men, women, and children streaming down the embankment to occupy the world's "greatest used car dealership."[73] This orchestral climax reveals the dark side of the symphony of global traffic, as the rotten trade in drugs demonstrates that the "comparative advantage" of economic specialization touted by NAFTA proponents may also characterize the violent economic situation of the black market.

The deadly oranges parallel an even more sinister infant organ trafficking ring. When Rafaela visits a neighbor in Mexico, she overhears the neighbor's son Hernando discussing a misplaced shipment of oranges as well as harvesting organs for a two-year-old. Her fear for the life of her son Sol—the "sun" of her world, but a child deemed expendable by supply-and-demand economics—spurs Rafaela's flight north, a flight that culminates in a battle between the mother and the organ smuggler. As Sadowski-Smith has noted, the battle between Hernando and Rafaela Cortes recasts the conquest of Mexico by Hernan Cortes, for while Rafaela is raped and beaten, she emerges as the victor.[74] Furthermore, during the battle she takes the form of an enormous serpent, turning on her attacker with fangs and fire. As mythic beasts, Rafaela and Hernando reenact the conquest of the New World, "gutting and searing the tissue of their existence, copulating in rage, destroying and creating at once—the apocalyptic fulfillment of a prophecy—blood and semen commingling among shredded serpent and feline remains."[75] When Gabriel finds a battered Rafaela by the side of the road and asks who attacked her, she replies, "I ate him . . . Is that possible?"[76] The fact that Rafaela devours Hernando while in the form of a snake "rewrites the myth of Aztlan, which is symbolized by the image of an eagle devouring a snake."[77] The battle also places drug- and organ-trafficking within a long history of destructive greed, of the earlier global traffic in gold, silver, and other natural resources of the New World. In fact, the theme of organ trafficking appears in contemporary literature worldwide as symbolic of the human cost of economic globalization. From Leslie Marmon Silko's *Almanac of the Dead* (1991) to Chris Abani's *GraceLand* (2004), literary works about the black market trade in human organs tend to highlight the cannibalistic tendencies of a neoliberal market.[78]

Yamahita's novel is ethically complex: the deadly oranges kill wealthy as well as disenfranchised people, and in a horrifying twist, the infant organs end up barbecued and eaten by a trio of homeless drug addicts on the Harbor Freeway. In *Tropic of Orange,* men and women are trapped by structural inequalities and the existence of arbitrary political borders. Yamashita's writing illustrates the ways in which large-scale structures like markets and political borders can have real consequences apart from human intention. After the attack, Rafaela follows the collapsed border to find her husband Bobby, only to discover that they are separated by the border itself; they fall away from each other as "the line in the dust became again as wide as an entire culture and as deep as *the social and economic construct that nobody knew how to change.*"[79] Emi is shot by a bullet meant for someone else, and the bullet that ends her life also triggers a military massacre of the homeless on the Harbor Freeway. The social and economic construct that separates people by political borders and social class indeed has far-reaching consequences, effects that nobody knows how to change.

Yamashita's novel leaves Sol intact and unharmed, as the promise of a LatinAsian future. Yet her novel also leaves the reader with a sense of the complexity of Los Angeles as a LatinAsian contact zone. Even as the Los Angeles freeways pulse with the circulating blood of the city, in a symphony of humanity whose beauty is most clearly understood by Manzanar Murakami, they hide the homeless and those who travel through the city on foot. And even as transnational border-crossings produce the hope and beauty personified in the multiracial two-year-old Sol, global traffic contains a darker side of drug-smuggling and organ trafficking, rotten trade that operates at the expense of the innocent. Yamashita's novel tackles the big question of responsibility for social and economic constructs "that nobody knows how to change." In the final page of the novel, she seems to suggest a solution in the reunion of the Ngu-Cortes family.

Though Bobby is left hanging fast to the Tropic of Orange, the border at "the Borders," he finally lets go, "arms open wide like he's flying. Like he's flying forward to embrace."[80] Ultimately, Yamashita abandons the liberal discourse of multiculturalism in favor of a much more complex metaphor. Her hypercontext maps a contact zone and serves as a new conceptualization of the traffic and trafficking of economic globalization.

ADOPTION AND ROTTEN TRADE: CRISTINA GARCÍA'S *THE LADY MATADOR'S HOTEL*

If Yamashita's work explores the idea of rotten trade, Cristina García's novel *The Lady Matador's Hotel* continues this literary investigation into a trade in "bads," tackling a sensitive subject throughout the LatinAsian contact zone: the international adoption of Third World "orphans." A scene from *Tropic of Orange* lays the groundwork for the unexpected (in the United States, at least) association of adoption with rotten trade. When investigative journalist Gabriel traces the infant organ smuggling ring to Mexico City, the text states that he finds the source of the organs in a family planning clinic, an adoption agency, an orphanage, and a shantytown of abandoned children: "Impoverished kids, orphaned kids, street kids, dead kids, disappeared kids."[81] The exact nature of the trade remains vague. Instead, Gabriel's discovery is described through a postmodern pastiche of images—orphanages, shantytowns, clinics, and the "disappeared"—that generate a range of textual associations; essentially, the text eschews realistic narrative for a set of signifiers that engage an entire discourse of first world power in Latin America. Thus, the organ trade is associated not simply with a black market presence but with a range of U.S. and European interventions in Latin America, from family planning clinics that may be linked to eugenics movements, to the United States-backed military dictatorship in Argentina that "disappeared" student protestors in the 1970s, executing them and kidnapping their babies for adoption in military families. Most strongly, the text indicts international adoption practices, linking the idea of rotten trade to the adoption of Latin American children—"impoverished kids"—by U.S. families through adoption agencies and orphanages. Yamashita's novel never makes this association more explicit; Gabriel returns to Los Angeles shaken, and the actual organs end up barbecued on the freeway. However, the critique of military power through international adoption is taken up further in García's novel *The Lady Matador's Hotel,* another multi-stranded narrative that juxtaposes U.S.-backed military genocide with adoption practices in a fictionalized Central American country.

Media narratives in the United States tend to frame international adoption as a charitable act that is mutually beneficial for adoptive parents and needy children. High-profile celebrity adoptions like Angelina Jolie's adoption of children from Asia and Africa as an offshoot of her work for the United Nations reinforce this image. Yet in Latin America, international adoption of Latin American children by parents in the United States is viewed in a much less positive light. Scholar Laura Briggs traces the disjuncture between U.S. beliefs in the power of First World families to "rescue" children from poverty and Latin American beliefs that international adoption violates the basic rights of the children's first families. In Latin America, Briggs reports, "international adoption with the United States has often been characterized as an extension of U.S. economic and military power and is frequently contextualized in a way that would be incomprehensible to most U.S. Americans—in relation to child kidnapping, prostitution, murder, and organ theft."[82] By 2005, Guatemala was the largest exporter of children per capita in the world, with 90 percent of international adoptions from Guatemala going to the United States.[83] As an industry valued at $50 million a year, it is not surprising that the adoption industry in Guatemala has been subject to significant corruption. In 1997, journalist Karina Avilés of Mexico City exposed a network of criminal activity related to international adoption in Guatemala, including reports of Mexican children bought under false pretenses and smuggled across the border into "orphanages" in Guatemala. Briggs summarizes Avilés's work:

> She identified a network of eighty Guatemalan professionals and officials—lawyers, social workers, judges—who benefited from these operations. Avilés told stories of kidnappers, birth mothers who sold children for as little as $250, homes where women stayed through their pregnancies with the understanding that their newborns would be adopted, and even prostitutes who "rented their wombs," in her phrase, becoming repeatedly pregnant and being paid for their offspring. . . . Avilés also wrote of the other side of the equation, a fantastic account of a hotel full of foreigners, each carrying an about-to-be-adopted, brown-skinned infant, an image worthy of Borges and repeated daily in Guatemala.[84]

These accounts are strikingly different from the images on adoption websites and in major U.S. news magazines, which effectively erase first mothers from the narrative in order to emphasize the "happy ending" of an adopted child saved from a life of poverty and raised in (U.S.) America.

Erased from the picture are not only the desperation and exploitation of first mothers but also any explanation of how women in Central America arrived at such a vulnerable state. This explanation is key to understanding García's work. Guatemala has only recently emerged from a decades-long civil war that was sparked by the CIA's overthrow of the elected government in 1954. The military's subsequent murder of civilians and attempted genocide of indigenous Mayan populations was funded by the United States, which provided money, CIA support, and "counterinsurgency" training for the Guatemalan military. During this time, Mayan children whose parents were killed were often abducted by the military and raised as soldiers or in the families of military officers; Briggs traces the origins of unregulated adoption in Guatemala to this practice.[85] Since then, investigations into adoption irregularities and human rights abuses in Guatemala have proven fatal for a number of activists and scholars, including a bishop who was beaten to death and a university professor who "disappeared" in 2000.[86] Guatemalan American novelist Francisco Goldman explores responsibility for these deaths in his fictionalized narrative *The Long Night of the White Chickens* (1998), the story of a Guatemalan girl raised in the United States who returns to Guatemala to run an orphanage and is subsequently murdered.

Elements of *The Lady Matador's Hotel* might also have come straight from Avilés's reports: most notably, the hotel itself, which contains dozens of foreign couples each waiting for a brown-skinned, about-to-be-adopted infant. In García's novel, these couples are a diverse group—a horse trainer from New Jersey, an interior designer from Dallas, a lesbian couple from San Francisco, and a Cuban American poet on the verge of separation from his wife. The only thing they have in common is what a local woman calls their "trophy children," along with a general obliviousness to the extreme corruption involved in their acquisition of these children.[87] In an interesting twist, the local adoption business in the novel is controlled by a German woman, a six-foot-tall lawyer named Gertrudis Stüber who considers it a compliment that her enemies say she "thinks and acts like a man."[88] Gertrudis is described using reptilian imagery; she wears crocodile pumps and red lizard boots and considers the mating habits of lizards preferable to the "silliness" of human passion.[89] She calls her adoption transactions an "'export' business" and refers to first parents as "breeder mothers" and "stud services."[90] As in Avilés's report, Gertrudis installs the mothers in homes throughout their pregnancies with the understanding that they will relinquish their infants to her when they are born. The process is big business; "her price for a healthy newborn: thirty thousand U.S. dollars."[91]

The fact that Gertrudis is German does not imply the innocence of local Guatemalan officials in the business of international adoption, even in this fictionalized world. Part of her business expenses go to bribe "a phalanx of judges and politicians paid to look the other way,"[92] and when a local senator proposes that the country follow the example of Korea, which has "stopped exporting its babies," he does so not out of concern for the children or their first parents, but because "he and the other politicians want a bigger cut of the lucrative adoption business under the guise of more regulation."[93] However, Gertrudis's German origin does serve at least two purposes in the novel. First, it indicates the transnational scope of capital in the age of globalization. The business sector in the novel is represented by the Korean Manufacturers' Association and more specifically by Won Kim, the Korean owner of a textile factory. Gertrudis's control of the adoption industry implies that more than just legitimate capital is international (although Won Kim's factory may not be entirely "legitimate," since he is under investigation for labor irregularities); transnationalism also includes the illegitimate trade in human beings. Second, her German origins, along with her chilling rationality, bring to mind the thousands of Nazi war criminals who fled to Latin America after World War II. German historian Daniel Stahl attributes the failure of these war criminals to be extradited and tried for their crimes to a "coalition of the unwilling," a phrase he uses to describe the reluctance of officials on both sides of the Atlantic to search for these men for fear that they would also be implicated in crimes against humanity.[94] In other words, the military regimes in twentieth century Latin America were not eager to finger men accused of systematic torture and murder while they were carrying out similar crimes; given the Argentine government's mass murder of students and intellectuals during the 1970s, it is safe to assume that some might even have been in sympathy with former Nazi officials. Gertrudis's more amenable husband Hans, who is also German, does not evoke Nazi associations, but Gertrudis herself is a reminder that not all international residents of Latin America have settled in the area for benign reasons.

The Lady Matador's Hotel thus functions as a scathing indictment of international adoption from Latin America, both of the business itself and of the naivety of U.S. couples, adoption agencies, and media that celebrate the "rescue" of Guatemalan children. The text takes a similar stance regarding military dictatorships in Latin America and the United States's backing of violent regimes: again, the idea of "rescue" that has been so crucial to Cold War justifications of intervention in the third world is shown to mask corruption, exploitation, and murder. In the same hotel where U.S. couples await their Latin American infants, a hemispheric military conference is taking place: "Top officials from twenty-two nations have come to compare notes on defeating insurgents, asserting their political relevance, swapping the latest torture and detainment techniques."[95] A major plotline of the novel centers on one of these officials: Colonel Martín Abel, a U.S.-trained military leader whose past missions included "rooting out the intellectuals, the professors and university students, the decadent artists and actors and writers who made up a dangerous fringe of society" and torturing them into submission.[96] Martín lifts weights obsessively, laughs at any hint of softness, and is proud of his brutality. In contrast, his would-be assassin, an ex-guerrilla fighter named Aura, wants nothing more than for the war to be over: "to be done with this forever."[97] Aura's brother was burned alive by Martín and his men as part of the attempted genocide of indigenous villagers during the civil war; working as a waitress in the hotel, she is in a prime position to kill him in revenge. Her brother, whose ghost haunts her, urges her to do it. Yet as much as she desires revenge, Aura detests violence: after she killed an informer during her time as a guerrilla fighter, "she didn't sleep for a month . . . no amount of washing removed the boy's stink from her skin."[98] As a Cuban American, García writes with the full awareness of the complexity of Cold War ideologies. Aura never fully identifies with her Cuban training in guerrilla warfare. However, if Cuban-style communism is unsatisfactory, it seems mild compared to the wanton violence and wholesale murder of villagers throughout Latin America by military regimes. Aura lists the brutalities inflicted on the people she loves by Martín and other officials during the war: not only her brother, burned alive in the fields, but her uncle, "jeep-dragged up the mountainside to a bloody pulp," her cousin, "killed by a rifle shoved between her thighs," and her priest, whose head was "impaled on a stick and left at the chapel door."[99] As with the novel's treatment of the adoption industry, the indictment of U.S. policy is indirect but scathing. While the corruption and violence occur in Latin America, the funding, training, and ideological excuses are coming from the north. Would-be parents from the United States unwittingly aid and abet a Nazi-like plot to "breed" infants for a waiting market; U.S. taxpayers enabled the murder of Guatemalans. In this novel, as in *Tropic of Orange,* ordinary U.S. Americans are not intentionally bad so much as they are unaware of the effects of policies and politicians they elect. Aura marvels at the short memories of her own people; she "is convinced that the entire country has succumbed to a collective amnesia."[100] This amnesia is even more profound for U.S. readers of the novel, who may never have been aware of the violence in the first place.

The ambiguous morality of both sides of the civil wars in Latin America is further explored through the figure of the lady matador herself, who embodies the conflict between humankind and its testosterone-fueled urges to violence. Suki Palacios is a Japanese-Mexican American woman from Los Angeles, a hybrid figure in more ways than one. A woman in an almost exclusively male occupation, she is an interloper in the world of bullfighting. Yet she is also extraordinarily sensual. Unlike Gertrudis, who also takes on a traditionally male role, Suki is a woman who attracts the admiration and desire of men and women alike. This sensuality spills from the pages of the book onto its cover, which illustrates the novel's opening line—"The lady matador stands naked before the armoire mirror and unrolls her long pink stockings"—an image both beautiful and erotic.[101] Like Aura, Suki considers the violence of her battles with the bulls to be a temporary condition. Her bullfighting is an interlude in her life, a part of her rage at the death of her mother from a bone disease; she "ultimately plans on becoming an orthopedist and finding a cure for what killed her mother."[102] Yet in the meantime, she revels in the artistic aspects of bullfighting. The Cuban American poet in the novel claims that although what she does is murder, "it's also transcendence."[103] Suki herself considers bullfighting to be an art that requires two sides: "Without the bull, the matador is nothing. There's no drama, no spectacle, no poetry."[104] Suki is the central figure of the novel—it is "her" hotel—and she encapsulates the terrible attraction of violence. Her battle parallels Aura's quest for revenge on Martín, whose hypermasculine form resembles a bull. When Martín sees Suki, he tells her, "Don't mistake me for one of your bulls." In turn,

Suki "holds up an imaginary cape, unsmiling. Martín is hypnotized by the sexy, twisted shell of her navel, and paws the ground with his bare feet."[105] The text reveals the play of Aura's match against Martín, as she tries to kill him in various ways before finally slitting his throat with an intimacy reflective of the final moments of a bullfight.

As a LatinAsian figure from the United States, Suki ties together all of the characters in the novel; as a matador, she also represents the act of writing itself. If her bullfighting is frequently likened to poetry, it is notable that poetry is of ambiguous value in the novel. On the one hand, the evil colonel Martín considers that "poetry by its very nature is subversive," a statement that seems to recommend it to the reader.[106] On the other hand, he continues, "It turns words inside out, confounds meaning, changes black-and-white to ambiguous shades of gray. *Never trust a poet.*"[107] The Cuban American poet in the novel is ineffectual, melancholy and guilt-ridden. And Suki herself is prone to conflicting thoughts, seeing "her mother's face like a mask over the bull's."[108] Such images suggest that the bull is a victim of circumstance even as her mother was a victim of the disease that claimed her life. In this view, Suki's revenge against the bulls for the death of her mother is misplaced, and the lovely words framing bullfighting as an art may be simply confounding meaning. Suki's last desire to "make death most eloquent" seems to comment on the writer's own desire to create beauty out of violence.[109] García has indeed crafted a beautiful narrative out of the devastation of Central America by decades-long civil wars, and the metanarrative of bullfighting may serve as a warning that the revenge exacted by Aura against the bull-like Martín provides an illusory satisfaction. Its poetic value is high, but it cannot resolve the decades of violence or its corrupt legacy.

In the end, *The Lady Matador's Hotel* offers no solutions to resolving the violent legacy of the past. It does not even provide narrative closure. In the final scene of the novel, the bull charges at Suki, and the outcome of the charge is unknown. Rather, the novel leaves the reader with a series of questions. To what extent are U.S. citizens responsible for the creation of a multimillion dollar adoption business that exploits women in Latin America? To what extent are U.S. military interventions in Latin America responsible for the attempted genocide of indigenous populations in Guatemala and elsewhere? Does violence necessarily need to be met with violence? Is there poetic justice in acts of revenge, or is this poetry simply an illusion rationalizing still more killing?

For the babies in the novel, the future is no less uncertain. One infant dies in the adoption process, resulting in the arrest of Gertrudis on charges of "kidnapping, extortion, obstruction of justice, and manslaughter," although given Gertrudis's power with the courts, it is unclear whether the adoption industry will actually halt or whether she will simply bribe her way out of the charges.[110] Another child is abducted by the Cuban American poet, who flees north on a bus with this infant whom he loves. The situation of baby "Isabel" is highly ambiguous; it encapsulates the radically different views of adoption on different sides of the U.S.-Latin American border. While the poet thinks of Isabel as his chance to redeem himself as a parent, the people he meets in the city assume the worst. "How much did you pay for her?" asks one man, and "Are you going to raise her yourself or sell her to a hospital?" Another woman remarks, "My sister says Israeli tourists bought her neighbor's boy, then had his body carved up for his kidneys and heart."[111] The poet believes there might be a fistfight, but the far graver danger of his situation is apparent in the real-world beatings of two U.S. women visiting Guatemala in 1994 on the mistaken premise that they were trafficking in children; one of the women died as a result of her injuries.[112] As Briggs observes, neither the rescue narrative nor the human trafficking narrative has sole claim to the truth. Not all children adopted from Latin America are "plucked from the arms of their victimized parents"; however, neither are they all "saved" from abandonment as relayed in the sentimental narrative of adoption prevalent in the United States.[113] The point, according to Briggs, is that within the United States, adoption narratives only work one way. Writers like Goldman and García provide valuable insight into the radically different stakes of adoption in Latin America.

If the future remains ambiguous for Suki and the children, it is even more uncertain for the other LatinAsian character in the novel, the newborn son of Korean businessman Won Kim and his fifteen-year-old indigenous Guatemalan mistress, Berta. The least developed of all the novel's storylines, the story of Won Kim is initially repugnant. The owner of a maquiladora, Won Kim pays his workers a fraction of the legal minimum wage, gives them few breaks, and fires employees who complain.[114] He has an unhappy relationship with his parents and contemplates suicide throughout most of the book, occasionally planning to kill Berta first.[115] The simple fact that he is keeping a fifteen-year-old girl in his hotel room is uncomfortably close to a rape and hostage situation; however, this is not the direction taken by the narrative. Instead, Won Kim's suicidal impulses are linked to his desire to break free from the past: not only the precedents set by his parents, but the country's past, which has left "unspeakable things behind his factory" during the war.[116] Won Kim's mistress does not speak of her own past; instead, she luxuriates in the textiles he orders for her, and she names their baby after him: Won Kim. In a surprise twist, the birth of his son sets him free. He even considers turning the factory over to the workers to form a cooperative. A butterfly enthusiast, Won Kim considers that he is like a butterfly larva; "the bitterest chapter of his life is already closed." Emerging from his chrysalis, he is vulnerable but full of potential. If he survives, he thinks, he "will reach the pinnacle of existence" and "finally, gloriously, fly."[117]

The birth of a LatinAsian baby in the novel thus serves as an unexpected symbol of a new era of hope. The novel does not underestimate the structural inequalities that characterize a LatinAsian contact zone. Yet the centrality of the LatinAsian lady matador, Suki Palacios, to the novel suggests that the intersection of three continents—North America, South America, and Asia—is increasingly important to the future of the Americas. To some extent, Suki stands outside of the novel's circuits of power: the rotten trade of arms and babies that links the north and south in a dark mimicry of transnational business. However, as a vital part of the narrative, her character not only brings together these elements but also brings awareness to the amnesia that Aura claims envelops the country. It is the "lady matador's" hotel, and it is her erotic image that graces the cover of the book, drawing in readers who then learn about the violent history of twentieth century Central America, the covert corruption of the international adoption business, and U.S. involvement in each. The lady matador also allows the text its hope for closure, the hope that Suki will indeed succeed in her last fight and retire to return to the United States as a healer. The LatinAsian characters in both Yamashita's and García's novels bridge several worlds; they are symbolic of new possibilities even as they bring awareness to the violence of the past.

CONCLUSION

American Studies beyond National Borders

This book began with the idea of the nation. Who is and is not considered "American," and what can we learn from the way the category has been deployed and interrogated in legal, historical, and literary discourse? It ends by looking beyond national borders to other ways of imagining the world. Specifically, what might academic disciplines like American studies gain if we consider the United States to be part of a LatinAsian contact zone, one that stretches east to Asia and south to Latin America? As the world becomes increasingly globalized through migration, capital, and new media, and as activists seek to forge alliances across national boundaries, the question of where "America" begins and ends becomes more pressing. Latina/o studies scholars like José David Saldívar turn to concepts such as "Americanity" and "trans-Americanity" to "broaden, open, and outernationalize our internally colonized horizons" and to bring together ethnic studies and postcolonial studies, especially within the Western hemisphere.[1] In Asian American studies, too, scholars have grappled with how to understand an increasingly transnational field without underestimating the continued power of the nation-state. In a special issue of *Modern Fiction Studies,* Stephen Hong Sohn, Paul Lai, and Donald C. Goellnicht discuss the complexity of defining Asian American literature given transnational flows between Asia and the United States, post-1965 demographic shifts, and sticky questions about race and authorship (how do we define "Asian American" without resorting to essentializing race?) These difficulties complicate the fields of Latina/o and Asian American studies but also enrich them by widening the scope of their inquiry. Rather than chastise Asian American studies for its theoretically undefined boundaries, for example, Sohn, Lai, and Goellnicht celebrate these flexible boundaries for creating a dynamic and imaginatively productive field. They call for critics to "develop shifting understandings" of Asian America as well as "of how our critical investments shape which authors and texts emerge as privileged subjects of analysis."[2]

In this conclusion, I ask how nation-states and borders may shape which authors and texts have been considered "Latina/o" or "Asian American." Can the boundaries of Latina/o and Asian American literature be productively extended past the borders of the U.S. nation-state? Can they be dislocated from race such that a Latina/o text may be written by an author of Asian ancestry, or a Latin American protagonist elucidate Asian American experiences? Most importantly, what can we learn about "America" and American history from including these transnational experiences? Specifically, I propose a different orientation to transnationalism in Latina/o and Asian American texts, one that is open to porous borders along both North-South and East-West axes. In the case of the Asian American literary canon, I also call for looking beyond English-language texts to those originally written in other "American" languages, including Spanish. Already, literary critics have expanded the definition of Asian American literature to encompass texts originally written in Asian languages; Sohn, Lai, and Goellnicht discuss the importance of the Angel Island poetry written in Chinese, observing that "texts that have been penned in languages other than English have been considered Asian American based on the setting of those texts in America."[3] Yet unexamined in this discourse is the definition of the term "America," which is most often conflated with the United States, or occasionally extended to include Canada in works referring to "Asian North American" identities.[4] The assumption that "America" refers only to North America, and more specifically to the United States, ignores the long history of Asians in Latin America. It fails to recognize the constant movement of people north and south across the United States-Mexico border, a movement that includes people of Asian descent. A growing body of historical scholarship on Asian Latin American populations suggests that it is time to take what historian Erika Lee calls a "hemispheric approach" to Asian American literary studies.[5] One might also propose a more racially open-ended Latina/o studies that does not simply accept U.S. racial formation of Latina/os as part of an ethnoracial pentagon separate from those of African, Asian, and indigenous ancestry, but takes seriously the presence of Asian migration between Latin America and the United States.[6] Such an approach need not only be hemispheric; it may also encompass the hybrid LatinAsian identities of Filipinos, who have a long history of migration between Asia and the United States and bear the linguistic and cultural traces of a Spanish imperialism that allies them to Latin America even as U.S. imperialism ties them to Anglo America.[7]

The most compelling theorization of LatinAsia may involve a serious consideration of these transpacific flows between Asia, Latin America, and Anglo America. In counterpart to Atlantic studies and Paul Gilroy's theorization of the "Black Atlantic," historian Gary Okihiro has theorized the Americas as "parts of a Pacific world that, like its Atlantic correlate, was a system of flows of capital, labor, and culture that produced transnational and hybrid identities."[8]

Since the initial formation of the Trans-Pacific Strategic Economic Partner Agreement in 2005 and its proposed expansion into the Trans-Pacific Partnership (TPP), scholars have further theorized the transpacific as a zone of interaction characterized both by trade and by deep historical conflicts.[9] Yet there has been little acknowledgement that the transpacific world has also produced literature that can give insight into this world, a literature that is at once Asian and Latin American, Asian American and Latina/o: literature that is both hybrid and transnational.

Writer-editor Russell Leong and historian Evelyn Hu-DeHart address the absence of scholarship on Asian Latin American literary production in an issue of *Amerasia* journal: *Towards a Third Literature: Chinese Writing in the Americas.* In order to avoid the pitfalls of understanding ethnic identity in terms of national boundaries (as wholly derived from either country of residence or country of origin), they propose a "third space" for Chinese literature in the Americas that allows for a hemispheric approach to Chinese America while also recognizing historically specific experiences. To this end, they ask three questions:

1. How do late-twentieth and early-twenty-first-century Chinese diasporic movements influence the literatures written by Chinese outside of China?
2. How does "Chinese American" literature (read: U.S. literature) fit into larger conceptions of a more inclusive Chinese literature of a multicultural Americas?
3. What should the role of transnational interpretation and translation be in forming a third literature of the Americas?[10]

While Leong and Hu-DeHart specifically address Chinese literature of the Americas, these questions also apply to other Asian American literatures. Karen Tei Yamashita and Ignacio López-Calvo have written extensively about Japanese communities in South America, Yamashita through her fiction and López-Calvo through literary criticism; both authors expand our definition of Asian America south to a plural and "multicultural Americas."[11] Recent work in South Asian American literature has also brought together works written by authors of South Asian descent living in the United States, Canada, and the Caribbean.[12]

This chapter ultimately addresses Leong's and Hu-DeHart's third question, which seeks to determine the role of transnational interpretation and translation in forming a third literature of the Americas, by suggesting that Asian and Asian American literary scholars might benefit from looking beyond Asian and English language cultural productions to incorporate all of "Asian America," including texts written in Spanish; likewise, Latina/o literary scholars might gain from looking beyond the ethnoracial pentagon to works written by Asian Latina/o and Asian Latin American authors. Specifically, I examine the short story collection *El tramo final* (1988), by Chinese Peruvian American author Siu Kam Wen, as a text that rewrites the history of a multicultural Peru in dialogue with

China and the United States. The life and works of Siu Kam Wen complicate ideas of Asian American identity and *latinidad,* dislocating race from cultural and national identity and stretching our idea of the LatinAsian imaginary to incorporate migratory movements along both East-West and North-South axes. They also challenge American studies scholars to imagine the Americas broadly as part of a transpacific world.

IN THE "NO-MAN'S LAND" OF SIU KAM WEN'S *EL TRAMO FINAL*

Siu Kam Wen has been described by one contemporary critic as "perhaps the most important Spanish language writer of the Chinese diaspora."[13] He describes himself as "chino-peruano-norteamericano," or Chinese-Peruvian-American, as his own history has involved multiple migrations between China, colonial Hong Kong, Latin America, and the United States; perhaps more revealingly, his personal blog is called "tierra de nadie," or "no-man's land," which is how he chooses to describe his literary landscape.[14] Siu's father was from Guangdong Province in China and moved to Peru in the 1930s, returning briefly to China to get married and conceive a son. The product of this marriage, Siu was born in 1951 in Zhongshan, China. At the age of six, the boy and his mother moved to Hong Kong; two years later he continued on to Peru, where he met his father for the first time. When he arrived in Peru, Siu spoke only Cantonese and Hakka, a dialect of Southern China.[15] His parents enrolled him in Lima's Chinese school, where he began learning Spanish as a third language. According to Siu's own account, he wanted to be a writer from a very early age; his decision to write stories in Spanish came later, as he explains in the introduction to a later version of *El tramo final*:

> When I sat down to write the first story of *El tramo final,* I was 29 years old. But that does not mean that my vocation was late. On the contrary, when I was only ten years old, I had already filled my school notebook with stories and even short novels. I wrote then in Chinese, which was the language that I knew best. But one day I had an epiphany, and decided to abandon Chinese and use Spanish from that moment on. I set myself to translating Chinese poems and classics into Spanish, trying to learn the language of this country. When I began night school . . . I already wrote very well, although there was no way to get rid of my accent, which will probably accompany me when I present myself before San Pedro [Saint Peter] and end up calling him San Pedo [Saint Fart].[16]

Despite the humor with which he describes his Chinese accent, Siu also relates feeling marginalized as a Chinese-Peruvian writer; specifically, he felt that his own life experiences, which were not representative of mainstream Peru, could not be of literary interest. Thus, Siu explains the "lateness" of his literary debut as the result of two factors: an excessive concern about style, because Spanish was his third language, and the feeling that the world in which he lived was not a valid literary subject. He explains, "I did not feel then that the world of the Chinese in Peru was of interest to anybody."[17] He was inspired to think otherwise after reading *The Fragmented Life of Don Jacopo Lerner*, by Isaac Goldemberg, a celebrated Peruvian-Jewish writer. If Peruvian literature could encompass Jewish subjects, he felt, perhaps it could also encompass the stories of the Chinese.

While studying at the University of San Marcos, Siu saw a poster advertising a short story contest organized by the Nisei Association of Peru, which must have supported his growing conviction of the possibility of an Asian Latin American literature. Returning home, he began writing the stories that would constitute *El tramo final*, or *The Final Stretch*.[18] Siu graduated with a degree in accounting in 1978 but was unable to obtain a job or Peruvian citizenship.[19] In 1985, he and his family moved to Hawai'i, where he has lived for more than a quarter century. Siu can thus be considered an "American" writer on at least two fronts: by virtue of his identification as South American and because his writing career has coincided with his long-term residence in Hawai'i in the United States. Nevertheless, when his first book *El tramo final* appeared in Peru in 1985, it evinced not only critical acclaim but also considerable astonishment. Literary critic R. A. Kerr reports that the original dust jacket of the book contained comments describing it as "el relato de un improbable chino" ("the story of an unlikely Chinese") and one questioning whether Siu Kam Wen actually existed: "no sabemos si en verdad existe, ya que está de moda inventar escritores orientales para encubrir autores conocidos" ("we don't know if he really exists, since it is fashionable to invent Oriental writers to conceal familiar authors").[20] Nevertheless, the book established Siu's reputation as one of the most important Peruvian writers of the 1980s, a generation marked by radical political transformation.[21] Peruvian writer and editor Gabriel Rimachi Sialer relates that the book was chosen as Book of the Year and recognized by writers and critics alike as "una de las 10 mejores entregas de la década del 80" ("one of the ten best works of the 1980s").[22] The book was reprinted in 2004, along with a companion volume, and was reissued in 2009 in its original form as part of a series of "Clásicos Peruanos Contemporáneos."

El tramo final, or *The Final Stretch*, consists of nine short stories that take place among the Chinese community of Peru. Siu deliberately designed the stories to encompass the perspectives of people of all ages and experiences, including stories about children, adults, and the elderly, as well as stories about Chinese-born Peruvians, Peruvian-born Chinese, and mixed-race individuals. He has also stated that he tried to include both culturally particular and universal themes, including old age, love and loss, marriage, identity, politics, and generational conflict. He describes his vision for the book using the metaphor of a Chinese fan, with each story representing a single fold of the fan: "Each story had to communicate its particular message, but read as a whole, they had to provide to the reader a complete picture of life in the microcosmic world of the Chinese in Peru."[23] Thus, the stories serve at least two purposes with respect to Chinese-Peruvian relations: they bridge a cultural gap by expressing the common concerns of Chinese and non-Chinese readers and they address the historical and cultural particularity of the Chinese community in Peru in the mid-twentieth century. For North American readers, they also shed light on transpacific migration patterns that have triangulated North America, South America, and Asia in a way that is seldom recognized in the United States.

In an interview, Siu has stated that he thinks of himself as someone torn between three worlds, three cultures, and three languages: he quotes one critic that describes him as an "escritor peruano de origen chino nacionalizado norteamericano" ("nationalized North American Peruvian writer of Chinese origin") and another who simply calls him an "escritor de nacionalidad confusa" ("writer of confused nationality").[24] Although Siu says that he agrees with the second critic's description, he also compares this multiplicity of origins to that of Vladimir Nabokov, the acclaimed Russian-French-American author whose literary works are generally considered to be among the most important of the twentieth century.[25] Through this comparison, Siu highlights not only the difficulties that such boundary-crossing entails but also the creative potential of national and linguistic origins that defy easy categorization.

RIPPING ASIDE THE VEIL: ASIAN CONTRACT LABOR IN THE AMERICAS

Despite literary critic Ignacio López-Calvo's declaration that Siu's opus "deserves more critical attention," little of his work has been translated into English or appeared in English language journals.[26] An exception is the aforementioned special issue of *Amerasia,* which includes critic Maan Lin's translation of one of Siu's later stories, "La primera espada del imperio" ("The First Sword of the Empire"), into both English and Chinese. Lin considers this classic Chinese swordsman story from the perspective of a Chinese diaspora: How does a Chinese native, living in Latin America and writing in Spanish, render Chinese storytelling conventions so that they are intelligible to a Spanish-speaking audience? And how does the translator then translate this tale into English, for a readership equally distant from these conventions, and also "back" into Chinese? Such questions fit Siu's work into the fascinating framework of diaspora studies, considering him primarily a displaced Chinese subject. In contrast, I will consider the implications of considering Siu's first collection of stories, set entirely in Peru (or en route to Peru), as part of an Asian American and hemispheric Latina/o studies canon. What do the stories tell us about the Americas and, more particularly, about Asian and Latina/o America?

First, Siu's work not only emphasizes the racial, linguistic, and cultural diversity of the Americas; it joins other works in rewriting American history to include a long and complicated relationship with Asian peoples. The story of Asian and Latina/o people in the Americas is predominantly a story of labor. Hu-DeHart and Kathleen López have called attention to the "practical erasure of Asia and Asians from the master narrative of Latin American/Caribbean history," an erasure they find particularly egregious given the four hundred year old history of Asians in Latin America.[27] Hu-DeHart and López stress the fact that Asia was an integral part of Spanish global trade for 250 years in a system that connected Europe to Asia through Acapulco, Mexico, and the Spanish Philippines.[28] Census records, petitions, letters, and other documents record the presence of Chinese, Japanese, and South Asian residents of Latin America as early as 1613. The nineteenth century saw a different kind of migration in much larger numbers, as the decline of the African slave trade in the Americas created a demand for contract laborers in agricultural, mining, and transportation industries. The so-called coolie trade—*la trata amarilla* in Spanish—brought nearly 225,000 Chinese men to the plantations of Cuba and Peru alone; New World appetite for cheap labor also drove the import of Chinese men to Louisiana, California, and Hawai'i in the nineteenth and early twentieth centuries.[29] At the same time, South Asian contract labor flowed to the Caribbean, particularly the British West Indies.

The connections between Asian contract labor in the United States, Latin America, and the Caribbean, as well as its relationship with the African slave trade in the Americas, are rarely acknowledged in area studies scholarship, a gap that cultural critic Lisa Lowe considers part of "more extensive forgetting of social violence and forms of domination" including slavery, informal kinds of slavery like indentureship and contract labor, and the genocide of native people. According to Lowe, the fact of Asian indentureship in the early Americas may be "forgotten" in historical narratives because it does not fit neatly into categories of freedom or enslavement; it blurs the boundaries between immigration and bondage.[30] Yet Asian contract labor also has much to tell us about the workings of an earlier period of globalization, one that was responsible for encoding race in various forms throughout the Americas. Siu's story "En altamar" ("On the High Seas") emphasizes the slipperiness of different levels of coercion in colonial endeavors by literally blending the stories of a Chinese coolie and a "free" migrant to Peru in the nineteenth century. Unlike the other stories in *El tramo final*, which take place in the mid-twentieth century, "En altamar" reaches back at least three generations before the author's own arrival in Peru to narrate the origins of the Chinese community in the Americas.

As its title suggests, "En altamar" takes place entirely on the high seas; it tells the story of two men travelling in separate vessels across the Pacific Ocean. The first man is one of 739 "coolies" shipped on a nine hundred ton frigate from the port of Macau to Callao in Peru. The name of the ship in the story, the *Luisa Canevaro,* as well as the number of passengers it carries, dates the story to 1872, when the real *Luisa Canevaro* made a passage that historian Watt Stewart calls "notorious" for the deaths of more than a quarter of its human cargo from dysentery.[31] When the story opens, the ship has already spent two and half months on its 9,000 mile journey, and over a hundred of the Chinese laborers on board have died. Previously, the captain, a foreign (i.e., non-Chinese) man with a "bushy black mustache and long sideburns," ordered one of the laborers thrown overboard "for no other reason than to prove to those yellow-complexioned men with the ridiculous pigtails who was the commander in the boat."[32] The hatches have been closed, and after one man throws himself into the sea at the port of Yokohama in an unsuccessful attempt to swim to freedom, the Chinese laborers have been forbidden to come up to the deck for fresh air. Packed into the filth of the ship's hold, the first protagonist has begun to rave in his delirium in a dialect no one else on board can understand.

The second man in the story also spends his voyage feverish and ill in the hold of a ship, although this vessel is a Chinese "junk" rather than a large frigate.[33] Unlike the first man, he has paid for his passage with his life savings of fifteen ounces of gold. Along with more than two hundred other Chinese passengers, he is herded into an area enclosed by barbed wire and given a voucher as a receipt. When the junk meets with strong winds and nearly overturns, many of the "refugees" fall ill and are ordered below deck to prevent contagion. The second protagonist is among the ill, and as the story opens, he too lies below deck, surrounded by people speaking a "Tower of Babel" of languages, including Cantonese, Amoy, Hakka, Swatow, and other Chinese dialects, as well as Vietnamese and French.[34] While the first man is imprisoned as a precaution for rebellion and loss of cargo—in other words, as part of his condition of slavery—the second man is imprisoned because of his poverty and illness. Yet he, too, meets with violence as the vessel is boarded by Thai pirates who raid the passengers and rape the women and girls.

As the story unfolds, the two men's fates become blurred, and the narrator makes no distinction between them; the unnamed men are simply written as "he," and as their illness progresses, the reader cannot be sure which of the men is feeling "penetrating pain" and a "searing cough, so violent that he was afraid his heart would be expelled from his body through his mouth."[35] The "vomit, sputum, feces, and urine" that cover the bottom of the junk could equally describe the hold of the frigate, and the only difference between the two men appears to be in their expectations of the future: the coolie hopes "to be able to die in time, before the boat docked," while the free man "did not have the least idea of where they were arriving, what would be their final destination, but as long as there was hope of being able to reach any place, he avidly clung to life."[36] The narrative dashes this hope, if not for the man, then for the reader, when the two vessels ultimately reach the same port of Callao, "where the masters of the great haciendas, the managers of the guano islands, and the builders of the railroads waited impatiently for the arrival of the new laborers."[37] The story ends with the cryptic information that in the end, both ships arrive safely; one of the men dies and one survives. The final sentence underscores the brutal situation that awaits them, as it presents the reader with a false choice: "I will leave to the discretion of the reader to decide which of the two, the coolie or the refugee, was the happy survivor."[38] The ironic use of the word "happy" ("feliz") to describe the fate of a nineteenth century laborer emphasizes the powerlessness of the two men, as well as the indistinguishable circumstances of their arrival in the Americas.

"En altamar" reimagines a largely forgotten period of history, the Pacific trade in Asian contract labor that supplemented and partially supplanted the Atlantic African slave trade in the mid-nineteenth century. It joins other Asian American and Latina/o texts such as Maxine Hong Kingston's *China Men* (1980) and Cristina García's *Monkey Hunting* (2003), as well as Jamaican writer Patricia Powell's *The Pagoda* (1998), in recovering a period of violence that has been virtually erased from dominant historical narratives of the Americas. Author Toni Morrison has named this recovery a critical exercise for any writer "who belongs to any marginalized category," to rip aside "that veil drawn over 'proceedings too terrible to relate'" and reimagine the lost interior life excised from slave histories.[39] Siu's story also acts as an interrogation of global capitalism and the binary opposition of freedom and enslavement that underlies modern humanism. Lowe describes the gap in current discourse about the nineteenth century trade in Asian indentured labor in terms of an "economy of affirmation and forgetting" that has as much to bear on current understandings of global capital as it does historical accounts.[40] In other words, Siu's story is not only a project of recovery, but it also interrogates the basis of global capitalism from the nineteenth century to the present: a basis founded on various degrees of coercion in which race and economic status act in conjunction with physical force to exert power over bodies of "others."

MULTIPLE MIGRATIONS AND *MESTIZO* CHINESE: IMAGINING ASIAN LATIN AMERICA

While "En altamar" traces the origins of the Chinese community in Peru, the other stories in *El tramo final* explore the daily interactions of various members of Peru's "Colonia China" in the mid-twentieth century. They show the effects of more recent labor migrations that connect Asia, South America, and North America in webs shaped by political and economic forces. For most of the characters in these stories, migration is not a simple trajectory from a native land to a new environment; like Siu himself, many of the stories feature characters who spend years in major colonial cities like Hong Kong or Macau, return to mainland China to marry or retire, or move on from Peru to other countries in the Americas when conditions in Peru become unstable. One such story is the title story, "El tramo final," or "The Final Stretch," which describes the life of Ah-po, or "grandmother" in the Hakka dialect of Chinese. Ah-po is a Hakka woman who "never learned to speak more than three or four phrases in Spanish," having spent her whole adult life in the *barrio chino*, or Chinatown, in Lima.[41] When her son, Lou Chen, makes enough money to move out of Chinatown into a luxurious mansion with his Peruvian wife and their two children, the old-fashioned Ah-po cannot fit into their new life. In her worn, hand-sewn Chinese pants, Ah-po is an embarrassment to her upwardly mobile son. Worse, she cannot communicate at all with her grandchildren Juan Carlos and Francisco José, who only speak Spanish. When she moves back into Chinatown, she temporarily finds happiness visiting the family's former tenants, who have two young daughters who attend the Chinese school and speak perfect Cantonese. However, this happiness is shattered when the former tenants decide to sell the business and migrate to El Salvador, joining the hundreds of Chinese residents then fleeing the tumultuous political situation in Peru and "emigrating to the United States, Australia, and Central America," or returning to Hong Kong or Macau.[42] The new shopkeepers are "Sén-háks," or recent immigrants who have spent enough time in Hong Kong or Macau to "acquire undesirable habits" that alienate them from the elderly woman.[43] Crossing the road to their shop one day, Ah-po is struck by an intoxicated driver and dies in the street. The poignancy of her fate is emphasized by the story's last line, which portrays the old woman "mentally extend[ing] her two arms towards the angels that descended from the sky, as a sign of welcome and of thanks."[44]

The extreme loneliness of Ah-po, stuck in one place as others move on, emphasizes the mobility of the other Chinese residents of Peru in the twentieth century and the multiple border-crossings that make up their lives. Her son reinvents himself, moving from Chinatown to the upper echelons of Peruvian society, while her friends and neighbors move from Peru on to other countries. Siu has said that he named his collection after the title of this story for two reasons: first, because when translated into Chinese, it was very "poetic" and second, because it was "appropriate," since in the mid-1980s political instability in Peru had resulted in "the whole world ... acting like rats on a sinking ship.... The Chinese population had lost so many of its members that it really seemed to be on its final stretch."[45] Latina/o studies scholars refer to "migration" rather than "immigration" to describe the movement of people within the Americas, because such movements often follow patterns commensurate with labor opportunities; Puerto Ricans, for example, who are U.S. citizens, often move back and forth in a "revolving door" pattern rather than a unilateral or permanent displacement.[46] This kind of migration is also characteristic of Asian populations in the Americas, who may move to the Americas and "back" to Asia, or to various

Asian nations or colonial centers before arriving in America, or from one nation to another within the Americas. Stories such as "El tramo final" call attention to these multiple migrations and complicate notions of migration endpoints or a simple hyphenated identity. They also tell the story of cosmopolitanism in a way that emphasizes its cost. While early global capitalism created conditions that blurred the boundaries between slavery and freedom, the movement of people in the twentieth and twenty-first centuries has also often entailed various levels of coercion and suffering, even when such movement has been ostensibly voluntary. In their recent volume *Transpacific Studies*, Janet Hoskins and Viet Thanh Nguyen call for a recognition that cosmopolitanism is "historically and culturally varied," the property not just of jet-setting elites but also of "populations whose travel has not been glamorous or celebrated."[47] Much of Siu's work deals with this unglamorous, even tragic side of cosmopolitanism, especially with the intergenerational conflict that often occurs when global capitalism and political upheavals necessitate several migrations over the course of a single lifetime.

The multiple migrations in the stories of *El tramo final* not only destabilize ideas about immigration; they also explore the process of racial formation in the Americas by challenging essentialized ideas of "race." One of the most fascinating stories in the collection, "La conversión de Uei-Kuong," or "The Conversion of Uei-Kuong," features an ethnic Peruvian who self-identifies entirely as Chinese.[48] Born to a Peruvian mother who died shortly after his birth and an unknown father, young Manuel Lau Manrique grows up in the household of his maternal aunt, who is married to a Chinese man. When he reaches the age of two, his uncle Lau takes him along with his two biological children and departs for China, without telling his Peruvian wife. In Pun-yi, a Cantonese-speaking area of China, the uncle rejoins his Chinese wife and raises the three children in a traditional Chinese manner, renaming his nephew "Uei-Kuong." When the boy shows an interest in farming, old man Lau is delighted, stating that "now is the age of the military and of landowners. Since they will never accept Uei-Kuong in the Wang-pu Military Academy, the best thing is for him to try to be a rich landowner."[49] Unfortunately, because of his landowning status, the uncle is executed at the end of the First Five Year Plan, and Uei-Kuong—now an adult—must escape to Hong Kong and then back to Peru.

Siu thus presents the reader with a plausible scenario in which an ethnic Peruvian could be adopted and live the formative years of his life in China. From the bystander's perspective, provided by a Chinese shopkeeper named Tío Keng, this Chinese-adopted Peruvian is difficult to categorize. Is Uei-Kuong a Chinese compatriot, or is he a *Kuei,* a Cantonese term literally meaning "ghost" or "demon" but referring here to Westerners in general?[50] As the story opens, Tío Keng is on a return trip from China, apparently the only Chinese adult on his flight. When Uei-Kuong taps his shoulder and asks to borrow his Chinese newspaper "in perfect and fluid Cantonese,"[51] Tío Keng is astonished. He cannot reconcile the voice with the man's features, which contain "not a single common physical feature that would mark him as a Chinese; not the eyes, which were deep-set; not the skin, which was coppery; not the nose, which was very pronounced."[52] As his friendship with Uei-Kuong develops, Tío Keng finds himself torn between his respect for the man's culture, which is conveyed largely through his perfect command of the Cantonese language, and Tío Keng's own prejudice against ethnic Peruvians. This struggle is most evident in Tío Keng's reluctance to hire Uei-Kuong to help him in his shop. Having experience with ethnic Peruvian employees who robbed the till or pilfered merchandise, Tío Keng has concluded that "Kueis are not reliable."[53] Despite his misgivings, Tio Keng ultimately hires Uei-Kuong, and the two men form a lifelong friendship.

Although Uei-Kuong's "conversion" from Peruvian to Chinese is nearly complete, his conversion back into mainstream Peruvian society proves impossible. He can barely communicate with his Spanish-speaking aunt, and he requires a Chinese Peruvian wife because he cannot understand mainstream Peruvian culture. Essentially, he lives the life of a Chinese migrant in Peru. Yet the story is more than a curious incident; it also serves as a reflection on the way that race is culturally encoded. Tío Keng's feelings towards his friend are "complicated and many times contradictory"; when Uei-Kuong speaks Cantonese, Tío Keng forgets his physical features and enjoys the man's agreeable, diligent, and culturally knowledgeable traits.[54] However, when Uei-Kuong falls silent or tries to speak Spanish, Tío Keng's prejudices come to the forefront; he describes his employee as "inscrutable" and falls back on his visual impression of the man's "dark face ... deep-set eyes and his pronounced nose. The illusion that Uei-Kuong was a Chinese man dissipated, and Uncle Keng was forced to accept the unwelcome reality that in the veins of his employee ran not a drop of blood of the Yellow Emperor, the mythological ancestor of the Chinese people."[55]

The use of the word "inscrutable," or in Spanish, "inescrutable," resonates with centuries of stereotypes about Asians in America: as Asian American studies scholar Elaine Kim describes, early images of Asians in the United States often portrayed "hordes" of identical Asians, each of whom wore a "yellow mask" that registered "no feelings and no expression."[56] By placing the mask—at least temporarily—on the face of Uei-Kuong, the Peruvian, Siu reverses the more typical roles of dominant society and the Asian immigrant. It is the man with the features of the dominant Peruvian society who is "inescrutable," not the characters visually identified as Chinese. In addition, by using the image of blood running through veins, an image both accepted as "unwelcome reality" and rejected by experience, the story at once concedes and questions the continuing importance of the body in racializing the other. On the one hand, the difficulties Uei-Kuong faces are due to the disparity between his physical features and his cultural identity; he must negotiate life being mistaken for someone that he is not. On the other hand, his "blood" ends up being far less important than other factors—especially language—in the measure of his "Chineseness." Race, in this story, is transparently a socially constructed phenomenon.

Uei-Kuong's story challenges what critic Colleen Lye identifies as a general move in Asian American studies towards "maximal ideological inclusiveness."[57] Can we consider Uei-Kuong to be Asian American? What can an ethnic Peruvian, born in Lima and living in Peru, tell us about Asian American experiences? Is the category "Asian American" in fact one with no fixed subject, as cultural critical Kandice Chuh has proposed? For Chuh, Asian American studies is a "subjectless discourse"; deconstructing the term itself, Chuh observes that the phrase "Asian American" both claims subjectivity and refers to the impossibility of that subject: that the idea of Asian American "is/names racism and resistance, citizenship and its denial, subjectivity and subjection."[58] In Siu's story "The Conversion of Uei-Kuong," the title character also claims a Chinese subjectivity that is impossible according to state assumptions about citizenship and nationality. Both Chinese and Peruvian states recognize Uei-Kuong as an ethnic Peruvian; as a *Kuei,* he is not eligible for the military academy in China, and his legally sanctioned refuge from political turmoil in China is Peru, his assumed homeland. His existence is also a source of astonishment to Chinese and ethnic Peruvians, who "could not bring themselves to understand why he did not speak Spanish but instead spoke a language as exotic as Cantonese."[59] Yet the story repeatedly rejects racial essentialism, in a way that reflects not only Uei-Kuong's situation, but that of all Asian Americans. Uei-Kuong's incapacity to master Spanish places him in the same situation as many other Asians in North and South America, including Ah-po in the title story. His tastes, too, are Chinese; on a visit from the countryside, where he has taken up farming, he savors imported Chinese tea and reminds himself to visit Lima's Chinatown to buy a tin of imported tea and a bottle of Hoisin sauce for flavoring.[60] Finally, his problems are the same as those of many Chinese migrants to Peru, chief among them the fear that his Peruvian-raised children are losing their Chinese language and culture. Referring to his oldest son, Uei-Kuong laments to Tío Keng that "however much I beat him he does not want to speak Cantonese at home . . . and he does not have respect for either me or his mother."[61] Just as an ethnic Chinese man might be linguistically and culturally American, this Latin American by birth is linguistically and culturally Chinese; the impossibility of his situation lies in the same tension that Chuh identifies in the term Asian American. A Peruvian raised Chinese residing in Peru, Uei-Kuong can never fully complete the conversion in the story's title; both Peruvian and Chinese, he can never fully be either.

Yet ultimately, the story insists that we adopt Chuh's idea that the category Asian American must be understood in terms of a "strategic *anti*-essentialism."[62] Siu recognizes the visual encoding of race, what López-Calvo calls "the affinity of the eye," but he rejects it as a primary racial epistemology.[63] The key scenes of the story conspicuously take place when Tío Keng's eyes cannot serve as his guide: when his eyes are closed on the airplane, when he talks to Uei-Kuong over the telephone, and when he deliberately breaks the "unwelcome illusion" that his employee is a *Kuei* by forcing him to talk.[64] Just as Chuh rejects the idea that Asian American can automatically refer to any subject, Siu's story rejects the idea of "Chinese Peruvian" as a particular subject, taking instead a shifting and relational view of Asian American subjectivity.

TOWARDS A LATINASIAN APPROACH TO AMERICAN STUDIES

Both Latina/o and Asian American studies have much to gain by taking a wider approach to the study of the Americas. The life of Siu Kam Wen, a Chinese Peruvian naturalized resident of the United States, illustrates the ways in which multiple migrations blur the boundaries of national, linguistic, and cultural identifications. His literary works also suggest that the concept "migration" might take the place of "immigration" in Asian and Asian American studies, as it has in Latina/o and Latin American studies, to refer to the movement of people across national borders. Here, we might return to María DeGuzmán's term "Latinasia" to describe the transnational convergence of Asians and Latin Americans or Latinos over the course of the last three centuries, the massive migration of Asian and Latina/o peoples throughout the Americas.[65] The cultural productions of LatinAsian peoples like Siu Kam Wen challenge United States-based definitions of racial and ethnic categories, as well as the disciplinary boundaries of Asian and Asian American studies and Latina/o and Latin American studies.

While this challenge might seem to stem from changes wrought by the recent globalization of labor and capital, Siu's story "En altamar" reminds us that the migration of Asian people through colonial ports like Hong Kong and on to the Americas is not a new phenomenon. Rather, migration between Asia and the Americas was part of the global trade in bonded labor that constituted an integral part of modern history. This migration continued in the twentieth century as a response to political and economic turmoil, and its characteristic pattern often included multiple destinations. As in the title story of the collection, movement between continents has not been a one-way, one-time occurrence; rather, Asian migrants have moved to colonial Asian territories, to Latin America and then back to Asia, and to multiple sites within the Americas. In "El conversión de Uei-Kuong," Siu Kam Wen even includes the fictional case of a Latin American native who makes the journey from Peru to China to Hong Kong and back again to Peru. The fact that this story, in the words of one critic, presents a situation of "dubious plausibility" does not make it less meaningful.[66] Rather, through the story of Uei-Kuong, Siu challenges the essentialism that still often undergirds dominant ideas of race, ethnicity, and nationality. By creating a Cantonese "*Kuei*" in Peru, told from the standpoint of an author residing in the United States, the story serves as another reminder that neither Latina/o nor Asian American studies can assume a particular racial subject, any more than they can assume a single "America" as their domain.

El tramo final ends with a scene in which a young woman boards a flight on Canadian Pacific airlines and never returns. Her erstwhile lover, the protagonist of the collection's final story "La doncella roja" ("The Red Maiden"), lingers in the airport in Lima long after the airplane has departed. He stands "looking at the place where the airplane had disappeared, first into a miniscule point and then leaving his view entirely."[67] Rosa, the girl who has left, is a half-Chinese, half-Peruvian girl who is going to marry a Harvard-trained Chinese American physician living in San Francisco. Latina, Asian, and American, Rosa can be understood to represent the movement of people across three continents; her flight from Peru on a Canadian Pacific airliner also symbolically encompasses both North and South Americas and the ocean that joins them to Asia. That Siu ends his collection with a migration is a testament to the shifting national affiliations of the subjects in his stories. To return to Siu's own analogy, like the folds of a Chinese fan, these individual experiences come together to form a more complete picture of a LatinAsian America, in this case one inscribed in Spanish.

Asian American and Latina/o literature, including the LatinAsian literature of the Americas, situates United States history within a global context. The literary texts examined in this book challenge dominant understandings of American history, placing the United States within the larger framework of the contact zone of the Americas, a zone that has depended on the labor and migration of Asian and Latin American people for generations. These literary works highlight suppressed aspects of the history of the Americas, including United States imperialism, nativistic racism during World War II, Cold War interventions in Latin America and Asia, and the politics of national borders in an age of globalization. Historical discourse is a narrative wrought with exuberances and silences, statements and omissions, comprised of stories we tell about ourselves and others. Asian American, Latina/o, and LatinAsian writers challenge the silences in dominant histories, calling into question the meaning of the United States as a nation-state in the global context of the Americas.

ACKNOWLEDGMENTS

This book began as a dissertation in the Department of English and Comparative Literature at the University of North Carolina at Chapel Hill, and I am enormously grateful to my dissertation directors, Jennifer Ann Ho and María DeGuzmán, for reading and commenting on multiple drafts of that project. The book is immeasurably stronger for their guidance; any faults, of course, remain my own. I would also like to thank the other members of my dissertation committee, Ruth Salvaggio, Minrose Gwin, and Laura Halperin, for their suggestions and enthusiasm; thanks especially to Ruth for the word "cartographies." The Department of English and Comparative Literature at UNC awarded me two dissertation grants, which allowed me eight months of research time and for which I am very grateful. I send thanks to the anonymous readers of the book manuscript, who provided valuable insights and detailed comments, and to Steve Alfaro for allowing me to use his beautiful art as a cover. Finally, thanks to Leslie Mitchner and all the staff at Rutgers University Press for their help and guidance throughout the publishing process.

I am fortunate to have colleague-friends at UNC and Duke who have both assisted me and inspired me with their own work. Thanks to John Ribó, Christina Lee, and Huiman Barnhart for their help with (often obscure) translation questions. My friends in the Literature of the Americas working group at UNC, especially Gale Greenlee, María Durán, Jameela Dallis, and Becka Garonzik, provided valuable companionship during the writing process. At the Thompson Writing Program, colleagues too numerous to name make working at Duke a pleasure. To these friends and others, thank you for celebrating this book with me.

Writing a book is a long-term endeavor, and credit must also go to those whose love and support have sustained me and shaped my understanding of the world. Thanks to Maya Socolovsky and Ellen Arnold for introducing me to Latina/o literature and Ethnic Studies and for their encouragement as I returned to academia after many years away. Thanks to the women in my Los Angeles mothers' group—Ariella Fiore, Liz Escobar Glover, Maria Juarez, Amy Hamamura Klosterman, Sabrina Lamberson, Christy Sauté, and Jen Tsai—and to my husband's family—the Thananopavarns, Boonsues, and Ostis—for making the LatinAsian cartographies of Los Angeles my home. To the many friends whose texts and phone calls have brightened my days, especially Jasmine Ueng-McHale, Patricia Bachiller, Vanessa Woods, and Leyf Starling, thank you for your friendship and for keeping me going. And finally, thanks to the women at Spanish for Fun Academy (especially Keila, Aury, Livia, and Graciela) for caring for my youngest child while I wrote and instilling in her a love of the Spanish language. To all of you—this book is for our children.

To my family, I send my deepest thanks. I am grateful to my in-laws, Srisook Boonsue and the late Chalemphol Thananopavarn, for always welcoming and supporting my academic endeavors. To my parents, Sally Bramley and the late Michael Bramley (whom I miss daily), words are not enough. From the bottom of my heart, thank you for always understanding my passion for education and justice. Your unwavering love and support have made all the difference. To my husband Paul, thank you for believing in this project and in me. We make a good team. And above all, thank you to my children: Adrian, Claire, and Eve. You are my inspiration and hope for the future. This book is dedicated to you.

NOTES

INTRODUCTION

1. Yamada, *Camp Notes,* 39.
2. Anzaldúa, *Borderlands,* 25.
3. Ibid., 26.
4. DeGuzmán, *Spain's Long Shadow,* 301.
5. Pratt, *Imperial Eyes,* 8.
6. Such sociological studies include George Yancey's *Who Is White? Latinos, Asians, and the New Black/Nonblack Divide* (2003) and Eileen O'Brien's *The Racial Middle: Latinos and Asian Americans Living Beyond the Racial Divide* (2008). For sociological and historical approaches that focus on particular Latina/o-Asian parallels, see Julian Go's *American Empire and the Politics of Meaning: Elite Political Cultures in the Philippines and Puerto Rico* (2008) and JoAnna Poblete's *Islanders in the Empire: Filipino and Puerto Rican Laborers in Hawai'i* (2014). Recent intersectional studies include Rudy P. Guevarra, Jr.'s *Becoming Mexipino: Multiethnic Identities and Communities in San Diego* (2012) and Anthony Christian Ocampo's *The Latinos of Asia: How Filipino Americans Break the Rules of Race* (2016).
7. Jones-Puthoff, "Is the U.S. Population Getting Older and More Diverse?"
8. White, *The Fiction of Narrative,* 112.
9. Jones-Puthoff, "Is the U.S. Population Getting Older and More Diverse?" This statistic can be constructed from Jones-Puthoff's chart that shows that the number of people identifying as "non-Hispanic white alone" was 197.7 million out of 313.9 million U.S. residents in 2012.
10. Kochhar, Fry, and Taylor, "Wealth Gaps Rise to Record Highs Between Whites, Blacks, Hispanics."
11. Manning, "Membership of the 112th Congress: A Profile."
12. "U.S. Census Bureau Statistics on Population Change," *C-SPAN* video, 30:01. June 14, 2013. https://www.c-span.org/video/?313378-4/us-census-bureau-statistics-us-population-change. The very category "non-Hispanic white alone" reveals the idea of the majority-minority as one of white racial anxiety. In the *C-SPAN* video, the Census Bureau representative explains this category in terms of tradition: "We actually use 'non-Hispanic white' as *sort of a traditional term* to represent the majority of the population of the country, which is 'non-Hispanic white alone,' not in combination with other races." While the concept might reflect the racial politics of the past, however, the term itself is far from "traditional"; the category "Hispanic" has only been in use by the U.S. Census since 1980, and the word "alone" has only been necessary since 2000, which was the first year in which citizens were allowed to self-identify as more than one race. On the contrary, the very combination of exclusive categories present in the term, one that requires a resident to identify with only one racial category, and *not* with one particular ethnic group, emphasizes its highly constructed nature. For additional reports emphasizing race and minority encroachment, see the U.S. Census Bureau's publications "Asians Fastest Growing Race or Ethnic Group in 2012, Census Bureau Reports," which contains the subheading *Six More Counties Become Majority-Minority* (June 13, 2013, http://www.census.gov/newsroom/press-releases/2013/cb13-112.html) and "Most Children Younger than Age 1 Are Minorities, Census Bureau Reports" which focuses on the number of states and counties that were "majority-minority" as of 2011 (May 17, 2012, http://census.gov/newsroom/releases/archives/population/cb12-90.html).

13. Pett, "It's So You'll Know Which Ones to Fear."
14. These words are taken from Emma Lazarus's poem "The New Colossus," which was inscribed on a bronze tablet and mounted on the pedestal of the Statue of Liberty in 1903. Lazarus, "The New Colossus," 525.
15. Omi and Winant, *Racial Formation in the United States*, 15.
16. St. John de Crèvecoeur, "Letters from an American Farmer," 27.
17. Quoted in Sollors, *Beyond Ethnicity*, 66.
18. Ibid., 66.
19. St. John de Crèvecoeur, "Letters from an American Farmer," 29.
20. Ignatiev, *How the Irish Became White.* Historian Paul Spickard also notes that "there is a fundamental difference between the experiences of peoples of color and those of White immigrants. . . . The assimilation model does not work for people of color. No amount of wishing will make it so" (*Almost All Aliens*, 14).
21. Omi and Winant, *Racial Formation in the United States*, 55–56. In 1997, the American Anthropological Association released a statement advocating the combination of the terms "race" and "ethnicity" into "race/ethnicity," on the basis that "both Hispanic and non-Hispanic respondents tend to treat the two questions as asking for essentially the same information." American Anthropological Association Response to OMB Directive 15: Race and Ethnic Standards for Federal Standards and Administrative Reporting, September, 1997. http://s3.amazonaws.com/rdcms-aaa/files/production/public/FileDownloads/pdfs/cmtes/minority/upload/AAA_Response_OMB1997.pdf.
22. Ngai, *Impossible Subjects*, 37–38.
23. Oboler, *Ethnic Labels, Latino Lives*, 31. See also Parikh, *An Ethics of Betrayal*, 17.
24. Ngai, *Impossible Subjects*, 8.
25. Parikh, *An Ethics of Betrayal*, 16.
26. Ibid.
27. Chuh, *Imagine Otherwise*, 8.
28. Ngai, *Impossible Subjects*, 17.
29. Pfaelzer, *Driven Out*, 8.
30. Ibid., 74–75.
31. Ibid., 75.
32. Ancheta, *Race, Rights, and the Asian American Experience*, 25.
33. Ibid., 25–26.
34. Quoted in Ancheta, *Race, Rights, and the Asian American Experience*, 66 (emphasis mine).
35. Ngai, *Impossible Subjects*, 18.
36. Lee, *The Making of Asian America*, 172.
37. Ngai, *Impossible Subjects*, 109.
38. Lee, *The Making of Asian America*, 186.
39. Ibid., 188.
40. After the Thind case, all South Asians in the United States who were citizens had their citizenship stripped, including Vaishno Das Bagai, a small business owner who was then forced to sell his property and his business due to California's alien land laws. Bagai was subsequently denied a U.S. passport to visit India and left essentially stateless. "Feeling trapped and betrayed," historian Erika Lee reports, "he committed suicide by gas poisoning in 1928," leaving behind a wife and three children (*The Making of Asian America*, 172).
41. Quoted in Ancheta, *Race, Rights, and the Asian American Experience*, 24.
42. Ibid., 34.
43. Takaki, *Democracy and Race*, 93.
44. Quoted in Takaki, *Democracy and Race*, 88.

45. Maki, Kitano, and Berthold, *Achieving the Impossible Dream*, 37.
46. Ibid., 195.
47. Ngai, *Impossible Subjects*, 8.
48. Ancheta, *Race, Rights, and the Asian American Experience*, 8. Ancheta describes numerous instances of anti-Asian violence based on the assumption that Asian Americans are foreigners, including the notorious killing of Vincent Chin in 1982. Chin, a Chinese American resident of Detroit, was celebrating his upcoming wedding at a bar when he was accosted and bludgeoned to death by two white automobile factory workers who blamed him for the loss of automobile factory jobs to the Japanese (*Race, Rights, and the Asian American Experience*, 7). The men pled guilty to manslaughter, but received just three years' probation and a fine; in a striking miscarriage of justice, they did not spend "a single night in jail for their bloody deed" (Takaki, *Strangers from a Different Shore*, 482). Chin was neither Japanese nor connected with the automobile industry.
49. Oboler, *Ethnic Labels, Latino Lives*, 18.
50. DeGuzmán, *Spain's Long Shadow*, xxv.
51. Ibid., xxi.
52. Quoted in Hietala, *Manifest Design*, 255.
53. Ibid., 255.
54. Ibid., 156.
55. Ibid., 156–157.
56. Oboler, *Ethnic Labels, Latino Lives*, 23–24.
57. Ibid., 26.
58. Quoted in Ngai, *Impossible Subjects*, 53.
59. Ibid., 54.
60. Oboler, *Ethnic Labels, Latino Lives*, 33 (emphasis in original).
61. *A Class Apart*, PBS American Experience.
62. DeGuzmán, *Spain's Long Shadow*, xxi.
63. Quoted in Oboler, *Ethnic Labels, Latino Lives*, 37.
64. Ngai, *Impossible Subjects*, 68.
65. Ibid., 60.
66. Molina, *How Race Is Made in America*, 34.
67. Balderrama and Rodríguez estimate one million repatriates as the "conservative middle ground," noting that enormous discrepancies existed between United States figures and those reported in Mexico. The official tally for the decade between 1930 and 1940, which did not count those who traveled without assistance or without contacting Mexican consulates, was 422,831. Balderrama and Rodríguez, *Decade of Betrayal*, 151.
68. Cacho, *Social Death*, 6–7. Cacho describes at length a brutal attack by eight white teenagers in 2000 against Mexican migrant workers in San Diego. Although all of the elderly workers were living and working in the United States legally, the teens assumed the workers were undocumented and would not report the crime. Cacho observes that the perpetrators grew up in an environment openly hostile to Latina/o populations, so they likely thought their violence would be condoned "because it was directed toward Latina/o workers assumed not be not just vulnerable as 'illegal' but deserving punishment as criminal." The teens received light punishment despite the passage of a law that required them to be tried as adults (36–37). Both this case and the murder of Vincent Chin highlight the physical danger and legal consequences of constructing Latina/os and Asian Americans as foreign; in this case, the category "illegal" added to the devaluing of human life.
69. Croucher, "The Success of the Cuban Success Story: Ethnicity, Power, and Politics," 369.
70. Ibid., 356.

71. Anderson, *Imagined Communities*, 203.
72. Ibid., 204.
73. Ibid., 205.
74. Ngai, *Impossible Subjects*, 5.
75. Ibid., 246.
76. Ibid., 247.
77. Wang, "Descendents of Chinese Laborers Reclaim Railroad's History." The absence of Chinese railroad workers from photographs commemorating the Golden Spike Ceremony was emblematic of a more disturbing lack of acknowledgement of their labor on the railroad. Historian Sucheng Chan reports that upon the completion of the railroad, nearly 10,000 Chinese workers were instantly rendered jobless, not even permitted to ride the railroad they had built back to the west coast without purchasing a ticket. Most were left to work their way back to California as migrant farmworkers and laborers (*Asian Americans*, 32).
78. Okihiro, *Margins and Mainstreams*, 155.
79. Ibid., ix.
80. Morrison, "The Site of Memory," 70.
81. Pérez, Emma. *The Decolonial Imaginary*, 6. Pérez extends this political project to literary production as well, as evident in her own novels decolonizing history, including *Forgetting the Alamo, Or Blood Memory* (2009).
82. Ibid.
83. Chu, *Assimilating Asians*, 7.
84. Lowe, *Immigrant Acts*, 6.
85. Anzaldúa, *Borderlands/La Frontera*, 24, 102.
86. Saldívar, *Border Matters*, 1.
87. Ibid., 13.
88. White, *The Fiction of Narrative*, 320.
89. Ibid., 326.
90. Ricoeur, *Memory, History, Forgetting*, 455. Ricoeur is responding to the *Historikerstreit*, the 1986 historians' debate about whether or not the Holocaust was a singular event. The ultimate question for Ricoeur is the connection between the work of historians and the actions of responsible citizens. In this sense, a dissensus may be educational and may result in "an enlightened public opinion that transforms the retrospective judgment on the crime into a pledge to prevent its reoccurrence" (*Memory, History, Forgetting*, 332). In a very different context, Asian American and Latina/o narratives about history may also create a dissensus that keeps American history alive for responsible citizens.
91. Moya, *The Social Imperative*, 39.
92. Ibid., 58.
93. Ibid. On the contrary, Jodi Melamed claims that in some cases, literary studies (and literature in general) can become a tool for those in the United States to "get to know" difference in a way that naturalizes racial privilege and is complicit with liberal capitalism. In this way, "literary multiculturalism" can be an institution for managing difference. Melamed contrasts this kind of "knowledge," however, with literary texts that challenge hegemony through what she calls a "race-radical tradition." It is this race-radical tradition that I trace throughout this book. Melamed, *Represent and Destroy*.
94. Rosaldo, "Surveying Law and Borders," 634.
95. Goellnicht, "Blurring Boundaries: Asian American Literature as Theory," 341.
96. Farmer, "An Anthropology of Structural Violence," 317.
97. Moraga and Anzaldúa, *This Bridge Called My Back*, 29 (emphasis in original).
98. Ibid.

99. Ricoeur, *Memory, History, Forgetting,* 329, 332.
100. Lye, Colleen, "The Afro-Asian Analogy," 1734.
101. Bonilla-Silva, *Racism Without Racists,* 188–190.
102. Pulido, *Black, Brown, Yellow, and Left,* 24.
103. Lowe, *Immigrant Acts,* 83.
104. Anderson, *Imagined Communities,* 149.
105. Craig and Richeson, "More Diverse Yet Less Tolerant?" 758.
106. Ibid., 759.

CHAPTER 1 UNITED STATES IMPERIALISM AND STRUCTURAL VIOLENCE IN THE BORDERLANDS

1. Williams, "The Frontier Thesis and American Foreign Policy," 379.
2. For academic volumes devoted to reinserting imperialism into American historiography, see especially *Cultures of United States Imperialism,* edited by Amy Kaplan and Donald E. Pease, which begins with Williams's statement and highlights the ways in which "imperialism has been simultaneously formative and disavowed" in American studies (5). Historian Howard Zinn has done much to popularize the study of U.S. imperialism in *A People's History of the United States* (1980), *A People's History of American Empire* (2008), and other works. More recently, literary scholars such as María DeGuzmán have explored Anglo-American empire in literature: see DeGuzmán's *Spain's Long Shadow: The Black Legend, Off-Whiteness, and Anglo-American Empire* (2005). It is important to note, however, that studies of American empire date back at least to the 1950s and include works such as Williams's *Roots of the Modern American Empire* (1969), Marilyn Young's *Rhetoric of Empire* (1968), Walter Lafeber's *The New Empire: An Interpretation of American Expansion* (1963), and Philip Foner's *The Spanish-Cuban-American War and the Birth of American Imperialism* (1972). The sheer volume of academic scholarship on the topic makes its absence from public historical discourse all the more disturbing; the disconnect between academic and public awareness also demonstrates the importance of novels, memoirs, and films that seek to intervene more directly in public discourse.
3. Texas State Board of Education, *Proposed Revisions to 19 TAC Chapter 113, Texas Essential Knowledge and Skills for Social Studies, Subchapter B, Middle School.*
4. Texas State Board of Education, *Proposed Revisions to 19 TAC Chapter 113, Texas Essential Knowledge and Skills for Social Studies, Subchapter C, High School, and 19 TAC Chapter 118, Texas Essential Knowledge and Skills for Economics with Emphasis on the* Free Enterprise *System and Its Benefits, Subchapter A, High School.*
5. The decisions of the Texas school board and the prohibition of ethnic studies in Arizona the same month coincided with the legislation of some of the harshest immigration laws in the last fifty years (for more on the wider impact of these education decisions, see Tamar Lewin, "Citing Individualism, Arizona Tries to Rein in Ethnic Studies in School"; James C. McKinley, Jr., "Texas Conservatives Win Curriculum Change"; and Barrett Sheridan, "Texas Cooks the Textbooks"). Arizona's immigration law SB 1070, for example, criminalized the failure to carry immigration papers and granted broad power to police to detain any person suspected of being in the country illegally. Legally, the law resembles the Geary Act of 1892, which required all ethnic Chinese residents of the United States to carry residency papers to "prove" their legal residence.
6. Farmer, "An Anthropology of Structural Violence," 309.
7. Ibid., 315, 317.
8. San Juan, Jr., *After Postcolonialism,* 27; Wong, *Reading Asian American Literature,* 225 n 27.
9. R. Saldívar, *Borderlands of Culture,* 4–5.
10. Paredes, *George Washington Gómez,* 5–6.

11. Palumbo-Liu, *The Ethnic Canon,* 2.
12. Bulosan, *America Is in the Heart,* 312.
13. Paredes, *George Washington Gómez,* 172.
14. Calderón and López-Morín, "Interview with Américo Paredes," 212. These events occurred in 1950, before the full elimination of legal barriers to the immigration of Asian war brides. The G.I. Brides Act of 1945 excluded "all persons ineligible for admission," a phrase that specifically meant Asians, who were constitutionally defined as aliens ineligible for citizenship (quoted in Zeiger, *Entangling Alliances,* 181). Although the Alien Brides Act of 1947 waived the racial component of the law, it granted this waiver only to couples who managed to apply for eligibility within thirty days of its enactment. The waiver was re-introduced in 1950, but again on a time-limited basis. According to historian Susan Zeiger, it was not until the McCarran-Walter Act of 1952 that Asian war brides were finally accorded the same rights as European war brides (*Entangling Alliances,* 182). This assertion is supported by figures from the U.S. Commissioner of Immigration and Naturalization that show just nine Japanese wives of U.S. servicemen admitted to the United States in 1950, compared with 4,220 in 1952 (see B. Kim, "Asian Wives of U.S. Servicemen," 99). Because of these laws, Paredes's wife had to stay in Mexico for a year while applying for a series of visas; Paredes traveled back and forth across the border while finishing his B.A. at the University of Texas, until his wife was finally able to join him the following year (Medrano, *Américo Paredes,* 43).
15. Daniel Aaron's *Writers on the Left: Episodes in Literary Communism* describes the appeal of communism among U.S. literary writers from 1912 to the early 1940s.
16. Paredes, *George Washington Gómez,* 195.
17. Bulosan, *America Is in the Heart,* 270.
18. Bascara, *Model-Minority Imperialism,* xxv.
19. E. Kim, *Asian American Literature,* 45.
20. Ibid., 56.
21. Bulosan, *America Is in the Heart,* 327.
22. Ibid., 327 (emphasis in original).
23. Bascara, *Model-Minority Imperialism,* 51.
24. E. Kim, *Asian American Literature,* 48.
25. San Juan, Jr., "Searching for the 'Heart' of America (Carlos Bulosan)," 264.
26. Alquizola, "The Fictive Narrator of *America Is in the Heart.*"
27. Bulosan, *The Cry and the Dedication,* 293.
28. Council on Books in Wartime, *A History of the Council on Books in Wartime,* 3.
29. Ibid., unpaginated introduction.
30. E. Kim, *Asian American Literature,* 45.
31. Bercovitch, *American Jeremiad,* 180.
32. San Juan, Jr., "Searching for the 'Heart' of America (Carlos Bulosan)," 226.
33. Francisco, "The Philippine-American War," 17.
34. Ibid., 19.
35. McKinley, "Remarks to Methodist Delegation," 22–23.
36. Kramer, *Blood of Government,* 168–169.
37. Constantino, "The Miseducation of the Filipino," 47.
38. Taft quoted in Kramer, *Blood of Government,* 237.
39. Kramer, *Blood of Government,* 266.
40. Marlon Fuentes' film *Bontoc Eulogy* (1995) excavates images, film footage, and historical documents about the 1904 World's Fair. A fictionalized description of the filmmaker's search for his grandfather, a Bontoc Igorot who inhabited one of the "authentic" villages at the Fair, the film demonstrates the connections between science, spectacle, and empire.

41. In keeping with other critical discussions of the text, I distinguish between Bulosan (the author) and the narrator of his memoir, who is called Allos in the Philippines and Carlos in the United States.
42. Chuh, *Imagine Otherwise*, 38. The quotation is from Bulosan, *America Is in the Heart*, 67.
43. Bulosan, *America Is in the Heart*, 40.
44. Ibid., 48.
45. Ibid., 26.
46. Assuming that the life of Allos parallels that of Bulosan, who was born in 1911, then the hunting trip, which occurred when Bulosan was a small boy, can be dated to 1916–1920. At that time, Bulosan's oldest brother had been away serving in World War I, which means he was approximately 18 years old in 1919. This makes Bulosan's father already an adult (parent) in 1901, in the midst of the Philippine-American War. If his nationalist fighting dates to his early adulthood, as the text suggests, it would almost certainly be a part of this war, which did not end abruptly but carried on for years in the form of guerrilla fighting and small bands of resistance.
47. Wesling, "Colonial Education and the Politics of Knowledge in Carlos Bulosan's *America Is in the Heart*," 60.
48. Ibid., 64.
49. Bulosan, *America Is in the Heart*, 29.
50. Ibid., 14.
51. Ibid., 23.
52. Ibid., 41.
53. Ibid., 45–46.
54. Ibid., 253.
55. E. Kim, *Asian American Literature*, 45–46. Elaine Kim describes Bulosan's decline into poverty, obscurity, and death: "Too frail and weak to work at strenuous labor, he had undergone eleven operations, some for lung lesions and others for leg cancers, before he died in 1956. One kneecap had been removed, and he walked with great difficulty. He drank heavily. . . . Finally, he collapsed in a Seattle street and apparently died of exposure." The lung lesions, for which he was continually hospitalized, were most likely the result of the tuberculosis he had contracted from family members in the Philippines. What Kim describes as "leg cancers" were probably tuberculosis infection of the kneecaps, a not uncommon manifestation of musculoskeletal tuberculosis infection and one that often requires surgical intervention or amputation.
56. Bulosan, *America Is in the Heart*, 69.
57. Calderón and López-Morín, "Interview with Américo Paredes," 215.
58. Paredes, "The Hammon and the Beans," 251–252.
59. Paredes, *George Washington Gómez*, 15.
60. R. Saldívar, *The Borderlands of Culture*, 158.
61. Ibid.
62. While waiting for Guálinto's birth, the boy's father and uncle pore over a newspaper mentioning "something about the duke of Austria getting shot" (Paredes, *George Washington Gómez*, 13), a reference to the assassination of Archduke Ferdinand of Austria on June 28, 1914. The naming of the baby occurs when he is seven months old, in the middle of a "heavy killing frost" (ibid., 14), which places the event at the beginning of 1915.
63. Montejano, *Anglos and Mexicans in the Making of Texas*, 117.
64. Ibid., 118.
65. Ibid., 122–125. The wide range of deaths estimated among Mexican and Mexican American residents indicates the lack (or unenforceability) of requirements for U.S. armed militia, Texas Rangers, and vigilante groups to account for killings of ethnic Mexicans. Judging from

the number of skeletal remains that appeared in the region in the decades following the uprising, historian Benjamin Heber Johnson sets a more recent estimate of deaths at "a number in the low thousands" (*Revolution in Texas*, 120).

66. Montejano, *Anglos and Mexicans in the Making of Texas*, 126.

67. Johnson, *Revolution in Texas*, 20.

68. Ibid., 3–4.

69. Ibid., 203.

70. As late as 2014, the Minutemen organization, a vigilante group of Anglos along the United States-Mexico border, was calling for 3,500 "non-militia volunteers," plus "uncounted militias from all over the country" to participate in a May 1, 2015 campaign they named "Operation Normandy" to echo World War II military actions. The aim of this operation was to "cover the porous areas of the 2,000-mile border from San Diego, Ca. to Brownsville, Texas." Naming Paredes's hometown of Brownsville places this operation squarely within a tradition of Anglo vigilantes along the United States-Mexico border stretching back to the nineteenth century (The Minutemen Project, "Operation Normandy").

71. Paredes, *George Washington* Gómez, 21.

72. J. Saldívar, *The Dialectics of Our America*, 51.

73. Paredes, "With His Pistol in His Hand," 19.

74. Paredes, *George Washington Gómez*, 117.

75. Ibid., 148.

76. Ibid., 150.

77. Ibid., 161.

78. Ibid.

79. Griswold del Castillo, *The Treaty of Guadalupe Hidalgo*, 11.

80. Quoted in Griswold del Castillo, *The Treaty of Guadalupe* Hidalgo, 111.

81. Paredes, *George Washington Gómez*, 162.

82. Ibid., 174.

83. Ibid., 175.

84. Ibid., 284.

85. Quoted in R. Saldívar, *The Borderlands of Culture*, 120.

86. Ibid., 181.

87. Paredes, *George Washington Gómez*, 270.

88. Ibid., 271.

89. Ibid., 274.

90. Calderón and López-Morín, "Interview with Américo Paredes," 225.

91. Paredes, *George Washington Gómez*, 273.

92. Ibid., 281.

93. Ibid., 282.

94. Ignacio et al., *The Forbidden Book*, 1–2.

95. In Brainard's novel, the protagonist's grandfather continually confuses the family's discussion of World War II with the earlier war; when his daughter corrects him by observing that "It's 1941, the Americans are our friends now," he replies, "Don't be foolish, child. Americans are tricky people" (*When the Rainbow Goddess Wept*, 9). His words are borne out by the subsequent action of the novel, which emphasizes the unreliability of American "aid."

CHAPTER 2 BATTLE ON THE HOMEFRONT

1. Torgovnick, *The War Complex*, 2.

2. Ibid.

3. In an introductory note to his Pulitzer Prize-winning book, *"The Good War": An Oral History of World War II* (1984), journalist Studs Terkel explains that his title phrase, "the good war," was commonly used by both his and the previous generation "to distinguish that war from other wars, declared and undeclared." Terkel added quotation marks to his title "because the adjective 'good' mated with the noun 'war' is so incongruous," but since the publication of his volume the term has stayed in use, both with and without quotation marks.
4. This quotation does not appear in the book, but is attributed to Brokaw on the book's back cover; it has also been used extensively in marketing campaigns for the book.
5. Brokaw, *The Greatest Generation*, xx.
6. Morrison, *Playing in the Dark*, viii.
7. Wong, "'Sugar Sisterhood,'" 200.
8. Even films that are ostensibly "about" minority experiences during World War II tend to follow this pattern; for example, the film *Windtalkers* (2002) is supposedly about Native American "code talkers" during World War II but stars Nicholas Cage as the white protagonist.
9. Ancheta, *Race, Rights, and the Asian American Experience*, 12.
10. Ibid., 173. It is important to note that the imperfect fit of nativistic racism into a black-white racial binary in the United States does not prevent the same binary from being used in its execution, as when Asians and Latina/os are compared to Africans or African Americans to incite white hostility.
11. Huerta, Introduction to *Zoot Suit and Other Plays*, 7.
12. Chicano Studies scholar Yolanda Broyles-González objects to the widely held notion that Valdez "founded" El Teatro Campesino, considering this idea overly male-centered and individualistic (*El Teatro Campesino*). Broyles-González prefers to emphasize instead the theater's roots in collective community activism and oral Mexican and Mexican American traditions. Still, Valdez's role as writer and spokesman for the troupe—and the individual author of poems, essays, plays, and films—should not be underestimated.
13. Jaskoski and Yamada, "A MELUS Interview," 97.
14. Ancheta, *Race, Rights, and the Asian American Experience*, 12.
15. Sanchez, *Becoming Mexican American*, 267.
16. Takaki, *A Different Mirror*, 393.
17. Steele, "Violence in Los Angeles," 20. The high proportion of Mexican Americans in the military was the result of a number of factors, including the conflicted but "muy patriotic" desire of Valdez's protagonist Henry Reyna (Valdez, *Zoot Suit*, 30). Steele also cites the relatively young age of the Mexican American population, their lack of draft deferment opportunities, and the lure of a job at a time of high unemployment and job discrimination as important factors in Mexican American participation in World War II.
18. The heroism of the 100th Infantry Battalion and the 442nd Regimental Combat Team has been the subject of many books, including Chester Tanaka, *Go For Broke: A Pictorial History of The Japanese American 100th Infantry Battalion and the 442nd Regimental Combat Team* (1997); Robert Asahina, *Just Americans: How Japanese Americans Won A War at Home and Abroad* (2006); C. Douglas Sterner, *Go For Broke: The Nisei Warriors of World War II Who Conquered Germany, Japan, and American Bigotry* (2008); and James M. McCaffrey's *Going for Broke: Japanese American Soldiers in the War against Nazi Germany* (2013), as well as an outstanding first person account of the war by Minoru Masuda, *Letters from the 442nd: The World War II Correspondence of a Japanese American Medic* (2008).
19. Historian Ronald Takaki (*A Different Mirror*, 381) observes the irony that Japanese Americans were not evicted from Hawai'i, even though Hawai'i was the closest to Japan and the site of the Pearl Harbor bombing, because they were vital to the local economy. Japanese Americans on the mainland, however, were viewed as competitors by white farming interests such

as the Grower-Shipper Vegetable Association in California, which lobbied for their incarceration, stating "If all the Japs were removed tomorrow, we'd never miss them in two weeks, because the white farmer can take over and produce everything the Jap grows." Despite this grand rhetoric, the white farmer needed help; the deportation of Japanese Americans in February 1942 was followed by the importation of thousands of Mexican nationals seven months later under the "bracero" program.

20. Torgovnick, *The War Complex*, 9.

21. Yamada, *Camp Notes and Other Writings*, 39.

22. Valdez, *Zoot Suit and Other Plays*, 30.

23. Torgovnick, *The War Complex*, x. The rhetorical use of World War II after 9/11 has also appeared in literature about the event. In his novel *The Reluctant Fundamentalist*, Pakistani writer Mohsin Hamid writes from the perspective of a Pakistani American in the months immediately following 9/11: "Living in New York was suddenly like living in a film about the Second World War. . . . What your fellow countrymen longed for was unclear to me—a time of unquestioned dominance? of safety? of moral certainty? I did not know—but that they were scrambling to don the costumes of another era was apparent. I felt treacherous for wondering whether that era was fictitious, and whether—if it could indeed be animated—it contained a part written for someone like me" (115).

24. Ibid., 16.

25. Valdez, *Zoot Suit and Other Plays*, 24.

26. Yamada, *Camp Notes and Other Writings*, 13.

27. *El Teatro Campesino*, 3.

28. Huerta, Introduction to *Zoot Suit and Other Plays*, 7.

29. *El Teatro Campesino*, 3.

30. Huerta, Introduction to *Zoot Suit and Other Plays*, 8.

31. *El Teatro Campesino*, 25.

32. Valdez, "The Actos," 12.

33. For more on the dramatic form of the play, see Ramírez, "Chicano Theatre Reaches the Professional Stage," 197–198 and Huerta, Introduction to *Zoot Suit and Other Plays*, 13.

34. Valdez, "Notes on Chicano Theater," 316.

35. Sanchez, *Becoming Mexican American*, 266.

36. Obregón Pagán, *Murder at the Sleepy Lagoon*, 126–128.

37. Although various styles could be seen as a precursor to the zoot suit, historian Luis Alvarez claims that the popularity of the zoot among African American jazz artists such as Cab Calloway, who wore it in the 1930s and early 1940s, was a major factor in its spread in big cities. Music and dancing were an important part of the zoot culture: "African American, Mexican American, Asian American, and white zoot suiters shared fashion trends, listened to the latest jazz and big band music, and danced the jitterbug or Lindy Hop together" (*Power of the Zoot*, 4–5). Like jazz, the zoot suit was also a symbol of disaffected youth. Alvarez tellingly describes the zoot as being worn by "African American hepcats in New York, Mexican American pachuca/os or Filipino youth in Los Angeles, or young Japanese Americans in internment camps" (ibid., 86).

38. Griswold del Castillo, "The Los Angeles 'Zoot Suit Riots' Revisited," 368.

39. Sanchez, *Becoming Mexican American*, 267.

40. Griswold del Castillo, "The Los Angeles 'Zoot Suit Riots' Revisited," 367–368. In another indictment of the media, the fact that they were called the "zoot suit riots," rather than race riots or racially-targeted violence against Mexican Americans, essentially accomplished the task of inverting blame for the events, suggesting that the riots were instigated by youths wearing zoot suits and failing to name race as a factor (instead using the zoot suit as metonymic code for Latino and African American youths). Critic Chon Noriega calls the result of this nomenclature the creation of the "first fashion crime in the United States"; rather than violating laws, those wearing zoot suits were considered in violation of the austerity of wartime clothing norms, deliberately distorting the form of the business suit and flaunting authority in a way that threatened nationalist sentiments and elicited racially charged reactions ("Fashion Crimes," 7).

41. Valdez, *Zoot Suit and Other Plays,* 25.
42. Paz, *The Labyrinth of Solitude*, 15.
43. Ibid.,16.
44. Alvarez, *The Power of the Zoot*, 7.
45. Valdez, *Zoot Suit and Other Plays,* 26.
46. Noriega, "Fashion Crimes," 1.
47. Broyles-González, *El Teatro Campesino*, 199.
48. Ramírez, "Chicano Theatre Reaches the Professional Stage," 193–195.
49. Valdez, "Notes on Chicano Theater," 316.
50. Valdez, *Zoot Suit and Other Plays,* 25.
51. Quoted in Huerta, *Chicano Drama*, 5.
52. Valdez, *Zoot Suit and Other Plays,* 38.
53. Ibid., 28.
54. Ibid., 30.
55. Ibid.
56. Ibid.
57. Alvarez, *The Power of the Zoot*, 1.
58. Valdez, *Zoot Suit and Other Plays,* 26.
59. Ibid., 28.
60. Ibid.
61. Ibid., 49.
62. Broyles-González, *El Teatro Campesino*, 202.
63. Alvarez, *The Power of the Zoot*, 66.
64. Valdez, *Zoot Suit and Other Plays,* 72.
65. Ibid., 84.
66. Ibid., 80.
67. Ibid., 81.
68. Ibid., 88.
69. Ibid., 94.
70. Lorde, *Sister Outsider*, 37.
71. Ibid., 39.
72. Ibid., 116.
73. Chang, "Reading Asian American Poetry," 81.
74. Yamada, *Camp Notes and Other Writings*, 56.
75. For histories of the Japanese American incarceration, see especially *Personal Justice Denied: Report of the Commission on Wartime Relocation and Internment of Civilians* (1997); Ronald Takaki, *Democracy and Race: Asian Americans and World War II* (1995); Gary Y. Okihiro, *Whispered Silences: Japanese Americans and World War II* (1996) and Okihiro, ed., *The Encyclopedia of Japanese American Internment* (2013); Eric L. Muller, *Free to Die for Their Country: The Story of the Japanese American Draft Resisters in World War II* (2001), *American Inquisition: The Hunt for Japanese American Disloyalty in World War II* (2007), and *Colors of Confinement: Rare Kodachrome Photographs of Japanese American Incarceration in World War II* (2012); Greg Robinson, *By Order of the President: FDR and the Internment of Japanese Americans* (2001) and *A*

Tragedy of Democracy: Japanese Confinement in North America (2009); Roger Daniels, *Prisoners Without Trial: Japanese Americans in World War II* (2004); and Alice Yang Murray, *Historical Memories of the Japanese American Internment and the Struggle for Redress* (2008).

76. Maki, Kitano, and Berthold, *Achieving the Impossible Dream*, 1.

77. Quoted in Murray, *Historical Memories of the Japanese American Internment and the Struggle for Redress*, 53.

78. E. Kim, *Asian American Literature*, 302 note 26.

79. Yogi, "Japanese American Literature," 134.

80. Inada, "Of Place and Displacement," iii.

81. Yogi, "Japanese American Literature," 133; Schweik 226.

82. Schweik, "A Needle with Mama's Voice," 227.

83. Yamada, *Camp Notes and Other Writings*, 13.

84. Ibid., 24.

85. Patterson, "Resistance to Images of the Internment," 107.

86. Ibid., 108–110.

87. Ibid., 111.

88. Murray, *Historical Memories of the Japanese American Internment and the Struggle for Redress*, 69. In a striking example of this concern with language, public notices originally used the term "evacuation" rather than "deportation" to describe the forcible removal of Japanese Americans from the West Coast. Later, worried that "evacuation" now recalled a traumatic experience, administrators replaced the term "evacuees" with "residents" and even "colonists." This concern with language has carried over into scholarship on the camps, as nearly every book on the subject carries a lengthy justification of the author's choice of terminology. For the most part, I follow historian Greg Robinson in his use of the word "camp" rather than "concentration camp," because of the inevitable association of the words "concentration camp" with Nazi death camps; I also avoid "internment" because of its implication that those who were imprisoned were enemy nationals, which was not the case. I diverge from Robinson in his preference for the term "confinement" over "incarceration." While Robinson argues that "these institutions were not penitentiaries," as implied by the word incarceration, in fact those placed in camps were criminalized, held without trial, and not free to leave. Robinson, *A Tragedy of Democracy*, vii–viii.

89. Yamada, *Camp Notes and Other Writings*, 20.

90. Ibid.

91. Ibid., 22.

92. Ibid.

93. Ibid., 26.

94. Of course, Mexican Americans who did serve in the military faced another impossible position, that of being ethnically associated with the "zoot suiters" regardless of their own actions. Historians emphasize the "double consciousness" that many Mexican Americans developed during this time as men and women who considered themselves patriotic Americans while experiencing discrimination at home. Griswold del Castillo, "The Los Angeles 'Zoot Suit Riots' Revisited," 57.

95. Muller, *American Inquisition*, 1.

96. Quoted in Muller, *American Inquisition*, 35.

97. Ibid., 35.

98. Yamada, *Camp Notes and Other Writings*, 29.

99. Inada, "Of Place and Displacement," 260.

100. Yamada, *Camp Notes and Other Writings*, 23.

101. Ibid., 31.

102. Ibid., 32.
103. Ibid., 32–33.
104. Yamada, "Asian Pacific American Women and Feminism," 74.
105. Ibid., 75.
106. Quoted in Obregón Pagán, *Murder at the Sleepy Lagoon*, 183–184. Obregón Pagán considers the sheriff's mention of a "cage" to constitute a veiled hint that the recent incarceration of Japanese Americans might also be employed as a solution to the alleged violence of the Mexican American population. Later in his report, however, Ayres made a distinction between "Malay" and "Mongolian" blood, claiming that Mexican Americans had more in common with Filipinos than with the law-abiding Chinese and Japanese Americans (Leonard, *The Battle for Los Angeles*, 92–93). Either way, the report, which was admitted as legal evidence in the trial, indicates the ways in which Mexican Americans and Asian Americans were often considered alien races, biologically and culturally incompatible with white Americans.
107. DeGuzmán, *Spain's Long Shadow*, 79.
108. Zinn, *A People's History of the United States*, 407–8.
109. Torgovnick, *The War Complex*, 4.
110. Ibid.

CHAPTER 3 COLD WAR EPISTEMOLOGIES

1. Choi, *The Foreign Student*, 51.
2. This comparison requires some additional unpacking within the context of the white South of the 1950s, in which south of the Mason-Dixon line was likely to have been identified as the side of freedom (for states' rights). In this context, Chang is identifying South Korea as the "right side," the side with which his audience can safely identify. The irony of the comparison is readily apparent to a reader outside of that context, who may note that the Mason-Dixon line actually perpetuated conditions of slavery and was drawn, like the 38th parallel, by white Americans who were not subject to oppression by slavery or colonization.
3. Choi, *The Foreign Student*, 51.
4. Ibid., 50.
5. Ibid., 234.
6. Crystal Parikh makes a similar point, claiming that Chang reconfigures the postcolonial slogan as "a *melancholic* constitution of the racialized subject called to account for himself in the terms of an American imaginary" ("Writing the Borderline Subject of War in Susan Choi's *The Foreign Student*," 54, emphasis in original).
7. The enormous military presence of the United States in Asia and Latin America during the Cold War begs the question of what exactly constitutes a "direct tie," as refugees and migrants from Central and South America, Thailand, Cambodia, and other areas of Asia and Latin America may certainly bear witness to the Cold War's creation of zones of violence, military dependency, and economic inequities. Here, by "direct" I refer specifically to the legal status that defined and legitimized refugee communities and war brides through the political ideology of the Cold War.
8. J. Kim, *Ends of Empire*, 148.
9. Rabe, *The Killing Zone*, 36.
10. Park, "Susan Choi," 61.
11. D. Kim, "'Bled In, Letter by Letter,'" 571.
12. Hirsch, quoted in D. Kim, "'Bled In, Letter by Letter,'" 571.
13. Koeppel, "Seoul-to-South Experience Refracted in Fictional Debut."
14. D. Kim, "'Bled In, Letter by Letter,'" 575.

15. The term "The Forgotten War" has been widely used to describe U.S. military action in Korea since the 1987 publication of military historian Clay Blair's influential monograph *The Forgotten War: America in Korea 1950–1953*. Today, the phrase can be found in such disparate sources as historical U.S. Navy documents, a PBS documentary, Korean American women's histories, and, most ironically, inscribed on war memorials in the United States. In a Foucauldian sense, the proliferation of discourse that insists on the repression of this war in the public memory indicates its importance for subject formation in the United States both during the Cold War and afterwards.
16. Harper, "Dancing to a Different Beat," 7.
17. Obejas, *Memory Mambo*, 14.
18. Ibid., 9.
19. J. Lee, "In North Korea, Learning to Hate US Starts Early."
20. Ibid.
21. Ibid.
22. LaFeber, *America, Russia, and the Cold War, 1945–2006*, 107.
23. Asian American studies scholar Jodi Kim has demonstrated how the war in Korea that occurred between 1950 and 1953—what Americans call the Korean War—occurred precisely when a local civil conflict and decolonization movement became embroiled in this battle between two superpowers (*Ends of Empire*, 146). After World War II, the defeat of Japan signaled the end of the long and brutal Japanese imperial occupation of Korea. However, the arbitrary division of the country at the 38th parallel and its joint administration by U.S. and Soviet powers created a neo-imperial relationship between Korea, the United States, and the Soviet Union in which a full decolonization was never achieved. Indeed, given the ongoing hostilities between the United States and North Korea, as well as the economic and military dependence of South Korea on the United States since the mid-twentieth centuries, Kim proposes that the Korean War be "interpreted as an arrested project of decolonization" (ibid., 156). As with the later war in Vietnam, this nationalist struggle for independence from an occupying power was lost in the Cold War rhetoric of containment.

Within the United States, the Korean War came to occupy such an important part of Cold War ideology that Judge Irving Kaufman specifically cited it in sentencing Julius and Ethel Rosenberg to death for espionage in April, 1951: "I consider your crimes worse than murder. . . . I believe your conduct in putting into the hands of the Russians the A-bomb years before our best scientists predicted Russia would perfect the bomb has already caused, in my opinion, the Communist aggression in Korea, with the resultant casualties exceeding fifty thousand and who knows how many millions more of innocent people may pay the price of your treason" (quoted in Schrecker, *The Age of McCarthyism*, 167). Historical investigation has since revealed that the case against the Rosenbergs was largely fabricated and that, furthermore, there was no "secret" that could suddenly have created nuclear technology in the USSR. However, Judge Kaufman's statements demonstrate the extent to which the war in Korea was perceived in the United States not as a local conflict, but as a regional manifestation of a global war between U.S. and Soviet ideologies.
24. Choi, *The Foreign Student*, 84.
25. Ibid., 67.
26. Ibid.
27. Ibid., 84.
28. Ibid., 164.
29. Ibid., 104.
30. Ibid., 84.
31. D. Kim, "'Bled In, Letter by Letter,'" 559.

32. Bow, *Partly Colored*, 169.
33. Choi, *The Foreign Student*, 85.
34. Ibid., 90.
35. Bow, *Partly Colored*, 169.
36. Choi, *The Foreign Student*, 16.
37. Ibid., 166.
38. Ibid., 167.
39. Ibid., 37.
40. Ibid., 56.
41. Ibid., 324.
42. Ibid., 229.
43. Ibid., 230.
44. Bow, *Partly Colored*, 170–171.
45. Choi, *The Foreign Student*, 44.
46. Ibid., 23.
47. Ibid., 16.
48. Ibid., 30.
49. Bow, *Partly Colored*, 175; Parikh, "Writing the Borderline Subject of War in Susan Choi's *The Foreign Student*," 57.
50. Bow, *Partly Colored*, 175.
51. Choi, *The Foreign Student*, 125.
52. Ibid. 26, 124, 122, 207.
53. Ibid. 221, 162.
54. Ibid., 271.
55. Ibid., 105.
56. Ibid., 210.
57. Ibid., 325.
58. Lowe, *Immigrant Acts*, 16.
59. Oboler, *Ethnic Labels, Latino Lives*, 82.
60. Ibid., 10.
61. Caminero-Santangelo, *On Latinidad*, 164.
62. Ibid, 167.
63. The 150,000 Vietnamese Americans in Orange County, California (the location of Westminster's "Little Saigon") comprise another community with political roots in conservative Cold War ideology. This community, originally founded by refugees after the fall of South Vietnam, is growing in political diversity like Miami's "Little Havana," but has traditionally voted Republican and was the site of massive protests in 1999 in response to a store owner who displayed communist icons (Tran, "From Refugees to Political Players").
64. Croucher, "The Success of the Cuban Success Story," 377–378.
65. Ibid., 369.
66. Ibid., 356.
67. Obejas, *Memory Mambo*, 37.
68. Ibid., 38.
69. Ibid., 29.
70. Ibid., 24.
71. For example, critic Kate McCullough analyzes the novel as a lesbian novel of transculturation; in her analysis, the violence between Juani and Gina takes center stage as it demonstrates the political determination of erotic and romantic desire ("Marked by Genetics and Exile," 577). This insightful reading of the novel simultaneously reveals its functions as

a lesbian intervention into colonial narratives and an "emergent moment in U.S. lesbian fiction" that situates lesbianism in a global rather than a domestic political context (ibid., 579). Caminero-Santangelo also focuses on Juani's and Gina's relationship, but rather as a failed example of the attempt to forge a coherent *latinidad*. For Caminero-Santangelo, the political conflict between Cuban exiles and Puerto Rican independence advocates demonstrates a "striking self-reflexiveness about the constructed and tentative (rather than essential) nature of Latina/o ethnicity" (*On Latinidad*, 180).

72. Obejas, *Memory Mambo,* 14.
73. Ibid., 173.
74. Ibid., 29.
75. La Fountain-Stokes, "Queer Ducks, Puerto Rican Patos, and Jewish-American Feygelekh," 196.
76. Obejas, *Memory Mambo,* 29.
77. *Oxford English Dictionary Online,* s.v. "duck, n.3." accessed November 28, 2014, http://www.oed.com/.
78. Barrett, "Sticking to the Facts, Tearing into the Truth, and Patching Together a Method to Find the History and Meaning of Duct Tape," 142.
79. La Fountain-Stokes, "Queer Ducks, Puerto Rican Patos, and Jewish-American Feygelekh," 205.
80. Barrett, "Sticking to the Facts, Tearing into the Truth, and Patching Together a Method to Find the History and Meaning of Duct Tape," 140.
81. Ibid.
82. Obejas, *Memory Mambo,* 27.
83. Ibid., 28.
84. Ibid.
85. Torres-Saillant, "Inventing the Race," 214.
86. Obejas, *Memory Mambo,* 30.
87. Ibid., 29.
88. Ibid., 29–30.
89. Ibid., 185.
90. Obejas, "Author Tells of a 90s Cuba."
91. Obejas, *Memory Mambo,* 76.
92. Ibid., 77 (emphasis in original).
93. Ibid., 78.
94. Ibid., 32.
95. Ibid., 35.
96. Ibid., 32.
97. Ibid., 122.
98. Ibid., 123.
99. Ibid., 145.
100. Ibid, 217.
101. McCullough, "Marked by Genetics and Exile," 577.
102. Obejas, *Memory Mambo,* 178–9.
103. Ibid., 180.
104. Ibid., 234.
105. Ibid., 237.
106. Choi, *The Foreign Student,* 164; Obejas, *Memory Mambo,* 76.
107. Truman, "Address to Congress," 33 (emphasis mine).
108. Ibid.

109. "US Expands 'Axis of Evil.'" *BBC News.* Last modified 6 May 2002. http://news.bbc.co.uk/2/hi/1971852.stm.

CHAPTER 4 GLOBALIZATION AND MILITARY VIOLENCE IN THE LATINASIAN CONTACT ZONE

1. Yamashita, *Tropic of Orange,* 128.
2. Ibid., 15.
3. Ibid. 128.
4. Ibid. (emphasis mine).
5. Ibid.
6. In the late 1990s, roughly the same time that Yamashita published *Tropic of Orange,* the Los Angeles City Council decided to designate various ethnic "towns" to enhance the tourist experience. Although some of these towns already existed due to historical segregation, like the city's Chinatown, newer boroughs actually had to be *created* by the City Council regardless of the overlapping and discontinuous demographics of the city. Thus, despite the location of the central Thai temple in the San Fernando Valley, in 1999 the Los Angeles City Council designated an area east of Hollywood as "Thai Town"; the (white) council spokeswoman claimed that the move would "bring neighborhood pride, economic development and promotion of tourism to the area" ("City Council Designates Area as 'Thai Town,'" *Los Angeles Times,* 28 Oct. 1999, http://articles.latimes.com/1999/oct/28/local/me-27216). The next year, most of the same area was also designated "Little Armenia." Dislocated from history and only partially connected with the demographics of these ethnic populations, Thai Town and Little Armenia do little to inform outsiders of the cultural or sociological conditions of Thai and Armenian people in Los Angeles. Rather, like Emi, the people remain invisible, their ethnicity on display for tourists only at restaurants where, in the words of the unnamed woman of the novel, one "can find anything in the world to eat, right here."
7. Yamashita, *Tropic of Orange,* 129.
8. Palumbo-Liu, *The Ethnic Canon,* 10.
9. Quintana, "Performing Tricksters," 224.
10. Palumbo-Liu, *The Ethnic Canon,* 2 (emphasis in original).
11. Pratt, *Imperial* Eyes, 8.
12. Ibid.
13. DeGuzmán, *Spain's Long Shadow,* 301.
14. Anzaldúa, *Borderlands/La Frontera,* 25.
15. Recall that Américo Paredes and his wife nearly settled in Mexico rather than Texas because racial exclusion laws in the early twentieth century prohibited his wife, a South American woman of Japanese descent, from entering the United States (see Chapter 1). Similarly, Chinese immigrants to the Americas during the nineteenth and twentieth centuries often settled on the Mexico side of the United States-Mexico border. As Evelyn Hu-DeHart has explained, "European immigrants largely found northern Mexico an unattractive destination for quite obvious reasons—the lack of available land for homesteading, marauding Indians, an uneducated, unskilled local population—leaving the space wide open for willing immigrants such as the Japanese, Lebanese and other Middle Easterners, and especially the Chinese, who were shut out of the USA after decades of steady migration to California and other points West since the middle of the nineteenth century" ("Immigration and Exclusion," 100).
16. Hu-Dehart, "Immigration and Exclusion," 91.
17. Ibid. Hu-DeHart describes three major types of historical Chinese presence in Spanish America: early mercantile settlements in Spanish-colonized Asia, the "coolie" labor in

plantation economies such as the one in Cuba, and the settler society that developed along the United States-Mexico border in response to U.S. Chinese exclusion laws. Asian presence in the Americas is not restricted to Chinese diasporic populations, however. Karen Tei Yamashita has done extensive work with the Japanese population of Brazil, which constitutes more than a million people in Brazil descended from contract laborers and settlers who arrived during the years 1908 to 1940 (see Yamashita, unpaginated forward material to *Brazil-Maru*).

18. "Los Angeles (city), California," United States Census Bureau, last modified 10 January 2013, http://quickfacts.census.gov/qfd/states/06/0644000.html.

19. Guevarra, *Becoming Mexipino*, 4. Guevarra observes that many factors facilitated the intersection of these two communities, including the fact that Catholicism is the dominant religion for both Mexicans and Filipinos. The groups also share the experience of Spanish colonialism, which gives them many cultural traditions in common, and some language affiliation, including Spanish surnames (9). In *The Latinos of Asia: How Filipino Americans Break the Rules of Race*, sociologist Anthony Christian Ocampo suggests that in some circumstances, Filipinos identify more with Latinos than with other Asian Americans; they are the "Mexicans of Asia" (11).

20. Holston and Appadurai, "Introduction," 13.

21. Gómez-Peña, *The New World Border*, 6.

22. Halpern, "Essay Ignored Rising Minority Numbers."

23. Ibid.

24. Pratt, *Imperial Eyes*, 242.

25. Lionnet and Shih, *Minor Transnationalism*, 2.

26. Ibid., 7.

27. Yamashita, "Interview with Tei-hsing Shan," 123.

28. Murashige, "Karen Tei Yamashita," 321.

29. Yamashita, "Interview with Tei-hsing Shan," 128.

30. Murashige, "Karen Tei Yamashita," 340.

31. Ibid., 341.

32. Irizarry, "An Interview with Cristina García," 175.

33. García, *Monkey Hunting*, 258.

34. Ibid., 209.

35. Ibid., 262–263.

36. The setting of the novel is never explicitly stated, but its history and defining characteristics strongly suggest Guatemala. In an interview, García clarifies her intentions: "I definitely had Guatemala in mind, but I also didn't feel like I wanted to limit it to a specific place, and I didn't want to worry about whether this street intersected with that street [in real life]. I wanted it to be a little bit of Everyplace, Central America. A sort of archetypal place where there's been civil war, a place that's been traumatized and is in the wake of that trauma. There's no shortage of that throughout the Americas" (Nutting, "*The Lady Matador's Hotel*").

37. García, *Lady Matador's Hotel*, 63.

38. Lionnet and Shih, *Minor Transnationalism*, 13.

39. Murashige, "Karen Tei Yamashita," 339.

40. *Oxford English Dictionary Online*, s.v. "hypertext, *n.*," accessed May 22, 2013, http://www.oed.com/.

41. See also Fredric Jameson, *Postmodernism: Or, the Cultural Logic of Late Capitalism* (1991).

42. Harvey, *The Condition of Postmodernity*, 279.

43. Yamashita, *Tropic of Orange*, 37.

44. Ibid.

45. See, for example, Rody, "The Transnational Imagination," 131.

46. Sadowski-Smith, *Border Fictions*, 59.
47. Ibid., 62.
48. Lionnet and Shih, *Minor Transnationalism*, 4.
49. Yamashita, *Tropic of Orange*, 11.
50. Yamashita, Interview with Tei-hsing Shan, 137.
51. Yamashita, *Tropic of Orange*, 47.
52. In García Marquez's short story "A Very Old Man with Enormous Wings" (1968), a bedraggled angel suddenly appears in a village, only to be met by indifference and cruelty on the part of the villagers and the Catholic Church. The character of Arcangel is physically similar to the angel in García Marquez's story. (His name is also a pun on Los Angeles as the "City of Angels"; notably, both Rafaela and Gabriel also have angel names.) In another reference to García Marquez, both "Very Old Man" and *Tropic of Orange* begin with characters sweeping crabs from a house. Thus, the crabs in Yamashita's novel reference García Marquez even as they foreshadow the importance of the Tropic of Cancer (the Latin "crab") in the novel.
53. Yamashita, *Tropic of Orange*, 48.
54. Ngai, *Impossible Subjects*, 156.
55. Hing, *Ethical Borders*, 37.
56. Quoted in Ngai, *Impossible Subjects*, 156.
57. Ibid.
58. Yamashita, *Tropic of Orange*, 132.
59. Hing, *Ethical Borders*, 10.
60. Ibid., 14.
61. Ibid., 16.
62. Yamashita, *Tropic of Orange*, 131.
63. Ibid., 132.
64. Ibid., 248.
65. Ibid., 259.
66. Ibid., 261 (italics in original).
67. Ngai, *Impossible Subjects*, 150–151.
68. Yamashita, *Tropic of Orange*, 259.
69. Hing, *Ethical Borders*, 15–16.
70. Scheper-Hughes, "Rotten Trade," 199.
71. Yamashita, *Tropic of Orange*, 141.
72. Ibid., 55.
73. Ibid., 121.
74. Sadowski-Smith, "The U.S.-Mexico Borderlands Write Back."
75. Yamashita, *Tropic of Orange*, 222.
76. Ibid., 226.
77. Sadowski-Smith, "The U.S.-Mexico Borderlands Write Back," 147.
78. Kazuo Ishiguro's novel *Never Let Me Go* (2005) also bears mentioning within this genre. Set in an alternate-reality England, *Never Let Me Go* explores the ethics of raising cloned humans in order to harvest their organs, a process that ultimately kills the donors. Because the children are cloned from lower class prisoners, prostitutes, and asylum inmates, the novel questions power structures within society, asking who is "expendable" and to what extent are people willing to violate moral precepts against murder to fulfill the economic logic of supply and demand? In Ishiguro's novel, the question of "expendability" is raised with respect to class; in Silko's, Abani's, and Yamashita's novels, it is explored as a critique of structural racism and international power, as third world, nonwhite children become unwilling suppliers of organs to the first world.

79. Yamashita, *Tropic of Orange*, 256 (emphasis mine).
80. Ibid., 270.
81. Ibid.
82. Briggs, "Making 'American' Families," 350–351.
83. Ibid., 356.
84. Ibid., 355–356.
85. Ibid., 358.
86. Ibid., 358–359.
87. García, *Lady Matador's Hotel*, 81.
88. Ibid., 14.
89. García, *Lady Matador's Hotel*, 107.
90. Ibid., 15.
91. Ibid.
92. Ibid.
93. Tony Paterson, "How the Nazis Escaped Justice," *The Independent.* Last modified 27 Jan. 2013, http://www.independent.co.uk/news/world/europe/how-the-nazis-escaped-justice-8468840.html. Stahl's book, Nazi-Jagd : Südamerikas Diktaturen und die Ahndung von NS-Verbrechen, was published by Wallstein in Göttingen, Germany in 2013.
94. García, *Lady Matador's Hotel*, 28.
95. Ibid., 29.
96. Ibid., 106.
97. Ibid., 104.
98. Ibid., 8.
99. Ibid., 9.
100. Ibid., 3.
101. Ibid., 76.
102. Ibid., 170.
103. Ibid., 125.
104. Ibid., 32.
105. Ibid., 28,
106. Ibid. (emphasis in original).
107. Ibid., 208.
108. Ibid., 209.
109. Ibid., 206.
110. Ibid., 176–177.
111. Briggs, "Making 'American' Families," 356.
112. Ibid., 362.
113. García, *Lady Matador's Hotel*, 59.
114. Ibid., 61.
115. Ibid., 122.
116. Ibid., 205–206.

CONCLUSION

1. J. Saldívar, *Trans-Americanity*, xiii.
2. Sohn, Lai, and Goellnicht, "Theorizing Asian American Fiction," 4.
3. Ibid., 4.
4. Until recently, the "America" in "Asian American" has referred primarily to the United States, with Canada a largely unexamined extension of the area. In their ground-breaking

annotated bibliography of Asian American literature, literary scholars King-Kok Cheung and Stan Yogi define their target body of literature to be "works by writers of Asian descent who have made the United States or Canada their home" (*Asian American Literature*, vi). Sau-ling Cynthia Wong addresses this ambiguity in her seminal work *Reading Asian American Literature: From Necessity to Extravagance* by considering the theoretical difficulties entailed in "the subsumption of 'Asian Canadian' under 'Asian American'" (16). More recent works have addressed the issue of Asian Canadians by using the term "Asian North American"; a notable example of this orientation is *Asian North American Identities: Beyond the Hyphen* (2004), edited by Eleanor Ty and Donald C. Goellnicht. Although this volume contains one essay on Karen Tei Yamashita's work, its theoretical orientation explicitly defines Asian North American in terms of the United States and Canada: "If a pan-Asian designation is to be used at all . . . we propose that 'Asian North American' is a more useful umbrella term because Asian subjects who reside *in the United States and in Canada* face many of the same issues regarding identity, multiple cultural allegiances, marginalization vis-à-vis mainstream society, historical exclusion, and postcolonial and/or diasporic and/or transnational subjectivity" (Ty and Goellnicht, 2, emphasis mine). Despite the fact that many of these issues also apply to Asian Mexicans, Asian Central Americans, and Asian people in the Caribbean, the term "Asian North American" does not directly address these groups.

5. E. Lee, "Orientalisms in the Americas," 235.

6. Many Latina/o studies scholars have addressed the racial diversity that exists within the highly constructed category of "Latino" or "Hispanic"; Silvio Torres-Saillant observes that the "Indian and Asian, too, not just the black and the white" inhabit "the sphere of the Hispanic" within the U.S. ethnoracial pentagon ("Inventing the Race," 124). In Torres-Saillant's view, the acknowledgement of this diversity is necessary in order to overcome intra-Latino racism and fight for "programs of compensatory justice" (ibid., 125).

7. See Guevarra, *Becoming Mexipino*, and Ocampo, *The Latinos of Asia*. As discussed in Chapter 4, the subjects of Ocampo's sociological study refer to Filipinos as the "Mexicans of Asia" (11). Guevarra has done extensive research into the factors that Filipinos and Latina/os have in common, including Catholicism, cultural traditions rooted in Spanish colonialism, and some affiliation with the Spanish language. His main interest, the convergence of the two communities into a "Mexipino" community in San Diego, is an important study of the cartographies of LatinAsia.

8. Okihiro, *Common Ground*, 17.

9. Hoskins and Nguyen, *Transpacific Studies*; Shu and Pease, *American Studies as Transnational Practice*.

10. Leong and Hu-DeHart, "Forging a Third Chinese Literature of the Americas," x-xii.

11. See especially Yamashita's *Brazil-Maru* (1992) and *Through the Arc of the Rainforest* (1990). Ignacio López-Calvo has done extensive work on Asian Latin American populations, including *Imaging the Chinese in Cuban Literature and Culture* (2008), *The Affinity of the Eye: Writing Nikkei in Peru* (2013), and *Dragons in the Land of the Condor: Writing Túsan in Peru* (2014).

12. See, for example, *Contours of the Heart: South Asians Map North America*, eds. Sunaina Maira and Rajini Srikanth (1998), and *The Fiction of South Asians in North America and the Caribbean*, eds. Mitali P. Wong and Zia Hasan (2004).

13. López-Calvo, *Dragons in the Land of the Condor*, 103.

14. Siu, *Tierra de Nadie*.

15. Lee-DiStefano, *Three Asian-Hispanic Writers from Peru*, 89.

16. Siu, *El tramo final*, 9. *El tramo final* has not been translated into English. The translation of this passage, from the Preface to the 2009 edition of the volume, is my own, as are all

subsequent translations from the text. I would like to extend my thanks to my colleague John Ribó for his assistance with these translations.
17. Siu, *El tramo final,* 9.
18. Ibid., 7.
19. Lopez-Calvo, "Sino-Peruvian Identity and Community as Prison," 73.
20. Quoted in Kerr, "Lost in Lima in Kerr," 54 (my translations).
21. López-Calvo, "Sino-Peruvian Identity and Community as Prison," 87.
22. Back matter to the 2009 edition; Gabriel Rimachi Sialer is the editor of the Casatomada publishing company.
23. Siu, *El tramo final,* 8.
24. Lee-DiStefano, *Three Asian-Hispanic Writers from Peru,* 127.
25. Siu, *Tierra de Nadie.*
26. Lopez-Calvo, "Sino-Peruvian Identity and Community as Prison," 77.
27. Hu-DeHart and López, "Asian Diasporas in Latin America and the Caribbean," 10.
28. Ibid., 9.
29. Ibid., 14–15.
30. Lowe, "The Intimacies of Four Continents," 204–205. In her book *The Intimacies of Four Continents* (2015), Lowe further develops the idea of the "particular plasticity of the figure of the *coolie* within liberal capitalist modernity," as Chinese laborers occupied a liminal position—neither free nor enslaved—that could be conveniently coded according to political context and needs (27). See also Lisa Yun's *The Coolie Speaks: Chinese Indentured Laborers and African Slaves in Cuba* (2008) for another fascinating account of how Asian indentureship in the Americas defies a "narrative of transition," as this labor was not an intermediate step in the progress from slavery to free labor, but rather contemporaneous and coproductive with slave economies.
31. Stewart, *Chinese Bondage in Peru,* 67.
32. Siu, *El tramo final,* 115.
33. Ibid., 117.
34. Ibid.
35. Ibid., 120.
36. Ibid., 119–120.
37. Ibid., 119.
38. Ibid., 121.
39. Morrison, "The Site of Memory," 70.
40. Lowe, "The Intimacies of Four Continents," 206.
41. Siu, *El tramo final,* 42.
42. Ibid., 40.
43. Ibid., 41.
44. Ibid., 44.
45. Ibid., 9.
46. Duany, "Reconstructing Racial Identity," 432.
47. Hoskins and Nguyen, *Transpacific Studies,* 26.
48. The text of *El tramo final* refers to Uei-Kuong and other non-Chinese Peruvians as *mestizos,* to distinguish them from Peruvians of indigenous or Asian heritage. Although *mestizo* technically means a person of mixed-race ancestry, in Peru it refers to the majority population. In 2006, 57.6 percent of the population of Peru self-identified as *mestizo,* while most of the remainder identified with indigenous groups. With regard to the *mestizo* population, Raúl Madrid observes that "there is a great deal of variation within this category," with many *mestizos* having a European appearance and few or no ties to indigenous culture ("Ethnic

Proximity and Ethnic Voting in Peru," 269). I refer to this mainstream population of *mestizos* as "ethnic Peruvians" to avoid confusion with other kinds of *mestizaje* more familiar to North American readers.

49. Siu, *El tramo final*, 98.
50. Ibid., 156.
51. Ibid., 95.
52. Ibid.
53. Ibid., 101.
54. Ibid., 104.
55. Ibid.
56. E. Kim, *Asian American Literature*, 6.
57. Lye, "Introduction," 4.
58. Chuh, *Imagine Otherwise*, 8.
59. Siu, *El tramo final*, 104.
60. Ibid., 113.
61. Ibid., 114.
62. Chuh, *Imagine Otherwise*, 10 (emphasis in original).
63. *The Affinity of the Eye: Writing Nikkei in Peru* (2013) is the title of López-Calvo's book on Japanese Peruvian writers; the title refers to a racial bond that may, in some cases, be based on little more than visual recognition of a common ancestry.
64. Siu, *El tramo final*, 114.
65. DeGuzmán, *Spain's Long Shadow*, 301.
66. Kerr, "Lost in Lima," 63.
67. Siu, *El tramo final*, 152.

WORKS CITED

Aaron, Daniel. *Writers on the Left: Episodes in Literary Communism*. New York: Harcourt, Brace, and World, 1961.

Alquizola, Marilyn. "The Fictive Narrator of *America Is in the Heart*." In *Frontiers of Asian American Studies: Writing, Research, and Commentary*, edited by Gail M. Nomura, Russell Endo, Stephen H. Sumida, and Russell C. Leong, 211–217. Pullman: Washington State University Press, 1989.

Alvarez, Luis. *The Power of the Zoot: Youth Culture and Resistance During World War II*. Berkeley: University of California Press, 2008.

Ancheta, Angelo N. *Race, Rights, and the Asian American Experience*. 2nd ed. New Brunswick, NJ: Rutgers University Press, 2010.

Anderson, Benedict. *Imagined Communities: Reflections on the Origin and Spread of Nationalism*. Revised edition. London: Verso, 1991.

Anzaldúa, Gloria. *Borderlands/La Frontera: The New Mestiza*. 2nd ed. San Francisco, CA: Aunt Lute Books, 1999.

Balderrama, Francisco E., and Raymond Rodríguez. *Decade of Betrayal: Mexican Repatriation in the 1930s*. Revised edition. Albuquerque: University of New Mexico Press, 2006.

Barrett, Joe. "Sticking to the Facts, Tearing into the Truth, and Patching Together a Method to Find the History and Meaning of Duct Tape." *Journal of Popular Culture* 28 (1994): 139–148.

Bascara, Victor. *Model-Minority Imperialism*. Minneapolis: University of Minnesota Press, 2006.

Bercovitch, Sacvan. *The American Jeremiad*. Madison: University of Wisconsin Press, 1978.

Bonilla-Silva, Eduardo. *Racism Without Racists: Color-Blind Racism and the Persistence of Racial Inequality in the United States*. 2nd ed. Lanham, MD: Rowman and Littlefield, 2006.

Bow, Leslie. *Partly Colored : Asian Americans and Racial Anomaly in the Segregated South*. New York: New York University Press, 2010.

Brainard, Cecilia Manguerra. *When the Rainbow Goddess Wept*. New York: Plume, 1994.

Briggs, Laura. "Making 'American' Families: Transnational Adoption and U.S. Latin America Policy." In *Haunted by Empire: Geographies of Intimacy in North American History*, edited by Ann Laura Stoler, 344–365. Durham, NC: Duke University Press, 2006.

Brokaw, Tom. *The Greatest Generation*. New York: Random House, 1998.

Broyles-González, Yolanda. *El Teatro Campesino: Theater in the Chicano Movement*. Austin: University of Texas Press, 1994.

Bulosan, Carlos. *America Is in the Heart*. Seattle: University of Washington Press, 1973.

Bulosan, Carlos. *The Cry and the Dedication*. Philadelphia, PA: Temple University Press, 1995.

Cacho, Lisa Marie. *Social Death: Racialized Rightlessness and the Criminalization of the Unprotected*. New York: New York University Press, 2012.

Calderón, Héctor, and José Rósbel López-Morín. "Interview with Américo Paredes." *Nepantla: Views from South* 1 (2000): 197–228.

Caminero-Santangelo, Marta. *On Latinidad: U.S. Latino Literature and the Construction of Ethnicity*. Gainesville: University Press of Florida, 2007.

Castillo, Ana. *Massacre of the Dreamers: Essays on Xicanisma*. New York: Plume, 1994.

Cha, Theresa Hak Kyung. *Dictee*. Berkeley: University of California Press, 2001.

Chan, Sucheng. *Asian Americans: An Interpretive History.* New York: Twayne Publishers, 1991.

Chang, Juliana. "Reading Asian American Poetry." *MELUS* 21 (1996): 81–98.

Cheung, King-Kok, and Stan Yogi. *Asian American Literature: An Annotated Bibliography.* New York: Modern Language Association of America, 1988.

Choi, Susan. *The Foreign Student.* New York: HarperPerennial, 1998.

Chu, Patricia P. *Assimilating Asians: Gendered Strategies of Authorship in Asian America.* Durham, NC: Duke University Press, 2000.

Chuh, Kandice. *Imagine Otherwise: On Asian Americanist Critique.* Durham, NC: Duke University Press, 2003.

A Class Apart. PBS American Experience. Produced and directed by Carlos Sandoval and Peter Miller. Camino Bluff Productions and Independent Television Service in association with Latino Public Broadcasting, 2009. DVD.

Constantino, Renato. "The Miseducation of the Filipino." In *The Philippines Reader: A History of Colonialism, Neocolonialism, Dictatorship, and Resistance,* edited by Daniel B. Schirmer and Stephen R. Shalom, 45–49. Boston, MA: South End Press, 1987.

Council on Books in Wartime. *A History of the Council on Books in Wartime, 1942–1946.* New York, 1946.

Craig, Maureen, and Jennifer A. Richeson. "More Diverse Yet Less Tolerant? How the Increasingly Diverse Racial Landscape Affects White Americans' Racial Attitudes." *Personality and Social Psychology Bulletin* 40 (2014): 750–761.

Croucher, Sheila. "The Success of the Cuban Success Story: Ethnicity, Power, and Politics." *Identities: Global Studies in Culture and Power* 2 (1996): 352–384.

De los Angeles Torres, María. "Encuentros y Encontronazos: Homeland in the Politics and Identity of Cuban Diaspora." *Diaspora* 4 (1995): 211–238.

DeGuzmán, María. *Spain's Long Shadow: The Black Legend, Off-Whiteness, and Anglo-American Empire.* Minneapolis: University of Minnesota Press, 2005.

Duany, Jorge. "Reconstructing Racial Identity: Ethnicity, Color, and Class among Dominicans in the United States and Puerto Rico." *Latin American Perspectives* 25 (1998): 147–172.

El Teatro Campesino: The Evolution of America's First Chicano Theatre Company, 1965–1985. San Juan Bautista, CA: El Teatro, 1985.

Farmer, Paul. "An Anthropology of Structural Violence." *Current Anthropology* 45(2004): 305–325.

Francisco, Luzviminda. "The Philippine-American War." In *The Philippines Reader: A History of Colonialism, Neocolonialism, Dictatorship, and Resistance,* edited by Daniel B. Schirmer and Stephen R. Shalom, 9–19. Boston, MA: South End Press, 1987.

Fuentes, Marlon. *Bontoc Eulogy,* film. New York, NY: Cinema Guild, 1995.

García, Cristina. *The Agüero Sisters.* New York: Ballantine, 1997.

García, Cristina. *The Lady Matador's Hotel.* New York: Scribner, 2010.

García, Cristina. *Monkey Hunting.* New York: Alfred A. Knopf, 2003.

García Marquez, Gabriel. "A Very Old Man with Enormous Wings." In *Leaf Storm: And Other Stories,* 105–112. New York: Harper Perennial, 1990.

Goellnicht, Donald C. "Blurring Boundaries: Asian American Literature as Theory." In *An Interethnic Companion to Asian American Literature,* edited by King-kok Cheung, 338–365. Cambridge, UK: Cambridge University Press, 1997.

Gómez-Peña, Guillermo. *The New World Border: Prophecies, Poems, and Loqueras for the End of the Century.* San Francisco: City Lights, 1996.

Griswold del Castillo, Richard. "The Los Angeles 'Zoot Suit Riots' Revisited: Mexican and Latin American Perspectives." *Mexican Studies/Estudios Mexicanos* 16 (2000): 367–391.

Griswold del Castillo, Richard. *The Treaty of Guadalupe Hidalgo: A Legacy of Conflict.* Norman: University of Oklahoma Press, 1990.

Griswold del Castillo, Richard. "The War and Changing Identities: Personal Transformations." In *World War II and Mexican American Civil Rights,* edited by Richard Griswold del Castillo, 49–73. Austin, TX: University of Texas Press, 2008.

Guevarra, Rudy. *Becoming Mexipino: Multiethnic Identities and Communities in San Diego.* New Brunswick, NJ: Rutgers University Press, 2012.

Halpern, Adrián R. "Essay Ignored Rising Minority Numbers." *Chapel Hill News* (Chapel Hill, NC), May 8, 2013.

Hamid, Mohsin. *The Reluctant Fundamentalist.* Orlando, FL: Harcourt, 2007.

Harper, Jorjet. "Dancing to a Different Beat: An Interview with Achy Obejas." *Lambda Book Report: A Review of Contemporary Gay and Lesbian Literature* 5 (1996): 1, 6–7.

Harvey, David. *The Condition of Postmodernity: An Enquiry into the Origins of Cultural Change.* Cambridge, MA: Blackwell, 1990.

Hietala, Thomas R. *Manifest Design: American Exceptionalism and Empire.* Revised edition. Ithaca, NY: Cornell University Press, 2003.

Hing, Bill Ong. *Ethical Borders: NAFTA, Globalization, and Mexican Migration.* Philadelphia, PA: Temple University Press, 2010.

Holston, James, and Arjun Appadurai. "Introduction: Cities and Citizenship." In *Cities and Citizenship,* edited by James Holston, 1–20. Durham, NC: Duke University Press, 1999.

Hoskins, Janet, and Viet Thanh Nguyen. *Transpacific Studies: Framing an Emerging Field.* Honolulu: University of Hawai'i Press, 2014.

Hu-Dehart, Evelyn. "Immigration and Exclusion: The Chinese in Multiracial Latin America and the Caribbean." In *Routledge Handbook of the Chinese Diaspora,* edited by Chee-Beng Tan, 89–107. Abington, United Kingdom: Routledge, 2013.

Hu-DeHart, Evelyn, and Kathleen López. "Asian Diasporas in Latin America and the Caribbean: An Historical Overview." *Afro-Hispanic Review* 27 (2008): 9–21.

Huerta, Jorge A. *Chicano Drama: Performance, Society, and Myth.* Cambridge, UK: Cambridge University Press, 2000.

Huerta, Jorge A. Introduction to *Zoot Suit and Other Plays,* by Luis Valdez. Houston, TX: Arte Publico Press, 1992.

Ignacio, Abe, Enrique de la Cruz, Jorge Emmanuel, and Helen Toribio. *The Forbidden Book: The Philippine-American War in Political Cartoons.* San Francisco, CA: T'Boli Publishing, 2004.

Ignatiev, Noel. *How the Irish Became White.* New York: Routledge, 1995.

Inada, Lawson Fusao. "Of Place and Displacement: The Range of Japanese-American Literature." In *Three American Literatures: Essays in Chicano, Native American, and Asian-American Literature for Teachers of American Literature,* edited by Houston A. Baker, Jr., 254–265. New York: Modern Language Association of America, 1982.

Irizzary, Ylce. "An Interview with Cristina García." *Contemporary Literature* 48 (2007): 175–194.

Ishiguro, Kazuo. *Never Let Me Go.* New York: Vintage International, 2006.

Jaskoski, Helen, and Mitsuye Yamada. "A MELUS Interview: Mitsuye Yamada." *MELUS* 15 (1988): 97–108.

Johnson, Benjamin Heber. *Revolution in Texas: How a Forgotten Rebellion and Its Bloody Suppression Turned Mexicans into Americans.* New Haven, CT: Yale University Press, 2003.

Jones-Puthoff, Alexa. "Is the U.S. Population Getting Older and More Diverse?" *United States Census Bureau.* 14 June 2013. Accessed 9 Aug. 2014. http://www.census.gov/content/dam/Census/newsroom/c-span/2013/20130614_cspan_popdiverse.pdf.

Kaplan, Amy, and Donald E. Pease, eds. *Cultures of United States Imperialism*. Durham, NC: Duke University Press, 1993.

Keppler, Udo J. "A Trifle Embarrassed." Cartoon. *Puck* 43 (3 August 1898): centerfold. *Library of Congress*. Accessed 11 Nov. 2014. http://loc.gov/pictures/item/2012647587.

Kerr, R. A. "Lost in Lima: The Asian Hispanic Fiction of Siu Kam Wen." *Chasqui: Revista de Literatura Latinamericana* 28 (1999): 54–65.

Kim, Bok-Lim C. "Asian Wives of U.S. Servicemen: Women in Shadows." *Amerasia Journal* 4 (1977): 91–115.

Kim, Daniel Y. "'Bled In, Letter by Letter': Translation, Postmemory, and the Subject of Korean War: History in Susan Choi's *The Foreign Student*." *American Literary History* 21 (2009): 550–583.

Kim, Elaine. *Asian American Literature: An Introduction to the Writings and Their Social Context*. Philadelphia, PA: Temple University Press, 1982.

Kim, Jodi. *Ends of Empire: Asian American Critique and the Cold War*. Minneapolis: University of Minnesota Press, 2010.

Kochhar, Rakesh, Richard Fry, and Paul Taylor. "Wealth Gaps Rise to Record Highs Between Whites, Blacks, Hispanics." *Pew Research Center*. Last modified 26 July 2011. http://www.pewsocialtrends.org/files/2011/07/SDT-Wealth-Report_7-26-11_FINAL.pdf.

Koeppel, Fredric. "Seoul-to-South Experience Refracted in Fictional Debut." *Commercial Appeal* (Memphis, TN), 4 October 1998.

Kramer, Paul A. *The Blood of Government: Race, Empire, the United States, and the Philippines*. Chapel Hill: University of North Carolina Press, 2006.

La Fountain-Stokes, Lawrence. "Queer Ducks, Puerto Rican Patos, and Jewish-American Feygelekh: Birds and the Cultural Representation of Homosexuality." *Centro Journal* 19 (2007): 192–229.

LaFeber, Walter. *America, Russia, and the Cold War, 1945–2006*. 10th edition. Boston: McGraw-Hill, 2008.

Lazarus, Emma. "The New Colossus." In *The Norton Anthology of American Literature*. 8th edition. Edited by Nina Baym, Volume C, 524–525.New York: Norton, 2012.

Lee, Erika. *The Making of Asian America: A History*. New York: Simon and Schuster, 2015.

Lee, Erika. "Orientalisms in the Americas: A Hemispheric Approach to Asian American History." *Journal of Asian American Studies* 8 (2005): 235–256.

Lee, Jean H. "In North Korea, Learning to Hate US Starts Early." *Associated Press*. Last modified 23 June 2012. www.yahoo.com/news/north-korea-learning-hate-us-starts-early-120658377.html.

Lee-DiStefano, Debbie. *Three Asian-Hispanic Writers from Peru: Doris Moromisato, José Watanabe, Siu Kam Wen*. Lewiston, NY: Edwin Mellen Press, 2008.

Leonard, Kevin Allen. *The Battle for Los Angeles: Racial Ideology and World War II*. Albuquerque: University of New Mexico Press, 2006.

Leong, Russell C., and Evelyn Hu-DeHart. "Forging a Third Chinese Literature of the Americas." *Amerasia Journal* 38 (2012): vii–vxv.

Lewin, Tamar. "Citing Individualism, Arizona Tries to Rein in Ethnic Studies in School." *New York Times*, May 13, 2010.

Lin, Maan. "Translating 'La primera espada del imperio' into English and Chinese." *Amerasia Journal* 38 (2012): 102–119.

Lionnet, Françoise, and Shu-mei Shih, eds. *Minor Transnationalism*. Durham, NC: Duke University Press, 2005.

López-Calvo, Ignacio. *Dragons in the Land of the Condor: Writing Túsan in Peru*. Tucson: University of Arizona Press, 2014.

López-Calvo, Ignacio. "Sino-Peruvian Identity and Community as Prison: Siu Kam Wen's Rendering of Self-Exploration and Other Survival Strategies." *Afro-Hispanic Review* 27 (2008): 73–90.

Lorde, Audre. *Sister Outsider: Essays and Speeches.* Trumansburg, NY: Crossing Press, 1984.

Lowe, Lisa. *Immigrant Acts: On Asian American Cultural Politics.* Durham, NC: Duke University Press, 1996.

Lowe, Lisa. "The Intimacies of Four Continents." In *Haunted by Empire: Geographies of Intimacy in North American History*, edited by Ann Laura Stoler, 191–212. Durham, NC: Duke University Press, 2006.

Lowe, Lisa. *The Intimacies of Four Continents.* Durham, NC: Duke University Press. 2015.

Lye, Colleen. "The Afro-Asian Analogy." *PMLA* 123 (2008): 1732–1736.

Lye, Colleen. "Introduction: In Dialogue with Asian American Studies." *Representations* 99 (2007): 1–12.

Madrid, Raúl L. "Ethnic Proximity and Ethnic Voting in Peru." *Journal of Latin American Studies* 43 (2011): 267–297.

Maki, Mitchell T., Harry H. L. Kitano, and S. Megan Berthold. *Achieving the Impossible Dream: How Japanese Americans Obtained Redress.* Urbana: University of Illinois Press, 1999.

Manning, Jennifer E. "Membership of the 112th Congress: A Profile." *Congressional Research Service.* Last modified 26 November 2012. http://fas.org/sgp/crs/misc/R41647.pdf.

McCullough, Kate. "Marked by Genetics and Exile:" Narrativizing Transcultural Sexualities in *Memory Mambo.*" *GLQ: A Journal of Lesbian and Gay Studies* 6 (2000): 577–607.

McKinley, Jr., James C. "Texas Conservatives Win Curriculum Change." *New York Times*, March 12, 2010.

McKinley, William. "Remarks to Methodist Delegation." In *The Philippines Reader: A History of Colonialism, Neocolonialism, Dictatorship, and Resistance*, edited by Daniel B. Schirmer and Stephen R. Shalom, 22–23. Boston, MA: South End Press, 1987.

Medrano, Manuel F. *Américo Paredes: In His Own Words, An Authorized Biography.* Denton: University of North Texas Press, 2010.

Melamed, Jodi. *Represent and Destroy: Rationalizing Violence in the New Racial Capitalism.* Minneapolis: University of Minnesota Press, 2011.

Minutemen Project, the. "Operation Normandy." *The Minutemen Project.* Accessed November 11, 2014. http://minutemenproject.com.

Molina, Natalia. *How Race Is Made in America: Immigration, Citizenship, and the Historical Power of Racial Scripts.* Berkeley, CA: University of California Press, 2014.

Montejano, David. *Anglos and Mexicans in the Making of Texas, 1836–1986.* Austin: University of Texas Press, 1987.

Moraga, Cherríe, and Gloria Anzaldúa, eds. *This Bridge Called My Back: Writings by Radical Women of Color.* New York: Kitchen Table: Women of Color Press, 1983.

Morrison, Toni. *Playing in the Dark: Whiteness and the Literary Imagination.* Cambridge, MA: Harvard University Press, 1992.

Morrison,Toni. "The Site of Memory." In *What Moves at the Margin*, edited by Carolyn C. Denard, 65–80. Jackson: University Press of Mississippi, 2008.

Moya, Paula M. L. *The Social Imperative: Race, Close Reading, and Contemporary Literary Criticism.* Stanford, CA: Stanford University Press, 2016.

Muller, Eric L. *American Inquisition: The Hunt for Japanese American Disloyalty in World War II.* Chapel Hill: University of North Carolina Press, 2007.

Murashige, Michael S. "Karen Tei Yamashita." In *Words Matter: Conversations with Asian American Writers*, edited by King-Kok Cheung, 320–342. Honolulu: University of Hawai'i Press, 2000.

Murray, Alice Yang. *Historical Memories of the Japanese American Internment and the Struggle for Redress.* Stanford, CA: Stanford University Press, 2008.
Ngai, Mae M. *Impossible Subjects: Illegal Aliens and the Making of Modern America.* Princeton, NJ: Princeton University Press, 2004.
Noriega, Chon A. "Fashion Crimes." *Aztlán* 26 (2001): 1–13.
Nutting, Alissa. "*The Lady Matador's Hotel*: An Interview with Cristina García." *Witness* 24 (2011). http://witness.blackmountaininstitute.org/issues/volume-24-number-2-2011-the-lady-matadors-hotel-an-interview-with-cristina-garcia.
Obejas, Achy. "Author Tells of a 90s Cuba." *NPR Books.* National Public Radio. Last modified 23 July 2009. http://npr.org/templates/story.story.php?storyld=106917751.
Obejas, Achy. *Memory Mambo.* Pittsburgh, PA: Cleiss Press, 1996.
Oboler, Suzanne. *Ethnic Labels, Latino Lives: Identity and the Politics of (Re)Presentation in the United States.* Minneapolis: University of Minnesota Press, 1995.
Obregón Pagán, Eduardo. *Murder at the Sleepy Lagoon: Zoot Suits, Race, and Riot in Wartime L.A.* Chapel Hill: University of North Carolina Press, 2003.
Ocampo, Anthony Christian. *The Latinos of Asia: How Filipino Americans Break the Rules of Race.* Stanford, CA: Stanford University Press, 2016.
Okihiro, Gary Y. *Common Ground: Reimagining American History.* Princeton, NJ: Princeton University Press, 2001.
Okihiro, Gary Y. *Margins and Mainstreams: Asians in American History and Culture.* Seattle: University of Washington Press, 1994.
Omi, Michael, and Howard Winant. *Racial Formation in the United States: From the 1960s to the 1990s.* New York: Routledge, 1994.
Palumbo-Liu, David, ed. *The Ethnic Canon: Histories, Institutions, and Interventions.* Minneapolis: University of Minnesota Press, 1995.
Paredes, Américo. *George Washington Gómez: A Mexicotexan Novel.* Houston, TX: Arte Público Press, 1990.
Paredes, Américo. "The Hammon and the Beans." In *The Latino Reader: An American Literary Tradition from 1542 to the Present,* edited by Harold Augenbraum and Margarite Fernández Olmos, 248–252. Boston, MA: Houghton Mifflin, 1997.
Paredes, Américo. *"With His Pistol in His Hand": A Border Ballad and Its Hero.* Austin: University of Texas Press, 1958.
Parikh, Crystal. *An Ethics of Betrayal: The Politics of Otherness in Emergent U.S. Literatures and Culture.* New York: Fordham University Press, 2009.
Parikh, Crystal. "Writing the Borderline Subject of War in Susan Choi's *The Foreign Student.*" *Southern Quarterly* 46 (2009): 47–68.
Park, Joonseong. "Susan Choi." In *Asian American Short Story Writers: An A-to-Z Guide,* edited by Guiyou Huang, 61–63. Westport, CT: Greenwood Press, 2003.
Patterson, Anita Haya. "Resistance to Images of the Internment: Mitsuye Yamada's *Camp Notes.*" *MELUS* 23 (1998):103–127.
Paz, Octavio. *The Labyrinth of Solitude: Life and Thought in Mexico.* Translated by Lysander Kemp. New York: Grove Press, 1961.
Pett, Joel. "It's So You'll Know Which Ones to Fear." *The Lexington Herald-Leader,* May 18, 2012. From The Cartoonist Group, http://www.cartoonistgroup.com/.
Pérez, Emma. *The Decolonial Imaginary: Writing Chicanas into History.* Bloomington: Indiana University Press, 1999.
Pfaelzer, Jean. *Driven Out: The Forgotten War Against Chinese Americans.* Berkeley, CA: University of California Press, 2008.
Pratt, Mary Louise. *Imperial Eyes: Travel Writing and Transculturation.* London: Routledge, 2008.

Pulido, Laura. *Black, Brown, Yellow, and Left: Radical Activism in Los Angeles.* Berkeley: University of California Press, 2006.

Quintana, Alvina E. "Performing Tricksters: Karen Tei Yamashita and Guillermo Gómez-Peña." *Amerasia Journal* 28 (2002): 217–225.

Rabe, Stephen G. *The Killing Zone: The United States Wages Cold War in Latin America.* New York: Oxford University Press, 2012.

Ramírez, Elizabeth. "Chicano Theatre Reaches the Professional Stage: Luis Valdez's Zoot Suit." In *Teaching American Ethnic Literatures: Nineteen Essays,* edited by John R. Maitino and David R. Peck, 193–207. Albuquerque: University of New Mexico Press, 1996.

Ricoeur, Paul. *Memory, History, Forgetting.* Trans. Kathleen Blamey and David Pellauer. Chicago: University of Chicago Press, 2004.

Robinson, Greg. *A Tragedy of Democracy: Japanese Confinement in North America.* New York: Columbia University Press, 2009.

Rody, Caroline. "The Transnational Imagination: Karen Tei Yamashita's *Tropic of Orange.*" In *Asian North American Identities: Beyond the Hyphen.* Edited by Eleanor Ty and Donald C. Goellnicht, 130–148. Bloomington: Indiana University Press, 2004.

Rosaldo, Renato. "Surveying Law and Borders." In *The Latino/a Condition,* edited by Richard Delgado and Jean Stefancic, 631–638. New York: New York University Press.

Ruiz de Burton, María Amparo. *The Squatter and the Don.* New York: Modern Library, 2004.

Sadowski-Smith, Claudia. *Border Fictions: Globalization, Empire, and Writing at the Boundaries of the United States.* Charlottesville: University of Virginia Press, 2008.

Sadowski-Smith, Claudia. "The U.S.-Mexico Borderlands Write Back: Cross-Cultural Transnationalism in Contemporary U.S. Women of Color Fiction." *Arizona Quarterly* 51 (2001): 91–202.

Saldívar, José David. *Border Matters: Remapping American Cultural Studies.* Berkeley: University of California Press, 1997.

Saldívar, José David. *The Dialectics of Our America: Genealogy, Cultural Critique, and Literary History.* Durham, NC: Duke University Press, 1991.

Saldívar, José David. *Trans-Americanity: Subaltern Modernities, Global Coloniality, and the Cultures of Greater Mexico.* Durham, NC: Duke University Press, 2012.

Saldívar, Ramón. *The Borderlands of Culture: Américo Paredes and the Transnational Imaginary.* Durham, NC: Duke University Press, 2006.

San Juan, Jr., E. *After Postcolonialism: Remapping Philippines-United States Confrontations.* Lanham, MD: Rowman & Littlefield, 2000.

San Juan, Jr., E. "Searching for the 'Heart' of America (Carlos Bulosan)." In *Teaching American Ethnic Literatures: Nineteen Essays,* edited by John R. Maitino and David R. Peck, 259–272. Albuquerque: University of New Mexico Press, 1996.

Sanchez, George J. *Becoming Mexican American: Ethnicity, Culture, and Identity in Chicano Los Angeles, 1900–1945.* New York: Oxford University Press, 1993.

Santiago, Esmeralda. *When I Was Puerto Rican.* New York: Vintage Books, 1994.

Scheper-Hughes, Nancy. "Rotten Trade: Millennial Capitalism, Human Values and Global Justice in Organs Trafficking." *Journal of Human Rights* 2 (June 2003): 197–227.

Schrecker, Ellen. *The Age of McCarthyism: A Brief History with Documents.* Boston: Bedford/St. Martin's, 2002.

Schweik, Susan. "A Needle with Mama's Voice: Mitsuye Yamada's 'Camp Notes' and the American Canon of War Poetry." In *Arms and the Woman: War, Gender, and Literary Representation,* edited by Helen M Cooper, Adrienne Munich and Susan Merrill Squier, 225–243. Chapel Hill: University of North Carolina Press, 1989.

Sheridan, Barrett. "Texas Cooks the Textbooks." *Newsweek,* May 21, 2010.

Shu, Yuan, and Donald E. Pease. *American Studies as Transnational Practice: Turning Toward the Transpacific.* Hanover, NH: Dartmouth College Press, 2015.

Siu Kam Wen. *Tierra de Nadie.* Web. Accessed 26 Nov. 2013. http://siukamwen.blogspot.com.

Siu Kam Wen. *El tramo final: cuentos.* Lima, Perú: Casatomada, 2009.

Sohn, Stephen Hong, Lai, Paul, and Donald C. Goellnicht. "Theorizing Asian American Fiction." *Modern Fiction Studies* 56 (2010): 1–18.

Sollors, Werner. *Beyond Ethnicity: Consent and Descent in American Culture.* New York: Oxford University Press, 1986.

Spickard, Paul. *Almost All Aliens: Immigration, Race, and Colonialism in American History and Identity.* New York: Routledge, 2007.

St. John de Crèvecoeur, Hector. "Letters from an American Farmer." In *Literature, Race, and Ethnicity: Contesting American Identities,* edited by Joseph T. Skerrett, Jr., 24–36. New York: Longman, 2002.

Steele, Richard. "Violence in Los Angeles: Sleepy Lagoon, the Zoot-Suit Riots, and the Liberal Response." In *World War II and Mexican American Civil Rights,* edited by Richard Griswold del Castillo, 34–48. Austin, TX: University of Texas Press, 2008.

Stewart, Watt. *Chinese Bondage in Peru.* Durham, NC: Duke University Press, 1951.

Takaki, Ronald. *Democracy and Race: Asian Americans and World War II.* New York: Chelsea House, 1995.

Takaki, Ronald. *A Different Mirror: A History of Multicultural America.* Boston: Little, Brown, and Co., 1993.

Takaki, Ronald. *Strangers from a Different Shore: A History of Asian Americans.* New York: Back Bay Books, 1998.

Terkel, Studs. *"The Good War": An Oral History of World War Two.* New York: Pantheon Books, 1984.

Texas State Board of Education. *Proposed Revisions to 19 TAC Chapter 113, Texas Essential Knowledge and Skills for Social Studies, Subchapter B, Middle School: Approved for Second Reading and Final Adoption.* May 21, 2010. http://www.tea. state.tx.us/index2.aspx?id=3643.

Texas State Board of Education, *Proposed Revisions to 19 TAC Chapter 113, Texas Essential Knowledge and Skills for Social Studies, Subchapter C, High School and 19 TAC Chapter 118, Texas Essential Knowledge and Skills for Economics with Emphasis on the* Free Enterprise *System and Its Benefits, Subchapter A, High School: Approved for Second Reading and Final Adoption.* May 21, 2010. http://www.tea.state.tx.us/index2.aspx?id=3643

Torgovnick, Marianna. *The War Complex: World War II in Our Time.* Chicago: University of Chicago Press, 2005.

Torres-Saillant, Silvio. "Inventing the Race: Latinos and the Ethnoracial Pentagon." *Latino Studies* 1 (2003): 121–153.

Tran, My-Thuan. "From Refugees to Political Players." *Los Angeles Times,* December 7, 2008. http://articles.latimes.com/2008/dec/07/local/me-vietnamese7.

Truman, President Harry S. "Address to Congress: March 12, 1947." In *Public Papers of the Presidents of the United States: Harry S. Truman, 1947,* 178–180. Washington, D.C.: U.S. Government Printing Office, 1963. Reprinted in *The World Transformed, 1945 to the Present,* edited by Michael H. Hunt, 33. Boston: Bedford/St. Martin's, 2004.

Ty, Eleanor, and Donald C. Goellnicht. *Asian North American Identities: Beyond the Hyphen.* Bloomington: Indiana University Press, 2004.

"U.S. Census Bureau Projections Show a Slower Growing, Older, More Diverse Nation a Half Century from Now." *United States Census Bureau.* Last modified 12 December 2012. https://www.census.gov/newsroom/releases/archives/population/cb12-243.html.

Valdez, Luis. "The Actos." In *Luis Valdez—Early Works: Actos, Bernabé, and Pensamiento Serpentino*, 11–13. Houston, TX: Arte Publico Press, 1990.

Valdez, Luis. "Notes on Chicano Theater." In *Twentieth-Century Theatre: A Sourcebook*, edited by Richard Drain, 315–319. London: Routledge, 1995.

Valdez, Luis. *Zoot Suit and Other Plays.* Houston, TX: Arte Publico Press, 1992.

Wang, Hansi Lo. "Descendents of Chinese Laborers Reclaim Railroad's History." *National Public Radio.* Last modified 10 May 2014. http://www.npr.org/sections/codeswitch/2014/05/10/311157404/descendants-of-chinese-laborers-reclaim-railroads-history.

Wesling, Meg. "Colonial Education and the Politics of Knowledge in Carlos Bulosan's *America Is in the Heart.*" *MELUS* 32 (2007): 55–77.

White, Hayden. *The Fiction of Narrative: Essays on History, Literature, and Theory 1957–2007*, edited by Robert Doran. Baltimore, MD: Johns Hopkins University Press, 2010.

Williams, William Appleman. "The Frontier Thesis and American Foreign Policy." *Pacific Historical Review* 24 (1955): 379–395.

Wong, Sau-ling Cynthia. *Reading Asian American Literature: From Necessity to Extravagance.* Princeton, NJ: Princeton University Press, 1993.

Wong, Sau-ling Cynthia. "'Sugar Sisterhood': Situating the Amy Tan Phenomenon." In *The Ethnic Canon: Histories, Institutions, and Interventions*, edited by David Palumbo-Liu, 174–210. Minneapolis: University of Minnesota Press, 1995.

Yamada, Mitsuye. "Asian Pacific American Women and Feminism." In *This Bridge Called My Back: Writings by Radical Women of Color*, edited by Cherríe Moraga and Gloria Anzaldúa, 74–79. Watertown, MA: Persephone Press, 1981.

Yamada, Mitsuye. *Camp Notes and Other Writings.* New Brunswick, NJ: Rutgers University Press, 1998.

Yamashita, Karen Tei. *Brazil-Maru.* Minneapolis, MN: Coffee House Press, 1992.

Yamashita, Karen Tei. "Interview with Tei-hsing Shan." *Amerasia Journal* 32 (2006): 123–142.

Yamashita, Karen Tei. *Tropic of Orange.* Minneapolis, MN: Coffee House Press, 1997.

Yogi, Stan. "Japanese American Literature." In *An Interethnic Companion to Asian American Literature.* Edited by King-kok Cheung, 125–155. Cambridge, UK: Cambridge University Press, 1997.

Yun, Lisa. *The Coolie Speaks: Chinese Indentured Laborers and African Slaves in Cuba.* Philadelphia, PA: Temple University Press, 2008.

Zeiger, Susan. *Entangling Alliances: Foreign War Brides and American Soldiers in the Twentieth Century.* New York: New York University Press, 2010.

Zinn, Howard. "The Greatest Generation?" *The Progressive* 65 (2001): 12–14.

Zinn, Howard. *A People's History of the United States.* New York: Harper Collins, 2003.

INDEX

ABOUT THE AUTHOR

SUSAN THANANOPAVARN is a lecturing fellow in the Thompson Writing Program at Duke University. She received her PhD in English from the University of North Carolina at Chapel Hill in 2015. Her work has appeared in the journals *Aztlán* and *The Lion and the Unicorn.* She lives in Chapel Hill, North Carolina, with her husband and three children.

AVAILABLE TITLES IN THE LATINIDAD: TRANSNATIONAL CULTURES IN THE UNITED STATES SERIES:

María Acosta Cruz, *Dream Nation: Puerto Rican Culture and the Fictions of Independence*
Rodolfo F. Acuña, *The Making of Chicana/o Studies: In the Trenches of Academe*
Xóchitl Bada, *Mexican Hometown Associations in Chicagoacán: From Local to Transnational Civic Engagement*
Maritza E. Cárdenas, *Constituting Central American–Americans: Transnational Identities and the Politics of Dislocation*
Adriana Cruz-Manjarrez, *Zapotecs on the Move: Cultural, Social, and Political Processes in Transnational Perspective*
T. Jackie Cuevas, *Post-Borderlandia: Chicana Literature and Gender Variant Critique*
Marivel T. Danielson, *Homecoming Queers: Desire and Difference in Chicana Latina Cultural Production*
Allison E. Fagan, *From the Edge: Chicana/o Border Literature and the Politics of Print*
Jerry González, *In Search of the Mexican Beverly Hills: Latino Suburbanization in Postwar Los Angeles*
Rudy P. Guevarra Jr., *Becoming Mexipino: Multiethnic Identities and Communities in San Diego*
Colin Gunckel, *Mexico on Main Street: Transnational Film Culture in Los Angeles before World War II*
Marie-Theresa Hernández, *The Virgin of Guadalupe and the Conversos: Uncovering Hidden Influences from Spain to Mexico*
Lisa Jarvinen, *The Rise of Spanish-Language Filmmaking: Out from Hollywood's Shadow, 1929–1939*
Regina M. Marchi, *Day of the Dead in the USA: The Migration and Transformation of a Cultural Phenomenon*
Desirée A. Martín, *Borderlands Saints: Secular Sanctity in Chicano/a and Mexican Culture*
Marci R. McMahon, *Domestic Negotiations: Gender, Nation, and Self-Fashioning in US Mexicana and Chicana Literature and Art*
A. Gabriel Meléndez, *Hidden Chicano Cinema: Film Dramas in the Borderlands*
Priscilla Peña Ovalle, *Dance and the Hollywood Latina: Race, Sex, and Stardom*
Amalia Pallares, *Family Activism: Immigrant Struggles and the Politics of Noncitizenship*
Luis F. B. Plascencia, *Disenchanting Citizenship: Mexican Migrants and the Boundaries of Belonging*
Cecilia M. Rivas, *Salvadoran Imaginaries: Mediated Identities and Cultures of Consumption*
Jayson Gonzales Sae-Saue, *Southwest Asia: The Transpacific Geographies of Chicana/o Literature*
Mario Jimenez Sifuentez, *Of Forest and Fields: Mexican Labor in the Pacific Northwest*
Maya Socolovsky, *Troubling Nationhood in U.S. Latina Literature: Explorations of Place and Belonging*
Susan Thananopavarn, *LatinAsian Cartographies*